Language, Learning, Context

In what way do educators understand the language they use to make sense of the educational environment?

How does language enable educators and how can they consciously make the most of its potential?

Using the right language and setting the correct tone in the school classroom has repercussions for all involved; whether it affects the linguistic development of a student or the effective delivery of a lesson, language plays an important factor in any educational context.

As such, this innovative book focuses right at the heart of learning, arguing that current theories of speech in classrooms do not, and cannot, capture the essentially passive aspects of talking. Until now, these verbal and physical expressions of communication have been left untheorized, leaving the potential of an entire secondary area of language untapped.

Exploring his argument along three clear, but interrelated, lines of investigation the author focuses on our understanding, on language itself, and finally on communication. Thus he argues:

- that language is unintentional and our understanding of it is limited
- as soon as we speak, language appears beyond us in a highly singular, situated context
- that communication cannot be reduced to the simple production of words.

Building on the work of linguistic philosophers such as Martin Heidegger, Donald Davidson, Paul Ricœur and Jacques Derrida, these salient points are further elaborated to fully develop the relationship between thinking and talk in educational settings.

This invaluable book makes recommendations for the praxis of teaching and will appeal to students, researchers, and practising science and mathematics teachers, as well as those with interests in language and literacy.

Wolff-Michael Roth is Professor of Applied Cognitive Science at the University of Victoria, British Columbia.

Foundations and Futures of Education
Series Editors:
Peter Aggleton *School of Education and Social Work, University of Sussex, UK*
Sally Power *Cardiff University, UK*
Michael Reiss *Institute of Education, University of London, UK*

Foundations and Futures of Education focuses on key emerging issues in education, as well as continuing debates within the field. The series is interdisciplinary, and includes historical, philosophical, sociological, psychological and comparative perspectives on three major themes: the purposes and nature of education; increasing interdisciplinarity within the subject; and the theory–practice divide.

Language, Learning, Context
Talking the talk
Wolff-Michael Roth

Re-designing Learning Contexts
Technology-rich, learner-centred ecologies
Rosemary Luckin

Education and the Family
Passing success across the generations
Leon Feinstein, Kathryn Duckworth and Ricardo Sabates

Education, Philosophy and the Ethical Environment
Graham Haydon

Educational Activity and the Psychology of Learning
Judith Ireson

Schooling, Society and Curriculum
Alex Moore

Gender, Schooling and Global Social Justice
Elaine Unterhalter

Language, Learning, Context

Talking the talk

Wolff-Michael Roth

Routledge
Taylor & Francis Group

LONDON AND NEW YORK

First published 2010
by Routledge
2 Park Square, Milton Park, Abingdon, Oxon OX14 4RN

Simultaneously published in the USA and Canada
by Routledge
270 Madison Avenue, New York, NY 10016

Routledge is an imprint of the Taylor & Francis Group, an informa business

Typeset in Galliard by
GreenGate Publishing Services, Tonbridge, Kent
Printed and bound in Great Britain by
CPI Antony Rowe, Chippenham, Wiltshire

British Library Cataloguing in Publication Data
A catalogue record for this book is available from the British Library

Library of Congress Cataloging in Publication Data
Roth, Wolff-Michael, 1953-
Language, learning, context : talking the talk / Wolff-Michael Roth.
p. cm. -- (Foundations and futures of education)
Includes bibliographical references and index.
1. English language--Study and teaching. 2. Communication in education.
3. Oral communication--Study and teaching. 4. Language arts (Elementary)
5. Classroom management. I. Title.
LB1576.R7546 2010
371.102'3--dc22   2009042244

ISBN: 978-0-415-55191-5 (hbk)
ISBN: 978-0-203-85317-7 (ebk)

Contents

Figures

Preface

Man speaks. We speak being awake and dreaming. We always speak; even when we do not utter a word, but listen or read, even when we neither listen nor read, but pursue some task or are absorbed in resting. We continually speak in some fashion. We speak because speaking is natural to us. It does not derive from a special volition. Man is said to have language by nature ... In speaking man is: man.

(Heidegger 1985: 11, my translation)

Every day we participate in conversations where we cannot foresee what we will have said between now and even a few seconds hence. Moreover, we do talk about issues that we have never thought about before; and we do so without stopping to think or to interpret what another has said. Yet, despite this inherent openness of conversations, the speed, and the inherent underdetermination of our contributions by anything that we can say to have known at the instant of speaking, most theories treat language (discourse) as something that is the result of the intentional spilling of mind. Existing theories merely articulate a dehiscence between mind and language that has a long tradition in metaphysics, a dehiscence that constitutes the history of metaphysics. But there are other ways to think/ write/talk about theory of language, one in which language and thought (mind) are no longer independent processes, let alone independent things.

The purpose of this book is to write—articulate and further develop—a theoretical position of communication generally, and language specifically, as something dynamic that *evolves* together with thought, and that provides resources for cobbling together responses to questions and ideas that we have never thought about before. In this theoretical position, language is not just about content or what human beings do to each other (speech as act). Thus, human beings do not just participate in communicative events but they also constitute the events in which they participate. That is, if my neighbor and I speak about the weather or about our gardens, then we not only produce contents of talk—i.e., text—but also the very *con*text of the conversation itself. When my wife asks me what I did, I will first respond by saying, "I talked to B-J" rather than in talking about the contents of our conversation. That is, when I account for what I have done, I first refer to the situation I had contributed to producing in talking rather than to the contents of the talk. Others may gloss this context as "small talk," "chit chat," or as "neighborly conversation," all of which recognize that the talk has done more than just transmitted content. In writing a different perspective on language, I am concerned as much with what goes *with* (i.e., con-) text as with the text itself.

Over the past two decades, and conducting research in a variety of different settings, I have built and elaborated a pragmatic non-intentionalist position on communication and language. This position is grounded in my reading of the dialectical and phenomenological literatures on language and discourse as it has emerged since the latter part of the twentieth century. Some of the key philosophers of language that my work has built on include Martin Heidegger, Donald Davidson, Paul Ricœur, Jacques Derrida, the circle around Mikhail Bakhtin (including P.N. Medvedev and V.N. Vološinov), and the conversation analysts/ethnomethodologists Harold Garfinkel and Harvey Sacks. In this way, my book allows me to address a number of aporia not currently addressed in theories of language, learning, and context.

This book presents an approach to language, learning, and context that substantially differs from current, intentionalist approaches to linguistic and discursive phenomena in the literature on learning. What the position taken here boils down to is this: one cannot make a distinction between knowing a language and knowing one's way around the world. There are not *explicit* rules for learning a language.

This position has (radical) implications for the school curriculum. If there are no explicit rules—Ludwig Wittgenstein already has argued against universal grammar before the linguist Noam Chomsky has resuscitated and promulgated it—then talking a language *is* learning a language. This is consistent with recent arguments we have made concerning teaching: we learn to teach in teaching not while learning rules *about* teaching. With this statement, I return to the subtitle of the book, *Talking the talk*. We learn to talk a language by talking; and in this book I outline how it is possible to participate in talking a language that one has not yet mastered. The phenomenon is captured in the image of laying a garden path in walking—we learn to talk in talking.

This book is designed to be useful not only to a small group of initiates but it is also intended for an intelligent and informed readership. My utmost attention has been to produce the individual chapters, and the book as a whole, as readable by a wide audience, all the while retaining academic integrity and high-level scholarship. I want readers to follow me along walking the walk while looking at how people in everyday settings and of different ages talk the talk.

Translation constitutes the possible impossible—a statement that goes to the heart of the matter in this book—which Paul de Man (1983), himself a fluent speaker of English, French, and German, beautifully shows in the failings of two translations (German to English and French) of a famous Walter Benjamin (1972) text on the task/abandonment of the translator. In this book I draw on foreign language texts (French and German) and provide my own translations for reasons that are at the heart of this book and elaborated in the section on translation in Chapter 1. Having grown up and lived in Germany for 25 years, worked in English for over 30 years, and spoken French at home daily for nearly as long, I am fluent in all three languages. (I also studied Latin for seven years, and know some Greek.) I frequently find that translations at times do not allow us to hear/read what we can hear/read in the original. In some instances, such as Mikhail Bakhtin's work in French and English, the problem apparently arose from poor translations, where the translator knows the language well but not so well the system of thought (Todorov 1984). Because of the different narrative and discursive requirements of different languages, there cannot be exact equivalents—e.g., "English calls for more explicit, precise, concrete determinations, for fuller more cohesive delineations than French … English … simply cannot let the original say what it says in French" (Lewis 2000: 267). The limits of translation are quite apparent in Derrida's (1982: 258) chapter "White mythology: Metaphor in the text of philosophy" where the title of the section "La métaphysique—relève de la métaphore" remains untranslated, accompanied by a 10-line footnote explaining why the subtitle is untranslatable. A "good" translation is not only linguistically adequate, but is also appropriate to the grammar of the said (e.g., the philosophy of the philosopher). Therefore, when a German or French source is cited, the translation is mine—not, however, without having checked it against some published translation, if it was available to me, in which case the specific translation is also noted in the reference section—to ensure that there is a consistent coherence in the thought expressed in this English text.

In this book I repeatedly draw on etymology. I use the online version of *The Oxford English Dictionary* (2009) as my main source; I also draw on the *Proto-Indo-European Etymological Dictionary* (Indo-European Language Association 2007) and on the *Indogermanisches Wörterbuch* (Köbler 2000). Etymologies are provided not to get at a true, or truer, sense of a word, but, in part, to point to the history and commonality among words and worlds that resonate far back in Western history, language, and philosophy (metaphysics).

The starting points for the different chapters have been my notes that initially led to a series of articles on language. These articles, which appeared in *Cultural Studies of Science Education, Educational Research Review,* and *Mind Culture and Activity* hereby are acknowledged as sharing early roots with my thinking articulated here, have been but crutches that now are preserved, repressed, and superseded—the three verb forms cover G.W.F. Hegel's *aufgehoben* and Jacques Derrida's *relevé*—by the theoretical position on language, learning, and context that I write/disseminate/articulate in this book. I thank all those with whom I have interacted over the past several years, both directly and indirectly (in double-blind review processes), for allowing and assisting me in elaborating this non-empiricist and non-intentionalist position that gives reason to the ways in which real people experience and articulate themselves in everyday settings. My special thanks go to Ken Tobin, who provided me with access to the data in Chapter 7 and who contributed to an article based on this work.

Victoria, British Columbia
September 2009

1 Walking the walk

Wie west die Sprache als Sprache? Wir antworten: *Die Sprache spricht* ... Der Sprache nachdenken verlangt somit, daß wir auf das Sprechen der Sprache eingehen. [How does language live/exist as language? *Language speaks* ... To meditate on language therefore requires that we enter into/engage with the speaking of language.]

(Heidegger 1985: 10, original emphasis)

In everyday educational endeavors—teaching, learning, or doing research—we use language without reflecting on its nature and without reflecting how language enables us to do what we currently do. We say: "Hello, how are you? Nice weather today, isn't it?" without reflecting even once about what we are saying and why. Yet we would immediately know if those words said by someone else make sense and are appropriate and true, that is, fitting in the present situation. Even among those who make language their main research topic, generally focusing on *what* we do with language—"making meaning," "learning," "positioning ourselves," or "producing identities"—few ask the question Martin Heidegger asks in my introductory quote: how is language *as* language? Even a simple question such as "what is language?" already presupposes not just the three words but a whole system of language and difference (Derrida 1972), including an understanding of an utterance *as* a question. Heidegger answers his question by saying that language speaks, a statement he elaborates, among others, by stating that in our meditation on language we need to engage with and enter into language.[1] Would it be possible to get a book on language, learning, and context off the ground without always already presupposing the existence of language? This question recalls a statement by Friedrich Nietzsche (1954b: 805) about the highest form of experience: the possibility to "read a text as text, without intermingling an interpretation," which is, he recognizes, "perhaps hardly possible." Would it be possible to investigate language without presupposing something that is even deeper than language, something that in any imaginable case (cultural-historically, individual-developmentally) precedes language: such as the unthematized experiences in a world always already inhabited *with* others?

The epigraph to this chapter comes from a book entitled *Unterwegs zur Sprache* (*On the Way to [Toward] Language*). Among others, Heidegger indicates with this title that it is not a self-evident thing to understand[2] and theorize language, as language itself is *in* the way as we are *on* the way to learn about it. To get to it, we have to speak/write in the same way as we think in order to get on the way to thinking (Heidegger 1954); my hearing/reading of speakers who appear in episodes/transcripts is of the same nature as that of the respondents in the episodes. As (applied) linguists and learning researchers interested in language, we always already find ourselves in language rather than independent of it. The simplest (linguistic) objects we can investigate already are a product of consciousness irreducibly bound up with language (de Saussure 1996). Moreover, this language that we are trying to understand and theorize is living—its understanding, in contrast to the understanding of a dead language, such as Latin—has to be treated, qua living, as something alive (Nietzsche 1954b). That means that we cannot, as do the experimental sciences or historians, presuppose the independence of researcher and research object, or object, method, and theory. This recognition is also central to ethnomethodology (e.g., Garfinkel 2002), a discipline investigating the mundane practices that reproduce and transform the world of our collective experience, the *everyday* world. Ethnomethodologists take as given that *any* social science researcher always, already, and ineluctably makes use of the very practices that they investigate and generally take to have an existence independent of them. But normally these practices are invisible. The researcher's problem is to make these structures, for example, of language and context, explicit, visible, and, thereby, to bring to consciousness the competencies that produce these structures.

This entire book constitutes a walk (an engagement of the way) toward a theory of spoken language that takes into account our everyday experience of speaking. It is offered as an alternative to the rationalized and intention-prioritizing accounts of language that have a large resemblance with computer language and with the way in which computers make available the contents—express, read/print out—of their memory to human beings. This relationship between computers and humans is governed by the formal logic underlying computer science. But human relations are different: "The relationship between Me and the Other does not have the structure formal logic finds in all relations ... The relation with the Other is the only one where such an overturning of formal logic can occur" (Levinas 1971: 156). Language is a mode of this relation. It is, therefore, important to uncover and disclose its nature so that we better understand the relation with the Other, for example, between students and their teachers, between friends, or between co-workers.

As I present in this book a perspective and mediation on language, learning, and context that differs considerably from the current educational canon—though my position is well founded in twentieth-century philosophical scholarship—I ground myself in everyday examples involving fragments of different conversations that I have recorded over the years in a variety of settings. I do this to walk the walk of talk, that is, to talk the talk—as the popular expression goes and as the subtitle to this book reads—because it is only in this manner that we can find our "way to language" and, therefore, to a viable theory of spoken language. I use these fragments to write/think about what they presuppose and, in so doing, both cover new terrain and show the limits of existing approaches to think language, learning, and context. I investigate language as it appears, that is, in the way "language lives/exists as language." I thereby follow[3] the way in which real human beings *actually* speak language, that is, the way language actually speaks through the speaking. But such writing always constitutes an oblique movement, in a way, for it "continuously risks to fall back into what it deconstructs" so that one has to "encircle critical concepts by means of a prudent and minutious discourse, marking the conditions, the milieu, and the limits of their efficacy, rigorously define their belonging to a machinery that they allow to undo in their constitution" (Derrida 1967a: 26).

To get us off the ground, ever so carefully so as not to fall into the traps that other theories of language have fallen, I presuppose my present audience to be capable speakers/readers of English, with the competencies to *overhear* everyday conversations, that is to say, to understand what speakers meant by saying what they said. Investigations of the texts produced in speaking lead us to the presupposed *con*texts—texts that go with (Lat. *con[m]*-) texts, texts that are ground against which the texts of interest appear as figure, texts with which the texts of interest are interwoven—that make any hearing of text possible. And understanding texts and *con*texts allows us to understand the phenomena denoted by the third concept in this book's title—learning—as the result of talking the talk.

My way to the essence/nature of language always already is on its way, as my use of language, my writing, my thinking, my overhearing of the interlocutors that appear throughout this book, all are grounded in, traversed by, and irreducible to that which is properly linguistic in language. This reflexive nature of language to our hearing/reading, speaking/writing, and thinking/being-conscious should never be left out of sight/hearing range. It is our dwelling in life/language that allows us to meditate on language rather than the other way around.

A mystery conversation

Communication generally, and language particularly, are amazing phenomena. On the one hand, communication is very fast and yet we participate in it even when there is no possibility for a time-out to reflect (e.g., about strategy and next moves). On the other hand, communication presupposes such an extensive background understanding and shared knowing, that it is astonishing that we accomplish what we do with the speed and precision that we actually do. This is true not only for adult conversations but also for conversations between children, or the conversations involving children and adults. Let us take a look at the following exchange and then unfold the pertinent issues concerning language and communication layer by layer to find out what is involved in conducting a simple conversation. This investigation takes us several rounds of inquiry—of *écriture*, writing, and the displacement it produces—as we have to slow down the reading of this situation to come to understand just what is going on.[4] Imagine finding the following "rough transcript" in which a research assistant only transcribed the sounds into sound-words that she heard. We now ask the question: what is being said here, not just the words, but what is the conversation about? Who are "T," "C," and "Ch," or rather, what category of people do they belong to?

Fragment 1.1a

```
01  T:   em an what did we say that group was about
02  C:   what do you mean like
03  T:   what was the what did we put for the name of that group
         whats written on the card
04  C:   squares
05  T:   square and
06  Ch:  cube
```

Many individuals finding such a sheet of paper may not know what to do with it and would discard it without any further thought. Even though we may not have available any other information—which in itself is significant to evolving a good theory of communication generally, and language specifically—we can find out a lot about what is going on here. In fact, in my graduate courses on interpretive methods, I often enact exemplary illustrations on the basis of such "found" transcripts about which I have no further information. I ask my students to provide me with just that—a "raw transcript" of a mystery conversation and no other information. I then read, slowly, reading/listening as I go along, making inferences in real time about what is happening, and unpacking the tremendous background knowledge that participants to such a conversation have and make available for hearing others *objectively*, available to everyone looking at the transcript.[5] I do so without actually "interpreting" what is said, practically understanding a conversation in the immediacy of the here and now. So what is being made available only in and with the words and in the absence of other identifying information, contextual details, identity of the speakers, intonations, and so on? The point is not to lay my interpretation or any one else's over the transcript but to find out the sense the participants themselves express to each other *in and through their talk*, and I, as a bystander, simply overhear how they are hearing each other's verbal productions, hearings that are made available again in verbal and non-verbal productions.

In the use of the interrogative pronoun "what" we might hear that T is going to ask a question ("an what did we say that group was about")—but to understand the conversation it is not important how we hear the utterance but how the other participant(s) hear it.[6] Because we are interested in interaction and learning of the situation to which the transcript is an index, we need to find out the *internal* dynamic. This requires us to know how the participants hear what others say, which is available only in how they react to an utterance or how they take up this and other preceding utterances in their own turns. In the present situation, the next turn begins with the same interrogative pronoun "what." Therefore, we are confronted with two interrogatives; one following the other rather than with a question–answer sequence. We may ask, drawing on our cultural and linguistic competence, under what condition would we hear a question followed by another interrogative? Two immediate answers are: when the second speaker has not heard (understood) what the preceding speaker said, or when the second speaker did not comprehend (understand) what the first speaker is asking. But already, we are ahead of ourselves, for I am invoking cultural competence. To understand a question as intended, we need to bring to bear the same cultural competence that the first speaker presupposes in asking the question in the way she or he did. However, how do we know about the intentions of others? The answer is: in and through talk. Yet, in the present instance, the first speaker does not ask just any question and does not ask the question in any form: both in form and content, the question takes into account the addressee and it takes into account possible answers. For it makes no sense to ask a child an adult question and it makes equally little sense to ask a "childish" question of an adult. Yet again, we are ahead of ourselves in our reading of the fragment.

To hear the first utterance as a question, especially as a question oriented to someone else, this someone else—who is the intended recipient and whose response is monitored—requires cultural competence. This cultural competence, the one operating within the transcript, also has to be the cultural competence that we, those who overhear the three individuals speaking, also have to have in order to hear the participants *in the same way* that they hear each other. But this analysis is accelerating again so that I have to slow it down once more.

Whatever the question is about—if indeed it is a question—has already been the content of a conversation. At least, it is described by one participant as having been the topic of conversation, "what *did* we say that group was about?" The question is not "what is that group about?" T uses indirect speech to bring something previously said to bear in the present situation. Indirect speech is when a speaker refers to something else that has been said, at a different time and perhaps at a different place, where the speaker may be the same ("we have said that," "I have said that") or someone else ("you have said," "X has said," "it has been said"), without actually directly quoting the person. We can gloss what is happening in the turn in this way: we had talked about the group and said that it was about something. What is this something?

In the second turn, C also appears to ask a question, which we would hear in the interrogative pronoun "what" and in the grammatical structure of the utterance, "what do you mean, like?" Again, to understand the evolution of *that* situation, it does not matter how *we* hear this utterance but how T and others in the situation hear and respond to it—as indicated in their uptake of whatever the utterance has made available. If indeed turn 02 is a question, and if it is heard as pertaining to the previous utterance, something about the former utterance has been unclear. The first utterance then is not a question but is itself turned into a problem in and by means of the second utterance, "what do you mean?" Is this really a question? And if so, what is it asking C? Is the question concerning the nature of "that group," that is, which of several possible groups (if so) is being indicated? Or is the question about something that the group itself denotes, serving as an index for a category of things? Our cultural competence tells us that "that" is an index, a verbal pointer to something available to the interlocutors. But, if it is an entity somewhere in the room, we precisely need to have available that room, the *con*text, the unarticulated text that goes with the text, to figure out what "that" refers us to. In fact, the context is like the ground against which the text appears as figure. No ground, no figure; if there is a figure, then it always figures against a (non-thematic) ground. Here, our cultural competence itself is a form of context that allows us to hear and understand even though we cannot detail and make explicit completely in what precisely this cultural competence consists (e.g., being able to hear the *same* voice across distant turns, to hear different voices distinguishing speakers in adjacent turns, or to hear the changeover of speakers tout court)—just as we do not detail and make explicit precisely the perceptual ground against which a perceptual figure takes shape.

When T takes the next turn, we hear nearly the same statement again—but only nearly the same. There appears to be a grammatically unfinished utterance, "what was the," which precedes a second part, "what did we put for the name of that group" (turn 03). So the "what was the group about?" has changed into "what did we put for the name of that group?" Assuming that the second question is about the same thing as the first, then the "what" is the "name of" the group—if the assumption is, in fact, justified. Such a hearing would be consistent with the third part of the utterance, "what's written on the card?" if the card is something like the name tag or "business card" of the group, whatever the group is in that situation. So if these three expressions—"what was that group about?" "what did we put for the name of that group?" and "what's written on the card?" —are but different versions of *the same question*, then we actually see translation at work. There is one question but it is formulated in different ways, some of which C does not understand (e.g., turn 01) and others which he may eventually understand—without this possibility looming at the horizon, it would make no sense formulating and reformulating the *same* question in different ways. In any event, the translation does occur at the heart of the English language and constitutes a translation from English into another such English by "playing with the non-self-identity of all language" (Derrida 1996: 123). I elaborate in Chapter 10 the hybridity, *métissage*, and heterogeneity announced in this statement central to the philosophy of difference that has been worked out in the works of such philosophers as Jacques Derrida, Jean-Luc Nancy, and Gilles Deleuze.

C goes next, uttering an elliptic "squares." The term "squares" is the plural form of the noun *square*. It is a possible candidate for a response if "what" is asking for a thing, its name expressing its quiddity. Tracking backward, and assuming the three *different* questions really are meant to be the *same* question, then the question is seeking something written on a card, which is the name of a group, itself being about something. "Squares" would fit the bill if the word were present on some card, recognizably denoting a group, and has been the topic of talk before. For readers of the transcript to understand, they need more than the *text* of the transcript—they need *con*text, additional text to go with the source text, to figure out what the text (transcription) does not say in and of itself. They would need part of the lifeworld, articulated or not, which those present take as unquestioned ground of their talk.

T takes the next turn at talk: "square." It is the same word that the previous speaker has uttered, only here in the singular. But why would T utter the *same* word as the previous speaker? In the repetition, therefore, something has changed. It is the same word, but it no longer has the same function. It may have a similar sound envelope that proficient speakers of English hear as the "same" sound-word despite the differences with its previous occurrence, and it may have the same dictionary sense. But, in any case, its role in the conversation has changed, if only because its preceding version now is part of the ground against which the repetition is heard. The word no longer has the same function in the conversation and competent speakers understand this change in function, for nothing would be communicated, etymologically and, therefore, literally to share *with* (Lat. *com-*), make *common*, if the word was a *mere* repetition. This is where most social analysts of transcript get it completely wrong—they take the same trace, sign-word, appearing in different parts of the transcript as *the same* when in fact later occurrences always already are heard against their previous occurrences as part of the no longer unarticulated ground (Bakhtine [Volochinov] 1977). This local history of the word itself has to be traced and taken into account rather than be obliterated in taking it to be the iterable captured in the dictionary sense.

Culturally competent speakers may immediately hear the repetition as a confirmation, which we may gloss in elaborating as "yes, that group was about *square(s).*" But there is more to it. The actual turn continues with an "and," followed by a third speaker who utters "cube." That is, by uttering "and" without continuing, T actually opens a slot that Ch fills in, and thereby completes, much like students fill the blanks left in their worksheets that teachers assign to them. There is an open slot, an incomplete statement, potentially open for someone else to complete, and it is T who opens this slot. In responding "squares and," T also exhibits attention to anticipated responses. Part of the response provided is correct, which we can hear in the repetition of the word "square." But this answer is also incomplete, as indicated by the conjunctive "and" that is left without a second word following it. There is something missing to be completed by whoever speaks next, which could also be T.

Some readers may think that I have *interpreted* the fragment. But this is not so. I have read the raw transcript as if I were overhearing a conversation; and I have done so in a step-by-step fashion, diachronically, as if actually listening to the conversation rather than as if reading a text with all words simultaneously and synchronously available. All diachronism has been removed in the transcript if it were not for the fact that in many Western cultures, reading proceeds from top left to bottom right, left page to right page, and so on, so that the temporality of diachronism can be recovered in the process of reading. I attempt to recover diachronism because I am interested in rendering the way in which the interaction participants themselves hear one another, which itself can be taken from the way they respond and in their responses take up or query the turns of others. To be able to overhear a conversation—of which I have nothing but the transcription of the sound into a device, written language, evolved for rendering particular hearings of particular sounds—I have to have cultural competencies of the same kind as the speakers have themselves. These competencies act as a *con*text that configure the hearing of the text before me. This includes hearing certain sounds as sound-words, which are recurrent in a culture and figure in its dictionaries, if these in fact exist, which is not the case for still existing oral cultures. If I had used the, for many (North American) speakers of English unfamiliar but otherwise widely used, conventions of the International Phonetics Association, the fragment might have looked as follows:

Fragment 1.1b

T: əm ən wɔt did wi: sei ðæt gru:p wɔz ə'baut
C: wɔt du: ju: mi:n laik
T: wɔt wɔz ðə wɔt did wi put fɔ: ðə neim ɔv ðæt gru:p wɔts 'ritn ɔn
     ðə ka:d
C: skweəs
T: skweə ən
Ch: kju:b

The question may be raised, "why might someone have used the transcription by the International Phonetics Association?" From my perspective, the answer is simple and makes a point. In transcribing the sound of the videotape as it appears in Fragment 1.1a, we already presuppose the cultural competence to hear a series of words rather than a sound stream, here transcribed in Fragment 1.1b. We already have to understand to physically hear the words as words, a point initially made by Heidegger nearly 80 years ago. Such a hearing of sound-words rather than sounds is part of a cultural competence that becomes rapidly clear in the two following examples. The first example I experienced when my wife, a native French speaker but then a beginner of the English language, became part of my research team responsible for the recording and transcription of recordings from science classrooms. At the very beginning, there were many parts of a soundtrack that she could not transcribe because she did not hear what was said, and this problem of hearing could be traced back to her lack of understanding of both English and science. This competency to hear words where others hear but sounds rides on top of another competence evident in the fact that the transcriber used the letters "T," "C," and "Ch" to attribute turns to different speakers. The transcriber already has available some other information, names of people, and, having learned in the past to distinguish voices, has now transcribed the videotape to produce a text, a written record of the sounds that participants have produced.

The second instance of cultural competence can be experienced—even by a proficient speaker of a language—listening to a "difficult" soundtrack where one can hear that someone is speaking—itself presupposing understanding of the situation even if the language spoken is foreign (Heidegger 1977b)—but where it is impossible to make out what the precise word equivalent to the sound is. That is, we recognize a sound as something that a human being could have produced so that we hear a particular word. But, and this is the crux of the story, this hearing of words already constitutes a translation. It turns out that sometimes someone else tells us what he or she hears, and, as soon as we are told, we can hear what, heretofore, has been a mystery word to us. The International Phonetics Association convention was designed to translate the sounds independent of the particulars of the language so long as sounds can be parsed into separate words. This separation is impossible, for example, when the gap between words is missing, such as when French speakers make a "liaison." For example, where a novice in French hears one sound such as in trwazã, a native speaker would transcribe it as two words, *trois ans* (three years). Already the difference between the singular *an* and the plural *ans* cannot be heard, it is undecidable; the difference becomes decidable only *in context* (here the numeral *trois,* three). Very different contexts are required for hearing diferãs as intended, which can be transcribed as both *différence* and *différance,* a (non-) word that Jacques Derrida has created to make both a philosophical point and postmodern furor.[7]

The reading of this first transcript fragment shows how we can listen to overhear others and understand the mechanism that makes for the unfolding of the conversation. If, instead, I were to interpret the utterance of each speaker, then in all likelihood I would not be able to understand the changes *internal* to the situation but only how my own interpretations—created outside of and superposed on the situation—link to each other. In fact, as I elaborate in Chapter 9, speaking is existentially grounded in hearing and listening, themselves grounded in understanding. What a speaker makes available to his or her interlocutor(s), he or she also makes available to us, to our listening and hearing. The interlocutor acts upon and reacts to what the other has made available, rather than to the purported contents of the mind that is not available in the situation but that I have interpretively laid on top of it. This does not prevent speakers from thinking about the intentions another person might have, but, in most instances, conversations are so fast that we cannot deliberate and thoroughly reflect upon what is said; we simply hear and participate, sometimes asking when we have not heard what the other has said or when we cannot make sense of the other's utterances. In such cases, we might ask, not unlike C in Fragment 1.1a, "what do you mean like?"

In the previous paragraph I state that, generally, there is no time-out to reflect and deliberate what another person has said. This, as we know, is the case for most conversations that we have in the course of a given day. When I meet my neighbor who says: "How do you do? What a nice day today?" then I do not have to stop and think what he might have said (meant). I hear and I know even without thinking any further what he has said and I respond without hesitation, "but there is still a chill in the air, the wind's coming off the ocean." But we also know that there are silences in conversations. (Silence, too, is an existential that allows us to better understand the nature of speech and language.) Are the individuals taking time to interpret? Or are there other processes at work that cannot be described by the deliberate expounding of a text? But again, I have moved too quickly and I need to slow down my reading of the fragment before I can move on.

What kind of situation might have generated the videotape that was the source of the transcription? Who might the speakers T, C, and Ch be? (And not knowing what kind of situation it was, we would have to make inferences that the speakers present do not have to make.) When we look at the fragment as a whole, we can see that there is something like a question (indicated by the interrogative "what"), followed by a question on the part of the respondent (indicated by the same interrogative "what"), succeeded by two more instantiations of fragments with the same interrogative "what" before the second speaker C offers a single word, repeated by the first speaker, who provides another slot ("and …?") that is completed by a third speaker. We may be reminded of the children's game *Do You See What I See?* in which children look around in the room or around the place where they find themselves and ask one another the question embodied in the name of the game. Here, the game is "what did we say that group was about?" Then there is a sequence of exchanges before C provides the searched-for item, confirmed by T, as indicated in the repetition of the item. But C does not provide the entire item, which T indicates by offering a slot, which Ch then fills—though the transcription breaks here so that we do not know whether this is the item that T was seeing/seeking/thinking about. This example is illustrative because it shows how children, in playing this game, enact its rules, turn sequences, even without knowing any speech act or language theory at all.

There are other possibilities as well. Those familiar with educational research may be reminded of more. There is a sequential pattern of turn-taking typical for schools, where the teacher is asking a question (i.e., *I*nitiates a sequence), a student provides an answer (i.e., *R*esponds), and the teacher assesses (i.e., *E*valuates) what has been said. This turn-taking sequence has become known under the acronym IRE (or I–R–E). When the student does not provide the already prefigured and sought-for answer, then there might be a more or less extended exchange until the answer slot is filled so that the teacher can evaluate it as correct. In the present case, this would mean that C has only partially answered correctly. In following the repeated word "square" with a (dangling) "and" that requires something else to be added by this or another student, the teacher would then have made available to students that the answer given so far is only partially correct and that more is required. We do not need to know what she thinks at that instant. What she wants, her intention, is written all over *the situation* and the resources it provides for marking, re-marking, and remarking the sense of any utterance made. But to recognize the resources *as* resources, cultural competence is required. Here, children already come with the competencies of understanding when their answers are incorrect or incomplete even if the respectiéve adult, parent, or teacher, does not articulate the evaluation as such.

"Words do not make a situation" much like a swallow does not make summer. If we had only words available, then interaction participants would be in the situation that we are in right now with the transcript that provides us only words. But we do not know what the conversation is about. There is something about squares and cubes, and the participants have talked about these things. "Square" and "cube" apparently are also the names of something, a group, written on a card. Whereas we can imagine possible situations that might have produced the talk, what we imagine is only possible. But interaction participants experience themselves in real rather than in possible situations. They are likely to know what "that group" is and "is about." They know *definitely* what "the card" is, as we can see from the turns of C and Ch, rather than having to hypothesize about it. T definitely knows what "the group" and "the card" are, because she/he can ask the question presupposing that "the group" and "the card" are available in the same way for C, Ch, and anyone else present to the conversation. The upshot of this analysis is that communication is not made by words. There is *more* to communication, and this more is likely to be found in other aspects of talk (language) not transcribed—e.g., the prosody—and in aspects of the *con*text that is an integral part of the communication. It is found there, available in situation (context), because the interaction participants apparently make use of it for marking, re-marking, and remarking sense definitively without the need to interpret. So what more is there? Let us return to the videotape and add a few more layers of aspects available to the interaction participants.

From mystery to classroom episode

Communication generally and talk—*parole*, spoken language—more specifically are frequently treated as if speakers were computers spilling the contents of their minds into "external representations," language, gestures, and the like. It is an Aristotelian conception of sound-words as the symbols of the states of the soul. At best, I take this to be a hypothesis open to empirical work. In over two decades of analyzing thousands of hours of videotape, I found overwhelmingly more disconfirming than confirming evidence for such a hypothesis. People act in their respective here-and-nows not as computers, cogitating every move before acting or speaking. Rather, people are situated in their familiar worlds; and it is precisely because these worlds are so familiar—always already populated with others, with significations, and with intentions—that they can presuppose these worlds to be available to others as well. These shared worlds are available objectively to all participants, where the adverb "objectively" means that interaction participants can point to and point out something materially concrete, including sound-words, that is, whatever is relevant to them, then and there. To do so, they draw on anything available in the situation as a resource, which, precisely because it is materially and objectively available, as an object, is so also to anyone else. This is clearly evident in the following when we take another look at the now familiar fragment, which leads us from it being a mystery episode to an actual classroom episode. The articulation of *con*text turns mystery into reality.

The episode in Fragment 1.1a was recorded in a second-grade class where the teacher opens the lesson by announcing that they are beginning a new unit called *geometry*. The teacher then invites the children to a task, where they have to get up from their place in a big circle to pull a "mystery object" from a black plastic bag into which they reach without looking. They then either group the mystery object with an existing set of objects, each collected on a colored sheet of construction paper, or begin a new group. The teacher takes the first turn by placing an object; the number of collections and the number of objects in collections subsequently increases over time and as each child takes a turn. The episode comes from Connor's turn. Connor initially places his cube in its own group but, upon the teacher's request to reconsider, eventually places it on the construction paper where there already are two other cubes (Figure 1.1). The teacher utters what we may hear as a question, "em, an what did we say that group was about" (turn 46). While she is speaking, the teacher stretches out her arm, points toward the objects on the floor, then toward what becomes the end of the utterance, makes a tiny circular movement with her index finger, as if circling the denoted group from afar. Although the pitch of her voice drops toward the end of the utterance, in the way it does in our culture for a declarative statement, we can *hear* her ask a question, grammatically achieved by the interrogative pronoun "what." (The transcription conventions are the same throughout this book and available in the appendix.)

Fragment 1.1c

46   T: em an ↑what did [₁we say that [₂group was about.]
                    [₁((points toward objects on the floor,
         Figure 1.1, maintained until turn 51))
                             [₂((makes tiny circular movement with
         index finger))
47   (1.00)
48   C: <<p>what do you [₃mean li[₄ke?>]]
                             [₃((touches "his" cube, Figure 1.2))
                                [₄((looks up to T))
49   T: ^[₄WHAt] ↑was the (0.15) ^WHAt ↑did
         we put for the name of that group.
50   (1.51)
51   whats written on the] [₅card.]
         ((still points))   ₁] [₅((Pulls hand back, no longer points))
52   (0.26)
53   C: <<pp>s::::::><<p>quares>–
54   T: ˇsquare [ˇan::d
                    [((Cheyenne has moved forward, jutting her index finger
         repeatedly to the card next to the cubes inscribed "square, cube"))
55   J: cubes.

Figure 1.1 Pointing to the groups of objects on the floor, the teacher asks Connor, currently in the center of the circle of children (omitted from the drawing), a question about "that group."

There is a pause of one second, which is, conversationally speaking, just about the standard maximum silence in conversations and more than most teachers tend to wait, before Connor, in a tiny voice, takes his turn, "what do you mean like." Here, then, rather than furnishing some entity that would correspond to the "what" that the teacher is asking about, Connor in turn asks what we may hear as a question, flagged both by the same interrogative pronoun "what" and by the pitch that moves upward as it nears the end of the utterance as it would in a question (see the question mark at the end of his utterance). He also touches "his" cube and then looks up gazing in the direction of the teacher (Figure 1.2). The teacher begins even before Connor has completed his turn. She uses the same interrogative pronoun, "what was the" but then briefly stops and begins again, "what did we put for the name of that group?" (turn 49). Again, our cultural competence allows us to hear a question even though, as indicated in the transcript by the period, the pitch of her voice drops toward the end of the utterance.

There is an even longer pause than before, a pause substantially exceeding the 0.7 seconds that teachers tend to allow before asking another student or before they themselves provide the answer. The teacher asks again for something using the interrogative pronoun "what," followed by a determination that describes the thing asked for to be written on the card (turn 51). Her arm, heretofore stretched out with the index finger pointing toward the objects on the floor, withdraws. There is a brief pause before, almost inaudibly, Connor begins with a long "s" sound that turns into "squares" (turn 53). The teacher repeats the word in its singular form, "square" and continues, "and?" (turn 54). We can hear the second word as a question because of the intonation, which first descends within the word and rises again as it completes the sound. Rather than Connor, it is Cheyenne who fills the empty slot following the teacher's "and" by pointing to the label next to the group where the words "square, cube" are inscribed (in Figure 1.2 covered by Connor's arm); Jane also answers, but articulates what we hear as the word "cubes." In the following sections, I articulate a variety of issues emerging from this episode that are subsequently elaborated in the remaining chapters of this book.

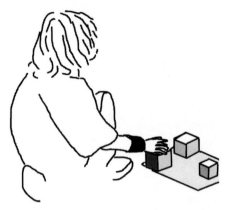

Figure 1.2 Connor touches one of the objects in "that group" and thereby exhibits his orientation to the teacher's request.

Communicating is talking, intonating, gesturing, seeing

In the previous section of this chapter, we see that the words, already translations of sound into a linguistic code—here the one that constitutes the English language—only get us a certain distance in understanding what is happening in the episode. Interaction participants have available more than sound to orient others, act toward others, engage them, and so on. They always already find themselves in a world full of resources for marking, re-marking, and remarking sense and signification; and this world has a history that the participants have experienced together. Some of these resources are produced in the course of speaking, though speakers often are not conscious of these productions (e.g., prosody, gesticulations, "body language"). Other resources are available in the setting and can be brought, through joint orientation, into the conversation to mark, re-mark, and remark the sense required for producing the situation for what it recognizably is and becomes. In this situation, what the interaction participants produce is a geometry lesson; and they do so recognizably, that is, anybody could have walked into the room and noted that this is a geometry lesson rather than some other lesson or some other form of gathering (especially given the fact that the meeting is held in a building called "school" with all the characteristics that such buildings tend to have in North America).

When the teacher begins turn 46, Connor looks at the group of cubes in front of him, thereby communicating his attention to them. (Readers note that we slid from the talk about "that" and "what" to the group of "cubes.") As the teacher utters the two first sounds ("an what"), Connor begins to lift his head so that his gaze meets hers. The teacher raises her hand and arm, which, while she utters "did we say," projects forward (Figure 1.3a). Connor now looks squarely at her as she utters "that group" and points (bottom image of Figure 1.3a) before continuing, "was about," and making a circular movement with the index finger while barely displacing the arm (Figure 1.3b). During the pause that follows, Connor's gaze returns to the objects, which he then touches as he utters his question (turn 48).

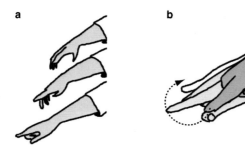

Figure 1.3 a The teacher projects her arm and hand forward until it points in the general direction of groups of objects on the floor (see Figure 1.1).

  b The teacher makes a circling gesture, which iconically represents a group.

This entire event, marked by the utterance "and what did we say that group was about," has lasted but 2.43 seconds. Yet it is a complex and coordinated phenomenon, not unlike a dance. There is an interchange of communicative resources that goes far beyond the presence of simple words; and, most importantly, the interchange goes both ways simultaneously, even though only one person is having a turn at talk at that instant and, thereby, concretizing the possibilities of language. That is, although it is *one* person's turn at talk, communication actually goes *both* ways and without interruption. This, as I elaborate in Chapter 4, has tremendous implications for how we have to think about communication generally, the effect on the Other, and the relationship of agency and passivity involved in speaking/listening.

At the instant that the teacher begins her turn at talk, Connor exhibits attention to the group of objects. As his head and gaze move upward, he not only comes to see his teacher and the movements of her arm and hand, but also he signals attention to her communicative effort. In being oriented toward Connor, the teacher, too, makes available that he has *her* full attention. As the words unfold from her lips, the hand and arm also begin to move, orienting Connor—and anyone else who may watch the scene—to something in the prolongation of her index finger. Using an index finger to point orients others, in almost all cultures, to something to be found in the setting or indicates some direction. That is, the teacher uses an indexical gesture to point to something in the material world. What might that thing (process) be that the teacher is pointing to? From the perspective of the audience, this is not necessarily clear. In the present instance, the teacher sits about two meters from Connor. Her pointing could orient him and other students to a variety of things. But because the audience can assume that the teacher communicates with a purpose, there is, therefore, something in the setting in the general direction of the pointing worth being pointed to. This thing, whatever it is, therefore *motivates* the pointing, and the pointing motivates the thing. This is a chicken-and-egg situation that the audience generally, and Connor more specifically, will pragmatically solve only to engage in some form of repair should it turn out that what they have been looking at is not what the pointing person has intended them to. This analysis, therefore, shows that it is not just the words or the gesture or the combination of the two that we need to take into account—as others have suggested, not surprisingly, after analyzing people who told stories in rooms without any features (e.g., McNeill 2002). The things that we perceptually identify as making this world, here the objects marked and those remaining unmarked and constituting the ground, themselves are an *integral* part of the ongoing communication. They constitute the *con*text, the text surrounding the text of talk, that allows participants to the setting to mark, re-mark, and remark the sense in and of the ongoing conversation.

Connor shows that he attends to the teacher's question, orienting himself toward the objects before him, that is, the group to which he has added his cube. He not only looks at the group of cubes, thereby following the teacher's gesture until it meets something consistent with "that group" and with the circular gesture, but also he places his hand on one of its constituents (Figure 1.2). After articulating and exhibiting his orientation, he withdraws his hand from the cube and raises his gaze to meet that of his teacher. He thereby exhibits a change in orientation away from "that group" generally (gaze, hand) and to the teacher (gaze, body orientation). His body orientation has not always been toward the teacher, but, during his turn with the object, he also makes repeated sideward glances to other students, right after talking, as if checking the impact his talk has had on his peers. He thereby exhibits attention to their attention as well.

But pointing itself is not clear: what is it that someone points to, especially when there is a (considerable) distance between the pointing entity (finger, head) and the referent (object referred to)? When the teacher responds to Connor's question about what she has meant by reiterating "what was the– what did we put for the name of that group" and while continuing to point, Connor returns his gaze to the objects in front of him. In the pause that follows, he looks up again in the direction of the teacher, who then provides him with another installment of the question in yet another form, "what's written on the card?" Connor exhibits attention to the question by orienting his gaze back to the objects at his feet. He utters "squares," while bringing his gaze back to meet that of the teacher, as if looking for a sign: about the correctness of the response he has given.

In the present instance, there are two more resources that orient Connor and other students toward some more specific thing: the teacher says "that group" and, immediately thereafter, makes a circular movement with her index finger (Figure 1.3b). Circles are figures that *en*close something. This gesture is therefore a presentation, iconically related to something that is closed, like a group is represented in a Venn diagram.[8] The gesture depicts something of a circular shape or at least closed nature. Here, that something may be a group of objects, because of the temporal proximity of "that group" and the figurative gesture drawing in the air an ephemeral closed curve. But this gesture is not merely iconic, indicating some closed entity: it also has indexical function (a) as each position of the finger corresponds to a position in or around the object to be found, and (b) it is pointing to something that is circular or closed.

In fact, it might slip from our attention that the teacher does not just point by means of gestures, she also points by means of her orientation. In keeping her body such that it squarely faces Connor and the group of objects to which he has added his cube, she orients participants and onlookers (e.g., analysts watching the videotape) in the general direction of the student. The body orientation, therefore, is consistent with the various forms of orienting Connor to "that group"; she exhibits full attention rather than split attention, as she might do when she simply turns the head to coordinate with the other teacher sitting to her right. In the latter case, her body articulates attention to the children, whereas her gaze seeks some form of information from the person with whom she has planned this lesson (a university professor co-teaching the unit). With her body and its orientation, the teacher, therefore, breaks the symmetry of physical space and provides a resource that others can use to re-mark and remark the sense of what the teacher marks with her communication. Pointing, iconic gesturing, body orientation, body position, and other aspects of the body are central to communication; these moments of communication constitute the topic of Chapter 3.[9]

Pointing does not only happen by means of the index finger and the stretched out arm. It also happens with specific words, which linguists have come to call *indexicals* and sometimes *shifters*. In Fragment 1.1c, the indexical "that" is repeatedly employed. It is an indexical that in our Anglo-Saxon culture frequently goes with a pointing finger or other bodily grounded pointing (e.g., the head). Another frequent indexical is "this." The two indexicals do not have the same function and are used in different contexts. "This group" would be an indicator of proximity, spatial or temporal, which can be contrasted with "that group," which is a more *distal* (i.e., distant) one. In the present episode, the teacher says "that group," which suggests that it is a group some distance away from her, which, as we can see from the drawing in Figure 1.1, is farther away than some other groups located closer to her—there are three other groups nearer to her position than the one labeled "square and cube." The term "that" is a shifter, because from Connor's position, the same group more accurately would be referred to as "this group," whereas other groups of objects are further away and, therefore, each could be referred to as "that group." But the shifting could also be in time, so that something more recently talked about would be indexed by the term "this group" whereas another group earlier talked about would be "that group."

There is more information available. When we listen to the speakers—for example, on the videotape—we notice that they do not speak like computers but that their voices have intonations varying across time and speakers. Some of the variations are captured in Fragment 1.1c, where we note some jumps, rising and falling intonations, and changing speech volume (intensity). Thus, we note, for example, that in the teacher's voice, the indexical "what" always differs from the surrounding talk. In turn 46, the pitch jumps by about 43 hertz, that is, by about 22 percent of its original value. Coming together with a spike in speech intensity, the word "what" stands out with respect to the remainder of the turn. Similarly, there are substantial changes in pitch and speech intensity associated with the first two instances of "what" in turn 49. These changes make this interrogative stand out against everything else—we hear them as emphases. They mark the interrogative.

It is the "what" that is emphasized, looking for something as an answer that can fill the slot. It is "what" rather than "where," "who," or "how." "What" is the ordinary interrogative pronoun of neutral gender, generally used with a thing or things, that corresponds to the demonstrative *that*. "What" therefore asks for something consistent with "that group," and it is the "what" that needs to be responded to rather than the fact that participants have already talked about it before. Intonation and its function in organizing social interactions is the topic of Chapter 7.

Intonation is used in other places as well, constituting a way of providing a resource for making distinctions. Thus, when the teacher utters "squares" with a falling and rising intonation, we can hear it both as an affirmation, a falling pitch generally characterizing statements, and as a question, a rising pitch generally characterizing questions. This intonation itself might suffice in a situation to both affirm and question a response. But in the present case, there is actually a duplication of the intonation preceding what comes to be treated as an open slot. Thus, the teacher utters "and," initially with a falling then rising pitch. Grammatically, the utterance is unfinished; there is something that needs to follow the "and." But the intonation is rising, as it would be in a question. Cheyenne provides the (what turns out to be the sought-for) answer by pointing to "the card" on which "square, cube" is inscribed, whereas Jane utters the second word not yet articulated verbally but perceptually available on the card. (Not presented here, the teacher subsequently provides signals that these answers are acceptable and accepted.) This case of the rising intonation is opposite to the one we have observed earlier, pointing us to the fact that grammar (interrogatives) and intonation play together to constitute how something is to be heard, for example, as a question or statement. Thus, we can hear a question being asked even if there is no interrogative (e.g., turn 54) and we can hear a question when there is an interrogative but with an intonation characteristic of a declarative statement rather than a question. The question "When is grammar?" is treated in great depth in Chapter 8.

"That," "this," "there," "here," and so on are not the only indexical expressions that exist in a language, and some others are used in this episode as well. Thus, who "we" (turns 46, 49) is depends on the present speaker and situation, thereby making this an indexical term. The "value" of the signifier "we," the persons thereby denoted, can be ascertained only in situation or by knowing the situation, which provides the *con*text that allows us to hear and evaluate this text. In any image, what we see, the gestalt, the figure, always appears against an indeterminate ground; in fact, figure presupposes an indeterminate ground. This is no different, though often not addressed in theories of communication, in the case of text, which requires indeterminate *con*text (i.e., ground) to produce its figurative effect. In the present instance, no *interpretation* is needed to know whom the signifier "we" denotes. Those saying and hearing the "we" immediately know who is included and who is excluded by the sound-word "we." Connor says "you," and those present know that he refers to the teacher, though he may be using the same sound-word to designate one of his peers only a little later. In a stronger sense, the other words, too, are indexicals figuring against a shared ground (the *con*text), because what is written on "the card" can be known only in the shared presence of the situation. Even though there are multiple cards on the floor, the participants know which of the cards is meant, as seen in Cheyenne's act of pointing, which picks out precisely the one that the teacher apparently wants and which contains the word that Jane sounds out.

Making context, doing schooling

Up to this point in the analysis of the episode, I merely focus on the concrete material resources that are available in the setting as signs that contribute to marking and re-marking sense so that others, too, may remark it. In fact, much of (educational) research on learning is conducted in this way. The episode represented in Fragment 1.1 can, therefore, be thought of as "social," because there clearly is a conversation unfolding in which multiple individuals take part. We may analyze this episode as if it were a self-contained unit and as if questions of the hows and whys of learning could be answered by merely finding out what happens here.

The approach outlined in the previous paragraph leaves unanswered why certain types of individuals do not tend to do well in schools. In the past, girls, for example, have not done so well in science or mathematics, and "socialization" is then used as external *con*text to explain that boys but not girls are encouraged to take things apart, to take risks, and to experiment. But this does not provide a good explanation, because it does not show how children's experiences outside school become a resource in and for their participation within school. Another case consists in what has come to be called the continual reproduction of working class in and through the practices of schooling that are consistent with a middle-class ethos (e.g., Eckert 1989). Again, it does not suffice to show how the students organize themselves differently from middle-class students in out-of-school situations to explain why there appears to be a cultural bias against them when it comes to learning. To be able to make a tight argument that links similarities and differences in root culture with school culture in concrete school-based interactions, we have to show how these different cultures bias against some but not other students. For the case of gender in mathematics learning, a good beginning has been made some time ago (e.g., Walkerdine 1988); but this work has not been continued to any considerable extent. What we really need is a form of analysis that allows us to bring society, with all of its inequities, to bear on the issues of language, learning, and context.

To begin such an analysis, consider this: the participants to the situation in Fragment 1.1c do not just talk for the sake of talking. They talk in a particular institutional setting that their talk simultaneously produces and reproduces. Connor, his teacher, Cheyenne, and Jane do not merely talk cubes and squares, they actually produce a lesson. This lesson is part of a societal activity called schooling.[10] In schooling, society has a mechanism to reproduce its culturally embodied forms of knowing. Those who work as teachers and administrators are part of the middle class, even though in more or less exceptional cases, they may have come from the working and under classes.[11]

In the research literature, institutional talk involving teachers and students generally is taken in a causal manner, meaning that the "teacher" and "students" behave in the ways they do *because* they enact the roles of teacher and student. For example, claims are rapidly made that a teacher "scaffolds" a student or a student group without showing, in careful and detailed analysis, what the participants to the conversation are *actually* doing. But this is not a very good way of thinking about schools, schooling, and the conversations that we find in them—and this not only because there are exceptions where teachers and students do not behave according to what we might think to be standard rule- and role-governed behavior. Thus, for example, analysts should be able to show, in a convincing manner, the scaffolding, or whatever is going on, in Fragment 1.1a without knowing who "the teacher" is. This is so, not only across different teachers and students, but also for the same individuals when they move from one setting in the school to another. It is, therefore, better to think about institutional talk as the phenomenon that brings about the institution. Schools exist only in and as a result of the talk-in-interaction that brings them to life. This is precisely the focus of Chapter 2, where I articulate how talking not only produces topics and contents but also, simultaneously, reproduces and transforms societal institutions.[12] In fact, the situation structures the linguistic forms in which the topic is developed, as I show in Chapter 6 concerned with the production of the auto/biographical genre during an interview involving a student and his teacher who is also a researcher.

The teacher in Fragment 1.1c has come to the school to do her job, which includes, on this day, the introduction to geometry. In her actions as a teacher, she orients toward schooling generally, and the task of introducing children to geometry specifically, much in the same way that we orient toward producing a nice meal when we go to the kitchen to make dinner. But this orientation does not *cause* specific outcomes. In the same way that we may end up with a spoiled soufflé or a burned pizza; the lesson of the day might fail, there might be chaos, children might get emotionally or physically hurt, and so on. But the participants do in fact orient toward *doing schooling,* which may include resisting and even undermining what the institutionally designated teacher explicitly intends to do. This orientation does not generally include an awareness of the inequities that are reproduced in and through the schooling process—which is why critical scholars in particular call for structural (Marxist) analyses that allow uncovering the hidden determination not available to our everyday coping with the world. The feminist sociologist Dorothy E. Smith (2005) therefore advocates institutional ethnography, which attends both to the world as experienced by people *and* the hidden determinations that, in fact, constitute the practices of power.

Looking at the episode provided in terms of the institutional roles would obscure our analysis in the sense that we would no longer be attuned to the reverse teaching that may occur. For example, Connor is actually teaching the teacher so that she understands what he needs: he makes salient that he does not understand the question she asks in turn 46, and, in her next turn, she makes several efforts to translate her question into another question, presumably asking for the same thing despite the difference in the form and constitution. Toward the end, we see that she at least somewhat succeeds, as Connor provides a partial response, which the teacher acknowledges only to open the opportunity for producing the complete response, which both Jane and Cheyenne achieve in different ways.

The teacher and students communicate as the need evolves. In this particular situation, the teacher asks Connor a question to allow him to complete the task, which is to place his mystery object appropriately, that is, consistent with the canon of geometry, and to provide a reason for the placement. Because this is supposed to be an introduction to geometry, the declared intent (she has said so prior to the lesson) is to have children provide reasons that are consistent with geometry rather than the reasons that they naturally provide, which, in this lesson, includes size and color. Connor responds. In this exchange they achieve an instant of schooling; and they do so in a recognizable way. To achieve schooling, the cooperation and collusion of all parties is needed. This may not be immediately apparent in this situation, but it would be with older students who may act in ways so that the intended curriculum (lesson plan) is not, and cannot be, achieved. Thus, in Chapter 7, I take a close look at a conflict between a student and her teacher, the solidarity that exists within the peer group, and the means that allow the conflictual situation to be abated and made to disappear.

Translating

In the previous section, I show how the teacher, by rearticulating her question differently, actually engages in an act of translation at the heart of the language that constitutes, for many in this class, their mother's tongue. Learning *a* language means learning *the* language, the mother's tongue; and learning *the* language means learning languages, as there is always the possibility of saying something differently, which is the very condition for saying it radically different, in another person's tongue, another mother tongue. Speech, more than awakening knowledge already within the children, teaches speaking and, therefore, teaches the teaching itself. Speaking with mathematicians, we use a different form of English than speaking with a car mechanic or with our family doctor. In each case, the language is specialized—made thematic in the notion of *Discourse* with a capital D—and, for newcomers, has to be translated so that it is understandable in the root language. But the root languages themselves, our mother tongues, are learned while speaking the mother tongue. The language of instruction in the tongue makes use of the tongue; and it does so in different senses of the word.

In the preceding sections, we encountered translation in at least two ways, paralleling the two types of limits and problems that come with translation: reading and teaching (Derrida 1986). The first type of translation occurs between languages, such as when the German texts of Martin Heidegger are translated into English and then are drawn on in texts of the new language where they are made available to speakers of another language. Another form of translation occurs when we—asked what we mean in the way the teacher is asked by Connor what she means—(re-) state what we really meant by saying what we said without actually having said so. Teaching generally has as its ideal that such translation is exhaustive, leading to an erasure of language itself, treated as a mere tool to express content and to mediate between minds. I begin with the second case.

First, following the teacher's question "what did we say that group was about?" Connor responds by asking, "what do you mean like?" With this question, Connor acknowledges that the teacher has said something, where the following events show that he has understood her as having asked a question. But here, he not only acknowledges that the teacher has said something but also queries the teacher about what she has meant. That is, he is, therefore, asking his teacher to translate what she has said into another form of English that renders *the same*, but in a different way. In turn 49, the teacher provides a translation of the question in turn 46. In fact, turn 49 makes sense only if it is understood as a translation of the earlier question, for Connor has asked the teacher what she means, indicating he does not know what she means, and now asks to articulate in a new way the "what" of the previous question. The verb "to mean" derives from the Proto-Indo-European root *men-*, to think, to mind, to be spiritually active. In some languages, it has given rise to uses equivalent to the English "to understand." The question "what do you mean like?", therefore, also asks what the teacher thinks/understands and to share this thinking/understanding with the student. True speech teaches; and here it teaches the teacher how to teach so that Connor can learn.

Excerpt from Fragment 1.1c

→ 46 T: em an ↑what did [₁we say that [₂group was about.]
              [₁((points toward objects on the floor,
          Figure 1.1, maintained until turn 51))
                            [₂((makes tiny circular movement with
          index finger))
      47   (1.00)
      48 C: <<p>what do you [₃mean li[₄ke?>]]
                          [₃((touches "his" cube, Figure 1.2))
                            [₄((looks up to T))
→ 49 T: ^[₄WHAt] ↑was the (0.15) ^WHAt ↑did
          we put for the name of that group.

The crucial point in the utterance is the "what," a neutral interrogative used to ask for something. The statement, therefore, brings to the fore that Connor understands there to be something that the teacher intends to communicate (the "what") but also that he does not understand what it is. That is, he points out that he understands her to have *intended* saying something but that—from his perspective—she has not said it. He is requesting her to express the same "what" differently, in different words all the while meaning the same. Some readers may suggest that this teacher did not express herself well—or alternatively that Connor has troubles of this or that kind that do not allow him to understand something already clearly expressed. But this would not get us to the heart of the fact that there is always another way of saying the same thing, some of which are understood and others are not. The crucial point is that we cannot ever be certain which of the different ways of saying something our interlocutors will understand.

The ideal of translation is that it leaves untouched the content—machine translations implicitly or explicitly are based on this presupposition. But specialists and scholars know that translation does not say the same but changes what is said and how it is said—as can be seen from the following (ever-too-brief) analysis. The first version (turn 46) appears to be asking for the referent of "that group," that is, the referent of whatever is denoted by the grouping of objects on the colored sheet. The second, translated version (turn 49) asks for the name of the/that group; that is, the question asks for a category name, the form of the sign that denotes the "about" articulated in turn 46. In the third, translated version (turn 51), the question asks for something that is written on the card next to the/that group. That is, the third version asks for something on the card, which is, through the translation and association with turn 49, taken to be *also* the name of the group that denotes something else asked for in turn 46. That is, the translation constitutes both a shift in signifiers (articulation of the question) and the signifieds. Moreover, it is not only the signified that has been changed but also the very signifying relation. That is, in taking the three versions to be translations of each other, translation augments, supplements, and displaces the respective sense of each utterance. In this translation, therefore, both the original and the target language (phrases) are changed—a point Walter Benjamin (1972) makes in a frequently cited text on translation between languages (the text is a preface to a German translation of the French poet Charles Baudelaire). But, in the present instance, all of this has happened *within* English so that we find here precisely the problems that we also encounter in translations from another language into English or from English into another language.

The translation turns out to be successful in the sense that Connor eventually answers, at least partially, in the prefigured way; and other students have understood the question as well as indicated in their providing the remainder that completes the question–answer pair. But the point is, as I emphasize throughout this book, that this slippage—where there is always another way of saying something, always another translation possible that more or less clearly expresses for the respective recipient what is to be communicated—*comes with the very nature of the word, which is that of non-self-identity.* A word not identical to itself, you may ask.[13]

This is precisely the point that scholars such as Jacques Derrida and Mikhail Bakhtin make throughout their works taken in their entirety. Both scholars, similarly grounded in semiology founded by the Swiss linguist Ferdinand de Saussure, articulate and exhibit the consequences of a sign (signifier/signified) that is different within itself. Any sign embodies a difference within itself synchronically (different for author and audience) and diachronically (different even if the signifier is repeated identically within seconds). This difference gives rise to the possibility of translation and to the impossibility of saying anything unequivo-cally, that is, in a way so that it cannot be misunderstood *in all cases.*

The non-self-identity of a word has serious and not yet recognized consequences for education, scholarship, and human conduct in all walks of life more generally. We are all familiar with situations where someone—e.g., a teacher, or professor—is blamed for not having expressed him/herself clearly enough to be understood. This blame will be upheld even though others in the same room hearing the same sound-words have perfectly well understood what the speaker was saying. What was said has been clear to some and unclear to others. In each case, the speaker is "blamed." Such a position does not capture the fact that a word is always already straddling the speaker/writer and listener/reader, in which case there are as many words as there are speaker/listener pairs. The very concept and phenomenon of language not only implies but presupposes such plurality. In the very utterance of the word, language changes, and with it, the way one word relates to others and, because of the mutual constitution of words, the nature of the word itself.

Second, translations of works on the philosophy of language do not neces-sarily facilitate the building of appropriate theories of language, learning, and context. An interesting case in point is where problems arise from the English word "meaning," which students are said to construct, make, deconstruct, and the like. Translations actually increase the problems of studying learning because other languages do not have an equivalent of this term. In French, for example, there exists the expression *vouloir dire* as in "qu'est-ce que tu veux dire?" (what do you want to say? what do you mean?). *Vouloir dire*, as a noun, sometimes is translated as "meaning," but in other books translated from French, "intention" is used instead. French authors—and scholars following them including Mikhail Bakhtin—use *référence, sens,* and *signification.*[14] In German, there is the verb *meinen*, as in "was meinst du?" (what do you mean?), but *Meinung* actually translates as "opinion, belief." Germans use the terms *Sinn* (Fr. *sens*, Engl. *sense*) and *Bedeutung*, the latter having in its semantic field the noun and verb *Deuten/ deuten*, that is, to point, and therefore would have its equivalent in "refer-ence." To confuse matters even more, a recognized German dictionary suggests *Bedeutung* as synonymous with *Sinn*. The most problematic issue arises when the same word in one language (French, German) is translated into different words in English, or different words with very different sense and connotations in the source language are rendered using the same word in the target language. Thus, Heidegger's *Bedeutung* sometimes is translated as "meaning," sometimes as "sense," and sometimes as "signification." It turns out that homonymy (using the same word to denote different things) and synonymy (using different words to denote the same things) not only have already been discussed by Aristotle but also have been recognized to constitute effects of the very possibility of language (Derrida 1972). Thus, we are faced with a truly babelish confusion, which any useful theory of *language*, learning, and context needs to deal with explicitly rather than brush it under the carpet.

The problems of translation come to be compounded when there are multiple translations in a series of languages leading to a continual shifting and slipping of words. Thus, for example, Mikhail Bakhtin read de Saussure in French, adopting the latter's French concepts. In *Le marxisme et la philosophie du langage* (Bakhtine [Volochinov] 1977)—the French version of *Marksizm I filosofija jazyka* (Volochinov 1929/1973)—the Saussurian terms *sens* and *signification* are retranslated into French. In the English version, however, the word meaning is everywhere, sometimes translating *sens* and at other times translating *signification*.[15]

Learning

By participating in the geometry lessons, Connor learns (e.g., Roth and Thom 2009). Preceding the featured part of his turn, Connor has placed his mystery object with the collection that it ultimately (at the end of the lesson) ends up in. But at this point, there has not been an explicit articulation of the predicate or predicates that make *this* object a consistent member of the collection named "square, cube." What the present part of the episode achieves, in and as a result of its sensuous work, is this: the production of an answer that allows the previously articulated predicates of the collection also to be predicates of the object at hand. The object turns from a mystery object into an object that belongs to a known group or collection that already has known predicates and two names. Or, to put it in terms of the theoretical edge McDermott (1993) proposes, a category already exists and through the children's work, becomes perceptually embodied in the collection labeled "square, cube." This category, therefore, has "acquired" another one of the mystery objects. It will continue to "acquire a certain proportion of [the category] as long as it is given life in the organization of tasks, skills, and evaluations" (McDermott 1993: 271) in the current lesson. This acquisition of another aspect of the world by language allows us to understand that "language, far from presupposing universality and generality, first makes them possible" (Levinas 1971: 45). It is language that enables universality and generality and thereby collects students' experiences rather than plurality of experiences that produces the universality and generality that comes with "concepts." In Chapter 2, I show that language itself provides the resources for capturing topics even if a person has never talked about them before.

In the present situation, the agreement between existing class and the mystery object arises from a series of sequentially uttered alternatives and in the course of sequentially uttered repetitions of (a) requests to state the name(s) of the collection, and then (b) assertions that the names/criteria are also suitable for the new object. It is only when the mystery object is identified as extending the existing collection of the squares/cubes that it turns from a mystery to a knowable and known object; and, by becoming a member of an existing collection and adopting its name, it also becomes a geometrical object from the perspective of the knowledgeable observer, analyst, curriculum planner, and teacher. For the students in this situation, the difference between learning a (geometrical) language and learning their way around the world (geometry class) thereby becomes undecidable.

A central part of learning to do geometrical classification is the association of objects with names. This is so because category names ultimately become metonymic devices for referring to and denoting geometrical classes of objects. Requesting and producing the names and predicates for the emerging collections of objects also is an important aspect of this lesson generally, exemplified in this episode specifically. Here, the classification episode continues as the teacher asks Connor what the indicated group has been said to be about (turn 46). After a one-second pause, Connor, however, asks her what she means. By querying "what do you mean like?" he not only queries her about the sense of what she has said but also he (a) marks what she has said as not meaningful, and (b) requests that the meaning be stated more clearly. Rather than bringing the teaching–learning sequence to a close, he extends and opens it up further by rendering problematic the content of the preceding talk. Here, he questions the nature of the question, that is, what she is asking him about is not yet evident. The teacher clearly replies using a category of an acceptable answer ("the name of that group"). But rather than asking "what … that group was about?" she now makes the request to produce the name of the group that the second, support-ing teacher has written earlier on a sheet of paper and has placed right next to the colored sheet with the cubes. When there is no response, the lead teacher exhibits preference for self-correction by saying, "what's written on the card." Connor utters "squares," which the teacher acknowledges by repeating. But she also denotes his response as incomplete "squares and …" This type of turn at talk constitutes a teaching strategy: an utterance incomplete by design, produced to allow students to self-correct by offering a slot ("…") that they can complete. As Connor does not answer, another student (Cheyenne) proffers the called-for sec-ond term ("cube," turn 56). In both instances, the teacher repeats and thereby positively evaluates the utterance of the previous speaker. It is precisely in such situations that students learn to associate new entities with given names, which, thereby, come to name categories that can accumulate further things and denote further situations in which the names turn out to be useful.

In this situation, although Connor has indeed clearly classified the object, the unfolding events make evident to everybody present that it is not an appro-priate classification in the normative framework hidden from the students but apparently attended to by the teacher. Learning means extending existing capaci-ties—here to classify according to different criteria (predicates) using different sound-words in different situations. Repeatedly, Connor exhibits bewilderment with the teacher's questions about the predicates of the group where his object should be placed ("what do you mean like?" [turn 48] and "like what do you mean?" [turn 64]). It is as if the bewilderment on his part is produced by the sup-pression of his classification and the predicate he uses while retaining a sense of what this game is about. These utterances are also instructions to the teacher con-cerning how to teach him. Here, he requests the teacher to explicate what she has meant to say before. That is, he explicitly instructs the teacher *what* is required for him to make the lesson contribution that will allow them to go on because they have arrived at an endpoint for which the accomplishment of the instruction "explain your thinking" is an adequate description. He thereby contributes to the work of teaching by instructing the teacher on how to teach to meet his current learning needs. Speech is magisterial in the sense of pedagogical—and, as this analysis shows, speaking as teaching goes both ways.

Toward a pragmatist position on language, learning, and context

Perhaps influenced by the predominance of the constructivist epistemology in scholarship, perhaps driven by a particularity of North American culture that celebrates the individual who can achieve anything she or he wants to achieve, educational discourses inherently theorize language, learning, and context within an intentionalist (mentalist) orientation. This position, which does not recognize the *passive* genesis of intention, is a central aspect of metaphysical philosophy, with its presuppositions concerning intention of a transcendental mind to express "meaning" in language (Derrida 1967b). There are things, referred to by the term meaning, that students are asked to intentionally construct; and, in the process, they also construct, intentionally, their identities. In fact, this intentionality comes with the noun "construction" and the verb "to construct," in part because of the nature of the terms. Transitive verbs involve agential subjects acting upon objects. We are said to construct something—e.g., knowledge or meaning—with something else. This something else, though often not articulated, cannot be anything other than what students already bring to class. And here we get into trouble—for what students can construct other than everyday knowing if all they can use are their everyday ways of knowing (talking, including their "misconceptions")? My first descriptions in the previous sections already show how complex language, specifically, and communication, more generally, are. In fact, they are so complex that any intentional processing and constructing can only run afoul, incapable of dealing with the mass of information to be tracked and processed. But in everyday coping, we act and speak, without time-out, and always appropriately with respect to the givens, making evident when we lack understanding so that this lack can be repaired. A pragmatist approach, such as the one implicit in my account of Fragment 1.1, appears to have much greater potential for theorizing language, learning, and context than the intentionalist accounts of language and discourse. Presenting a pragmatist approach, which goes against the grain of much of current educational thinking on the topic, is the purpose of this book as a whole.

The essence of my claim may be glossed in this way: *current theories of talking in school classrooms do not and cannot capture essential aspects of the human experience of communicating generally and talking more specifically.* This is because existing approaches to language, learning, and context deal only with the intentional aspects of everyday experience and leave untheorized the essentially unthematized and passive aspects. For example, in everyday situations—including those in science, mathematics, or language immersion classrooms (where students learn school subjects in a second language that is not their mother tongue)—we (speakers) hardly, if ever, have the full script of what we will be saying. Rather, what we are saying emerges from our mouths and prior to what we are aware of. That is, we (speakers) do not select words in the way computer models of cognition do to place them in slots predetermined by a fixed—some say inborn—grammar, but the words generally appear just in time and as needed. Thus, although we have the intention to participate and talk, we are passive with respect to the actual utterance or, for all that matters, with respect to the intention, which we have not itself intended. We, therefore, end up contributing to, and significantly developing, a topic even though we are not planning our utterances ahead of time. This is an important point because although we contribute daily to conversations that we have not planned ahead in our heads, existing theories of language use do not explain how this is possible. The fact that this phenomenon is possible at all lies in the nature of language, learning, and context that I develop in this book.

There is a second dimension to the essential passivity of being in the world that needs to be theorized to understand everyday talk. In speaking, we mobilize *cultural* language and linguistic resources; and we realize/concretize *cultural* possibilities of talking. What we say, therefore, is not entirely our own, because the words we produce have come to us from the culture in which we live; and what we are saying has to be intelligible to those who listen, which means that what we say is constrained in two directions. What we say cannot be so new at all, because the words always already have come from an Other and are designed for an Other who is to understand—it makes no sense to produce gibberish if we intend communicating with another person. Competently speaking, therefore, is not much different from competently navigating other parts of our everyday worlds, where we do not have to stop, think, and reflect, prior to taking action. Thus, speaking is both (a) highly singular, contextual, and situated, and (b) highly conventionalized, intelligible, shared, and historical. But *what* is said cannot be *just* mine—because language expresses the general (Hegel 1979a).

In the preceding sections, we already see that communication cannot be reduced to the production of words. While talking, we also produce a variety of signifiers other than words that listeners take into account without necessarily being conscious thereof (the signifiers or the taking into account). Variations in pitch, speech intensity, and speech rate provide listeners with resources to understand the *what* of the speaker's telling. Pointing and imaging gestures are also pervasive features of communication, in all cultures and even among the blind, who cannot see another's gestures. Thus, we—if sighted—hear a sentence differently if a person produces (ephemeral) quotation marks in the air than if those quotation marks were not present. Body orientation, location, and body configurations are other aspects of the situation that speakers and audiences take into account during conversation. And, most importantly, they take their settings as a topic or background resource in the communicative event. It was a cultural–historical psychologist (Vygotsky [1978]) who suggested that we must not and cannot reduce the communicative situation to words; rather, the communicative situation constitutes a whole that only partially and one-sidedly (i.e., falsely) is represented by one or the other of its dimensions.

There are other contradictions in current theories and treatments of language, learning, and context in school settings. Talk generally is theorized from the perspective of individual intentions, though theorists from very different disciplines have been pointing out for decades that communicative situations are irreducible to individual contributions. In speech act theory (Austin 1962), for example, a *pair* of speaking turns constitutes the minimal unit, the element to be analyzed, rather than the individual utterance. The members of the Bakhtin circle conceptualize speech in the same way. That is, the speech act minimally is distributed across two speakers.[16] In Chapter 4, I expand this unit to consist of at least three turns. This has the consequence that a conversation cannot be broken down into independent contributions as this is being done in the vast majority of educational research (e.g., attributing stretches of interview talk to a student, a teacher, independent of the evolving nature of the talk and independent of the constitutive relations of interlocutors). Rather, there is coherence between consecutive contributions and there are *necessary* rather than arbitrary connections throughout a conversation. In traditional psychological, and even, cultural treatments available in the literature, contributions are often treated as if *independent* individuals were making them (a consequence of taking an intentional and agential research stance and omitting, neglecting, being oblivious to the passive dimensions of participating in conversations). As such, a conversation merely would be the sum total of the utterances participants produced independently and as a consequence of the contents of their minds. Moreover, there is a historical connection where speakers take preceding talk into account but inherently cannot take into account what is going to be said later. Most transcript analyses do not heed to the diachronism at work in conversations, instead treating all text as emanations of rather fixed minds. In Chapter 3, I provide an analysis that irrevocably shows why we have to account for diachronism because thinking itself changes with communication.

There are further aporias—quandaries, perplexing difficulties, insurmountable problems—within current theorizing of language, learning, and context in education. These include, for example, the inner (inherent) contradiction of communication during lessons, where lecturers (teachers, professors) incessantly talk about, and use/refer to, concepts and phenomena unfamiliar to students, who do not speak the (theoretical) discourse that an understanding of the phenomena requires. The difficulties are deepened when students are asked to learn social studies, science, mathematics, or history in a second language, which is the case in immersion classrooms and when new immigrants only at the beginning of their linguistic competence in the language of instruction attend school in their new country. That is, current theories of talking some (school) subject matter *cannot* capture the opportunities and constraints that arise from the increasing linguistic heterogeneities in school classrooms due to the globalization of culture. How should we think about such heterogeneity, always subject to further *métissage* and hybridization? I begin to provide answers to these and related questions in the two final chapters of this book.

2 Making context in talking

Contexting—the present participle of the old English verb "to context" in the sense of "to weave together"—might have been a more apt title for this chapter had it not been for the fact that it is (nearly) obsolete today. It would have been more apt because the main point of the present chapter is that in talking, conversationalists not only produce topics but also the very situation that they are said to be in—a mathematics class, an interview, a lecture, and so forth. That is, in producing texts, conversationalists also produce contexts (in the modern usage), and, in talking, they weave the two together. For Aristotle, *logos* as speech makes something to be seen; in fact, *logos* lets us see something from itself (Heidegger 1977b). But something, a figure, can be seen only against some (unseen, indistinct) ground, which is the source and condition for seeing. Figure and ground are created simultaneously in seeing, in the same way that text and context are created in speaking.

In Chapter 1, I point out how Connor, the other students in his class, and their teacher come together in a particular building that they call their school to *do schooling*. But schools, as institutions, do not exist like boxes into which we walk. If there is nobody else around and we walk into a school, there is nothing to be observed that contributes to the reproduction and transformation of cultural knowledge, the purpose for which schooling has evolved as a human activity in its own right. Schooling comes to life when people act and interact in particular ways: some as students, others as teachers, and still others as administrators. As part of their everyday life, these people interact and communicate. As they talk "business" (mathematics, science, history, English, grammar), they do the business of talk; and they produce the very business that contextualizes them in an activity. That is, social life does not constitute a box: "Through their actions in real places and under real and quite specific conditions of action, social actors instantiate those elusive and invisible structures of social science lore" (Boden 1994: 13). We make institutions in institutionally relevant talking—much as the way we lay the proverbial garden path in walking.

In Fragment 1.1c, we hear the teacher ask a question about something that those present ("we") have said a group was about. Connor accountably displays that he is attending, first by orienting his gaze to the speaker, his teacher, then by looking down in the direction of the objects at his feet recognizably grouped because they all appear on the same sheet of paper, then by placing his hand on the object. By asking what she means, Connor makes available for everyone present to notice not only that he has been attending to his teacher's talk, but also that he is trying to understand. His question is an account of his attending—an engagement in and a production of an instant of schooling. In her question, the teacher asks Connor to do something; to name what "that group" is about. In his response, Connor both accountably responds and assists the teacher in identifying what is needed to move this lesson along. But in this, both not only ask about "what that group is about" and what the other means by "what that group is about," but they also contribute to making a lesson that others can recognize as a lesson in geometry. That is, through their accountable actions—here talk and gestures—the members in this setting contribute to the production of this lesson, which is a concrete realization of schooling generally, and of schooling in this building more specifically. In the process, the participants create the facticity of this lesson such that they and others can report it as an actual event that has happened in the here and now of that school, identifiable in its specificity, for example, by the date and time stamp on the video.

> It is, in other words, in their accountable activities that human actors both produce and expect agency in immediate and distant others who, *through their actions*, constitute the organizations of their society. Through their local activities and accounts, moreover, they create the facticity of "matter of factness" of the world, which they then treat as real and constraining. In phenomenological terms social agents give to their collaborations a kind of retrospective illusion of solidity and facticity.
>
> (Boden 1994: 14, original emphasis)

In Chapter 1, we see that Connor and his teacher specifically, and all human beings generally, produce not just *a* societal situation but also *this* societal organization; they do so on the fly—each second could have been different as life is not determinate like a machine or straightjacket—and through their local and contingent engagement. Such organizations generally, and each concrete situation specifically, therefore, do not surround us like boxes but, if we want to think of them as boxes at all, these boxes are made as we are going about our business. That is, if we think in terms of agency and intentionality, then we have to think about and theorize not only the texts that we produce but also the *con*texts that our texts both presuppose and collaterally produce. The upshot of this is that we can always create the institutions differently from how they are at that instant.

In much of the literature on language, learning, and context, however, the setting is treated like a box into which participants enter but which does not mediate the events and that are not shaped and reshaped by the role-specific actions of those present. The roles are assumed to be fixed—although we have already seen with Connor, second-grade students can and do *actively* contribute to the teaching–learning process by teaching teachers how to be taught. Instead, the conversations of students and their teachers generally are transcribed and featured as if the topic of their talk was all that there is to it. Lessons tend to be taken as a given; and the talk making the lessons tends to be analyzed as if it were about the content alone. In the same way, interviews tend to be taken as a context in which the participants talk about the content that the interviewer has outlined beforehand as the topic of interest. The context is not taken into account and can be seen from the fact that it does not matter to the analyses that knowledge or identity or beliefs are elicited in interviews rather than in some other situation. Knowledge, identity, beliefs, literacy, and so on, are taken as characteristic features of the individuals that move unscathed, together with the latter, across the varying situations that make a life. Thus, one eminent scholar suggests that

> [i]t is almost as if we "videotape" our experiences as we are having them, create a library of such videotapes, edit them to make some "prototypical tapes" or a set of typical instances, but we stand ever ready to add new tapes to our library, re-edit the tapes based on new experiences, or draw out of the library less typical tapes when the need arises.
>
> (Gee 2005: 25)

But we know that in everyday coping, such as when I talk to my neighbor across the street, such videotapes, if they were to exist, do not come to play. We *generally* do not have videotapes running before our eyes, or libraries in our head. Instead, thrown into the world, we act, and in acting, we contribute to producing the situation for what it is. In talking, we produce a neighborly conversation or we have an argument (about whether I should or should not pay for the repairs on the fence) or we come to be shed with insults, in response to which we may shrug shoulders (thereby further enraging the neighbor) or return a shower of insults. We do not have to reflect on the fact that we produce *con*text all the while we produce the text of our talk. That is, we produce a nice neighborly conversation about our advances in the garden, an argument, and so on, all the while talking about the weather, vegetables, or fences. We make and remake situations *in*, *through*, and *for* communicating. Here, the different prepositions are chosen deliberately. We make a situation *in* communicating; we make the situation *through* or *by means of* communicating; and we make the situation *for the purpose of* further communication. Thus, the difference between talk that produces text and talk that produces *con*text is undecidable.

In this chapter, I provide two exemplary analyses. In the first, I show how an interview is made while the conversationalists are talking about something of interest to science educators and scientists. But, because the speakers reproduce what they have come together to produce, some readers might be tempted to understand the situation in terms of roles. I, therefore, provide a second example that shows how the conversationalists change the agreed-upon context—a think-aloud session to elicit expertise—into something radically different: a tutoring session. That is, conversationalists may *reproduce* the agreed-upon context or they may *transform* it; and we can never know beforehand with absolute certainty what they actually do until we are faced with the final results of their doing.

Making an interview

At the outermost, most-encompassing level of analysis, an interview concretely produces and reproduces a societally motivated activity formation (interview as possible activity), while producing a text that the researcher can analyze. Without this outer level as a frame, discursive action cannot be understood. The utterance, "what time is it?" has a very different sense and leads to very different responses when directed (a) by one pedestrian in the street to another, (b) by a teacher in an elementary school class to her students who are learning to read a clock, (c) by an attendee in a movie theatre during the performance to another attendee, or (d) by a student to the professor during a science lecture. In these four examples, possible hearings of the utterance are that of a genuine question, a formatted question, a nuisance, or an attempt to disrupt/bring to a close the lecture. There are then immediate consequences that follow from this joint orientation to the production and reproduction of the interview qua interview: (a) the conversation and its transcript have to be considered as a *collaborative* product that subsumes but cannot be reduced to individual contributions, and (b) (discursive) actions on the part of the interviewer provide the interviewee with resources to interpret the extent to which an answer is sufficient. I use Fragment 2.1 to point out these dimensions in the way that these are apparent in an interview conducted with a seven-year-old.

To set up the episode, the (male) interviewer has asked the child if she is willing to participate in an interview answering a few questions that the interviewer has about everyday phenomena. This setup—which is part of informing the potential participant and gaining informed consent and, therefore, cannot be recorded—nevertheless frames what comes thereafter. The child is comfortably seated on a rattan couch (Figure 2.1). The interviewer begins not just by asking a question but, in fact, by telling that he is going to be asking a question and, furthermore, that the question is going to be a "very simple" one.

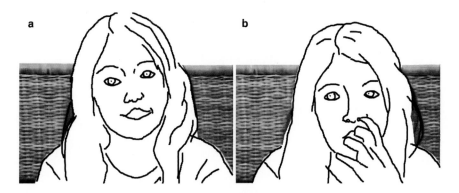

Figure 2.1 During this brief interview, the seven-year-old AJ is comfortably seated on a rattan couch.

  a The child squarely looks to the camera and audience.

  b The child orients to the interlocutor.

Fragment 2.1 shows that this interview reproduces a typical pattern in which the interviewer asks the questions and the research participant responds. Here, the utterances are set up as questions by the interrogative adverbs "why" and "what" (turns 01, 05, 09) and, sometimes, by the upward movement of the pitch toward the end of an utterance unit that is typical for questions (turn 09). The child *constitutes* the interviewer's utterances as questions by following with the adverb "[be]cause," which thereby also becomes a conjunctive in the constitution of a question–answer pair. That is, Fragment 2.1 first and foremost is about successfully producing and reproducing question–answer pairs "typical" of interview situations in the way that participants understand and presuppose the sharing of an understanding.

Fragment 2.1

→ 01 I: so the question is very simple. (0.24) .hhh could you explain me:?
              'why:: (0.55) 'why: we have day and why we have night;
    02   (1.28)
    03 AJ: kay (2.06) ((licks lips with smack)) be (0.16) cause .hhhh (0.84) we
              need 'day to pla:y: anweneed night to sleep. (0.69) .hhh and then if
              we dont have 'day we dont have the flash light or we can bump to
              <<dim>something or something>; (0.47) .hh=yea; (1.04) we can
              bump to something;
    04   (0.75)
→ 05 I: 'why is it hotter (0.19) in the summer.
    06   (0.67)
    07 AJ: because we orbit the ↑`sun
    08   (2.63)
→ 09 I: what about the winter we dont orbit the sun? (0.35) during the
              winte:r?
    10   (0.23)
    11 AJ: no. (0.47) so the snow will melt.

It is precisely the setup of the situation as an interview that allows the participant to treat an interviewer utterance as a question even when it does not end—as is normal for questions—with a rising pitch (turns 01, 05). Yet in both instances, competent speakers of English can hear AJ respond, which means that she does not merely respond but, in fact, completes question–answer pairs, and thereby reifies the interviewer utterances as questions rather than as something else (statements, insults, requests). The situation here is similar to that captured in the saying "it's nothing until I call it [a ball, strike]" attributed to the baseball umpire Bill Klem. A performance is nothing until the next performance indicates what the preceding one has done, the effect it has produced. This may appear or sound strange to the non-initiate reader, but consider the following, which is a typical move by an ethnographer trying to understand a situation by making it strange.

We can gain a better understanding of my statement "it's nothing until I call it," if we ask "what would have happened if the response were to have been different?" Imagine AJ had responded in this way: "your so-called question is not simple at all. Can you ask me another one?" The interviewer would have been confronted with a situation where the formulation of the situation provided, "an easy question," would have been questioned. Subsequent actions may have included asking AJ something like "why don't you try anyhow!" or "let me ask the question in a different way," or "let me ask you a different question then." *Formulating* is a technical concept denoting the fact that speakers not only talk but also, in talking, tell others what they are doing in talking. The interviewer says to AJ, "so the question is very simple" and thereby formulates a simple question to be forthcoming.

An even more difficult situation would have emerged for the interviewer if AJ had said, "this is boring. Can we go and play now?" In this case, the interviewer would have seen the very interview put into question. He would have had to accede, giving up the hope to get any useful data, or he would have had to try to persuade the child (with or without bribe) to continue. In the former case, the child's action would have not only called into question the interview situation but also, together with the adult's actions, dissolved the very situation that their talk was intended to produce and reproduce.

These considerations show how the talk not only produces text but also the *con*text (situation) that the talk/text presupposes. We need to understand and theorize the "interview" as a precarious situation that requires collusion. That the precariousness often does not become an issue should not be taken as evidence against the formulation but, in fact, as evidence for the great collusion that exists on the part of participants in any societal activity to make it work. That things could and, in fact, do go otherwise can be observed daily in "difficult schools," such as those that I have researched in US inner cities, where teachers find it difficult, if not impossible, to teach and where students learn little, if anything, stated in the official curriculum. Such situations are also found in "malfunctioning" marriages or relationships, where the very conversations *within* the societal configuration (marriage, relationship) lead to the break up and dissolution of what has been the context and setting of the talk at the outset. In fact, if we were not allowing the possibility that events could be otherwise, we would eliminate the possibility of freedom or the necessity to make difficult decisions because, in any case, social action would be mechanical and rule governed and, for this reason, precisely violating most ethical rules (Derrida 1993).

Some readers may think that the particular turn-taking routine between AJ and the interviewer goes without saying. But this is not the case as I show in the next section, where questions from the "interviewee" turn an expert/ expert study into a tutoring session, though not without the cooperation of the researcher. This shows that we cannot take Fragment 2.1 as something that goes without saying, but that we have to take it as an *achievement* that requires the collaboration, even collusion, of the participants. The nature of the session precariously depends on the reproduction of the question–answer pairs distributed over predetermined but unstable role assignments, which also are up for grabs, as the next section shows. The present session involving the interviewer and AJ is reproducing a conceptions/conceptual change protocol only under the condition that the participants collude to make it such and then *actively* produce it by contributing in the way they do even though they cannot know what any of the subsequent utterances will be confronting them with.

The interview, therefore, has to be considered as the outcome of the work that participants muster to bring about the recognizable reproduction of a societal phenomenon. They achieve this feat despite all the pauses, restarts ("why? why" [turn 01], "bump to something" [turn 03], "the winter" [turn 09]), extended in- and out-breaths, unfinished (when compared with written) sentences, run-together sounds ("anweneed" [turn 03]), solecisms, half-pronounced words ("kay" [turn 03]), prosodic miscues (in turn 05, pitch drops as at end of proposition rather than rising, as in question), ungrammaticalities (when compared with writing), and so on. Pragmatically and collectively, the participants achieve the production of what they and others recognize as a(n) (conception, conceptual change) interview even though any single one of these features threatens their mutual understanding. It is precisely because of these threats that the event has to be considered as *actively* produced and, therefore, as something achieved. It is precisely because any human being *always* can act otherwise that we need to theorize phenomena such as that in the fragments provided in this chapter as *actively* and *recognizably* reproducing interviews as and for what they are rather than as something else.

In interaction, role assignment does not causally *determine* what follows but itself requires the reproduction of the roles in and through talk. Roles are resources and products of interaction. Participants actively orient to the reproduction of these roles because any utterance has the potential to undermine it. Because interviews require the collaboration (collusion) of the participant, the resulting (recorded and transcribed) text is a collective product that cannot be reduced to individual contributions without considering under what conditions such a reduction is possible and what it presupposes (e.g., knowledge independent of the socially and historically contingent talk that realizes it). This is further evident from the fact that the interviewer orients to and *designs* each question *for* his participant AJ; and he does this in a way to facilitate the reproduction of the question–answer pair and the associated role assignment of interviewer–interviewee. With other interviewees, he might ask the "same" questions differently; with adults, he would most likely ask the question differently unless he wants to risk being charged of asking "childish" questions. The interviewees also orient their utterances to interviewers in ways that presuppose the intelligibility of their utterances. That is, what any participant says is *said for* the production of the present situation *as* interview specifically. Thus, whatever student participants in conceptual change interviews say is presupposed to be intelligible, and is understood by science educators even if it is subsequently categorized as "misconception." That is, what students say is reasonable and intelligible even though learning scientists might subsequently characterize a stretch of talk as misconception, and even though teachers might penalize students with low marks for having talked/written in a particular way said to "express" a misconception.

To bring this point further into relief, consider the sequence from turn 05 to 11. Turns 05 and 07 constitute a typical question–answer pair, whereby the second utterance is an answer only because it relates to the previous utterance in a particular way. That is, AJ is not simply spilling the contents of her mind, but is collaborating/colluding in reproducing an interview situation, so that she says what the *situation* appears to require not what might be in her head independent of the current situation. Similarly, the interviewer asks questions that make sense to conceptions/conceptual change researchers *and* to the interviewee, so that both reproduce phenomena that exist beyond them as general cultural possibilities of acting/talking within certain settings. We can think of the two as individual thinkers, who "become rational only to the extent that their personal and particular acts of thinking figure as moments of [some] unique and universal discourse" (Levinas 1971: 44). Because of this orientation to the production of speech *for* the Other, the utterances and intentions of different speakers come to be enfolded in one another and no longer are independent. They therefore have to be studied from a unit of analysis that exceeds the individual.

From the analysis so far, it is clear that to understand the internal dynamic of the interview, we need to take turn pairs as the minimal unit of analysis. This may not suffice, however, as the following considerations show. In producing turn 09, the interviewer does not only complete turn 07 as an answer that requires further elaboration but also sets up turn 11, the elaboration of the content AJ produces in turn 07. That is, the interviewer simultaneously *completes* the turn 07 and *sets up* turn 11. *He*, therefore, is doubly responsible for AJ's performance, first in completing her utterance as a response to a previous question *and* in proffering a first part of another question–answer pair. (For more on responsibility and ethics in talk see Chapter 4.) That is, because of the particular turn-taking routine and role assignment that the two reproduce throughout the session, AJ's performances are not independent from the interview situation in general, its temporal (i.e., contingent) unfolding, and the interview protocol in particular. It is because of this situation that interviewees come to talk about topics and concepts that they have never talked/thought about before and yet engage, for the purpose of reproducing the interview as such, in talking about it even at length—an issue that I take up in Chapter 5.

The unfolding event provides the interviewee with resources for understanding whether an utterance has fulfilled attendant expectations or not—something we have already seen in the teacher's turn following Connor's partially correct answer. This, too, is apparent from Fragment 2.1. Thus, after AJ completes the utterance that constitutes turn 02, which accomplishes turns 01/03 as a question–answer pair, the interviewer moves to a different topic. In so doing, he does more than simply move to the next question prescribed in the protocol. He also indicates to the interviewee that whatever she has done is sufficient for the purposes at hand and that, therefore, the event can proceed to its next stage. The converse is the case in the turn pair 07/09. Here, the second turn of the pair questions the veracity or general applicability of the previous turn, and therefore its completeness. Thus, AJ proposes "because we orbit the Sun" as a candidate answer to the question, derived from the documentary *A Private Universe,* "why is it hotter in the summer?" (turn 05).[1] The interviewer then offers a contrasting season (i.e., winter) in the context of which the orbiting as the reason for the summer heat is to be evaluated. In so doing, the interviewer directly questions the applicability of the previous reason for explaining the temperature during all seasons. For the purposes of the interview, turn 07 is rendered incomplete or insufficient by the follow-up question, thereby telling AJ that more is required to complete the sought-for question–answer pair. After turn 11, the interviewer moves to yet another topic, thereby again telling AJ that now her response is sufficient, having completed the question–answer pair. Depending on the situation, such continuation can be understood as signaling satisfaction not only in terms of completing a turn pair but also in terms of the correctness of the statement proffered (see Chapter 1). In the end, the topic and interview situation are completed simultaneously.

To summarize, in this section I show how interviews not only elicit information but also, and especially, produce and reproduce themselves. This reproduction, to be successful in the face of all the possible threats, requires the collaboration (collusion) of the participants. This collusion leads to orderly turn-taking patterns, collective rather than individual elaboration of some rather than other topics, orientation to and language use for the other, and implicit evaluations of performances. The upshot of this analysis is the fact that contributions to interview talk cannot be taken apart into independent contributions. We have to seriously question, "under what conditions do researchers legitimately attribute parts of interview texts to interviewees as if they had used their turns to spill their minds?"

How a think-aloud protocol becomes a tutoring session

We do not often think about organizations and situations as actively produced, and thereby reproduced at each instant, requiring the collusion of the participants. The fundamental order of conversations is oriented to the need for mutual commitment, including listening/hearing, rather than to reproducing statuses and institutional relations, which goes a considerable "way toward neutralizing institutional considerations" (Rawls 1989: 161). Although we intuitively know that "good lessons" depend on the collusion of teacher and students, assessment systems, whether these are course evaluations at the university or evaluations of how well a school does, imply that teachers are solely responsible for the lessons and the outcomes, often measured by student performance. When lessons do not take their intended courses, or when students do not do well, then one or the other party is blamed. In some instances, the blame is laid on a lack of skill on the part of the teacher, which may lead to requirements such as engaging in professional development; in other instances, the students and their context ("low socio-economic status," "inner-city school") are made responsible. In the previous section, I propose questioning "what if something else had happened?" as a way of making salient the collusion and collaboration required in bringing about situations specifically, and organizations more generally. It is precisely at the instant when the anticipated social organization is not reproduced (realized) that we can observe the work that goes into making it generally (perhaps almost always) occur (e.g., Garfinkel 1967). In the present section, I exhibit how microprocesses lead to a radical change in the planned activity, which is thereby turned into something else clearly unintended and unforeseen in the research protocol.

As part of a larger research project concerning graphs and graphing in the sciences, I had hired an undergraduate physics and anthropology co-op student to help me study how scientists read/interpret/think about graphs. We had chosen the think-aloud protocol, which is a method frequently used in expert and usability studies. This involves getting the research participants to say aloud what they are thinking while engaging in the task of interest; if the participants stop talking for a while, the researcher asks the participant to think aloud. In the following, I show aspects of one session that turned from a think-aloud session into a question–answer and eventually into a tutoring session. Interestingly, the person doing the tutoring was the physics undergraduate student (Daniel) and the tutee was a veteran physics professor (Annemarie) with over 30 years of notable and noted teaching experience, including a university teaching award. The videotape shows Annemarie sitting with the task sheet in front of her (Figure 2.2), holding a pencil in her right hand that frequently points to particular locations on the graph. This graph features a birth-rate and a death-rate curve as a function of population size. The two curves intersect in two places and participants are asked to talk about the implication for the population.

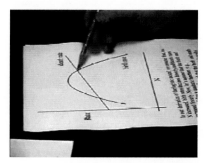

Figure 2.2 Annemarie has the task sheet before her, the pencil in her hand placed on the intersection of the death rate (straight line) and birthrate (curved) of a population, which vary as a function of the population size (horizontal axis).

Challenges involved in following a think-aloud protocol

During the first three minutes on the population graph task in front of her, Annemarie has done what, after the event, from an a posteriori perspective can be said to have been consistent with the think-aloud protocol that had been explained to her beforehand. She has read the text, which both presents the task and asks her to talk about what happens to the population (given the birthrate and death rate) in various regions of the graph defined by the two intersection points of the birthrate and death-rate curves. The end of this first period is realized in turns 31–33, where, after making the statement that the birthrate is increasing faster than the death rate, and following a pause of nearly one second, she poses the question, "is that right then?" (turn 33). As I suggest in the previous chapter, as analysts, we are interested in understanding the dynamics of a communicative situation so that what matters is not how *we* interpret an utterance but how participants themselves hear what they tell one another. We do know from the analysis of the sound-track that the pitch is rising toward the end of that utterance, generally marking a question; the grammatical structure realized in "Is that right?" also is that of a question. (For more on grammar in interactions see Chapter 8.)

Fragment 2.2

```
      31  A:   death rate increasing (0.69) and the birthrate increasing and the
                birthrate is increasing (0.57) faster (0.95) than the death rate.
      32       (1.71)
  →   33       so they=re both increasing but the birthrate invar is faster increasing
                than the death rate so presumably that means that the population is
                increasing. (0.93) is that right then?
      34       (0.88)
      35  D:   hhum
      36       (0.43)
      37  A:   round [this] region?
      38  D:          [khmm]
      39       (0.73)
      40  D:   u:m; yea=if you=take (.) well (.) shall=i=think=i=use the half
                if=you=take the birth minus the death (.) rate (0.63) `well the birth
                plus the death (.) rate which is negative, you=re gonna get (0.13)
                some positive (0.98) growth rate; right?=
      41  A:   =^yea ^[i=]m looking at the slopes of the curve[ss].
      42  D:     <<p>[so]>                                    [uh]=<<p>okay.>
```

We notice a pause of 0.88 seconds (turn 34), then hear a level-pitched sound transcribed as "hhum" (turn 35), followed by more pausing (turn 36). Obviously, what Annemarie is doing does not correspond to the protocol. She is uttering what can be heard as a question, and, consistent with the role of a researcher in a think-aloud protocol, Daniel does not provide an assessment. But there is a tension. Annemarie has uttered something that can be heard as a question. If he does not respond, then there is a break of the social conventions according to which a question requires a response, even if it is in the less preferred negative. The ethics of face-to-face conversations, as I elaborate in Chapter 4, demand a response if there is a question; or, if there is no response, at least an explication is required. Here, we can hear the "hhum" as Daniel's acknowledgment of the fact that it is his speaking turn right now, which he has taken without saying anything substantially. It may also be heard as a hesitation or as a resistance to respond. To understand *this* conversation and its evolution, we need to see how Annemarie, in her own subsequent turn, is taking up the pauses and Daniel's interjection.

Annemarie breaks the silence, uttering "round this region?" (turn 37) with a rising intonation that culturally competent speakers tend to hear as a question. In fact, it is both a specification of an area and a question. When heard in the context of her preceding words, it is a specification of the region she is currently attending to and, therefore, that she has been talking about what happens to the population "round this region." The utterance, then, does two things: it specifies the content of the earlier question *and* it reiterates the question as question.

While she is producing the utterance, Daniel releases another rasp-like sound. But, then another pause develops. He does not follow the invitation to realize a question–response pair. But then, suddenly and with a very high speed, including sound-words barely separated and difficult to be parsed, he describes what happens in the area specified if the death rate is subtracted from the birthrate; a statement that he changes to one that states the death rate as added to the birthrate. In this case, there is a positive growth rate (turn 40), a statement that is consistent with an increase in the population in the way Annemarie has stated previously (turn 33).

Annemarie then states that she is looking at the slopes of the curves, which contrasts the description that Daniel has just provided in terms of the values of the two curves rather than values of their slopes at each point. Daniel acknowledges and Annemarie then continues, only to ask him again and again whether what she has said is right.

In this situation, there clearly emerges a possible breach of the session as arranged—and this is so all the while Annemarie is doing nothing but asking whether she is right. In talking about the issue at hand, she actually challenges the intended session, threatens it, and thereby opens up the possibility that it turns into a different kind of session. We can see Daniel resisting, not giving in to providing an assessment concerning the correctness of Annemarie's reading of the graph. But he is also in a difficult situation in that he has been asked a question, to which social norms require him to act or explain why he does not want to provide it. He does so in uttering a non-committal assessment, simply restating what he has heard Annemarie say: what happens when the birthrate is larger than the death rate. But Annemarie then tells him that she has been looking at the slopes of the curves, which is different from what he has been explaining to her (to look at the heights of the curves).

This situation, therefore, already exhibits how the anticipated think-aloud session is under threat. To realize it, both parties to the setting have to collude. In this instance, Annemarie's question threatens the research on graphing expertise, which, if it does not unfold so that it can be labeled subsequently as a "think-aloud protocol," then the transcription of the videotape potentially does not count as such—it is something else, not a think-aloud protocol and may have to be eliminated from analysis. However, the situation has been rescued as Daniel achieves a non-committal translation of what he has heard Annemarie say. This is so even though it becomes evident that Annemarie has provided an explanation based on a different feature of the graph from the one Daniel expects (based on his conversations with the researcher, based on what other participants have said).

Doing tutoring

Following a first query for a hint, Daniel responds by restating the problem only to be interrupted by Annemarie, who makes another attempt at articulating an explanation of the graph. Then she stops and asks for another clue (Fragment 2.3, turn 01). Without hesitation, Daniel *formulates* both that he thinks (process) and that he thinks she possibly confuses some things (content). He suggests that she is thinking, or rather talking about the "birthrate as the slopes of those curves" (turn 02). Just as he continues with a contrastive "but," Annemarie overlaps saying "yes" (turn 03). There is a brief pause, an indication that Annemarie has stopped, which allows Daniel to take another turn. Here, he provides a description of the curves, which express rates of change (turn 05). Between the articulation of "but those curves" and the conclusion "are the rates of change," there is a pause, giving emphasis to the "are." Thus, rather than ("but") talking about the slopes, Daniel suggests that the curves *are* the rates of change. That is, Annemarie does not, in fact, have to look at the slopes of the curves to find the rates of change of the population, but all she has to do is look at the curves themselves, which *are* rates of change.

Fragment 2.3

```
01   A:   [give me] a clue.
02   D:   yea=i think whats confusing you– is you=re thinking (0.40) of
          (0.34) you=re tal (0.30) you=re talking about (0.34) the birthrate
          (0.87) as the slopes of those um (0.18) curves you are talking about
          (0.39) b[ut]
03   A:                [ye]s:
04        (0.22)
05   D:   but those curves:: (0.33) are the rates of change.
06        (0.82)
07   A:   oh; okay
08        (0.28)
09   D:   s:o, the (0.45) the sl[ope ]
10   A:                            [this] is the rate of change of birth? (0.23)
               °i see.°
```

There is a considerable pause. Annemarie realizes the possibility for a next turn to talk by beginning with the interjection "oh" (turn 07). This interjection generally expresses—depending on intonation (which realizes one of the possible dictionary senses)—surprise, frustration, or disappointment. She follows with an "okay," allowing us to hear her say something like "oh, this is how things are." Daniel takes the next turn beginning with a conjunctive "so," which may open an inference, and then continues by denoting the slope (turn 09). But here, Annemarie begins to speak while overlapping him, thereby accessing another turn to talk, in which she restates what Daniel has pointed out earlier, but which she just now appears to realize—as announced and formulated by the interjection indicating surprise. This hearing is further confirmed by the "I see" (turn 10), which we can understand both literally (she now does see the graphs as expressing the rates of change) and metaphorically (she now recognizes and comprehends the state of affairs). In fact, the situation is a bit more complicated as Annemarie does not simply state an observation, "this is the rate of birth," but the pitch of the utterance increases toward what will be the end of the phrase preceding the pause and a subsequent clause complete in itself. It is as if she is asking herself, expressing her questioning of herself before responding to the question.

Asked to gloss the episode transcribed in Fragment 2.3, we may respond by saying that we are confronted with (listening to) a tutor identifying the problem of the tutee and then explicating how the task feature needs to be looked at. The tutee, Annemarie, acknowledges recognition of differences and then articulates the curves as "rate of change of birth." But in saying "I see," Annemarie, in and with the statement, expresses recognizing something that apparently she has not recognized before. There is still the possibility of confusion and misunderstanding, but there is no evidence currently available whether the two are aware of these differences—Annemarie, in fact, says that "this" is the rate of change of birth, which is different from birthrate. The birthrate is the rate of increase in a population rather than the rate of change of births, which in biology refers to the numbers that are always given with respect to the total number in the population, that is, as a birthrate.

As the events unfold, Daniel continues to point out features that assist Annemarie to progressively realize how the graph is expertly explained. In these events, we can see that the think-aloud protocol really has become a tutoring session. But neither Annemarie nor Daniel was constrained or forced to act in the way that they have done. Daniel could have concluded the protocol and asked Annemarie to continue with the next task; Annemarie could have suggested that she has said all that she can and that she is ready to move on. She did not ask explicitly to be tutored to read this graph, and yet this is what the two achieve. They do so without explicit agreement, which could have been enacted in this way. Daniel says, "I can show you how to do this graph," and Annemarie could have accepted the offer by saying, "I would be interested in finding out about how to interpret this graph." In any event, if we had access to but the second part of the taped session, without knowing its internal history, we would have likely said that this is a tutoring rather than a think-aloud session or some other form of activity.

The irreducibility of text and context

Many social scientists analyze verbal transcripts from interviews, classroom situations, and other occasions where people talk. They use the transcripts to support claims about the individuals that physically produced the sound. That is, they reduce the conversation to a chain of utterances each attributable to the speaker rather than to speaker, audience, and situation. In this chapter, I present two phenomena that undermine the presuppositions underlying the mainstream approach to analyzing verbal data whereby any piece of text is attributed to the person who has physically produced it. The point here is that members to a setting do not just produce contents of talk but, at the same time, make the very context in and for which the content is produced. Without context, sentences float entirely free and their sense cannot be narrowed in any useful way. Even with context, the sense of an utterance is irreducible, for "no sentence has absolutely determinable 'meaning': it always is in a situation of the word or in some measure of the text as a whole, which borders and entrains it, in an always-open context that always promises still more sense" (Derrida 1988b: 116). Participants produce context together, in collusion with all other participants. This, therefore, constitutes a double intertwining of text and context—a double-bind situation—that cannot be reduced. Any reduction comes with a penalty—generally a theory that does not stand up to close scrutiny of real situations unfolding under real conditions. But, and this is the companion "law," even if interlocutors produce the context together in talking, they cannot ever saturate the context: there always is another way of—even a need for—saying something differently.

Linked to the first point is a second one: members to a setting generally collude in the reproduction of the activity that they are in. We are, therefore, not surprised to hear a literary theorist state that talk "produces the empirical conditions it assumes" (Fish 1982: 709). Thus, AJ colludes with the interviewer and, as a result, the two achieve an interview, and, with it, a transcript that subsequently is used as data in the research literature—to undermine the claim about individual conceptions and misconceptions (see Chapter 5). On the other hand, the members to a setting may not actually reproduce the activity that they had gotten themselves into: a think-aloud protocol turns into a tutoring session. We see that Daniel hesitates at first but then works together with Annemarie turning the think-aloud protocol into something else. But because they produce the situation together, they also produce shared context for hearing subsequent text that is not only contextualized but also contextualizing what has happened and what is to come.

We learn from these two examples taken together that any situation may unfold as expected or may turn into something else. The collaboration and collusion of a sufficient number of members is required to achieve this, which, in the two situations featured, means the only two individuals present. A *general* theory of talk in and for interaction needs to make it possible for the activity to change into something else. It also needs to take into account that the speakers *make the situation*, so that the talk is not only about content (text) but also about reproducing and transforming the context. This context includes other features of the setting, including other participants, and the very nature of culturally recognizable formations, including lessons, interviews, and lectures. But the difference between the two achievements of talk is undecidable so that we cannot proceed analyzing transcripts as if the talk was about content only. Talk produces both the warp and the weft of the resulting tissue, thereby contexting text and context, figure and ground. Therefore, if nothing exists outside of (con-) text (*hors-texte*), as Jacques Derrida has frequently said, in different situations, and at different occasions (e.g., Derrida 1967a: 227), then *text* is meant in this way, as the contexture of text and context in the tissue of life.

3   Speaking|thinking as distributed process

In Chapter 1 we see that communication exceeds the use of words. Communication, therefore, cannot be reduced to language because (a) there are modes other than language involved, and (b) translation even within one and the same mode (e.g., language) changes what is articulated. In this chapter, I present a more comprehensive approach to communication, of which the verbal utterance becomes but a one-sided expression. Moreover, talking does not follow thinking. Speaking and thinking are each processes that unfold in time, intersect with one another, mediate each other in their evolution (Vygotsky 1986). Thought *becomes* in speaking—that is, it is not merely expressed following prior thinking but thought becomes thought in speaking. Thought is produced in speaking in the same way as the proverbial garden path is laid in walking. The difference between the two processes—thinking and speaking—thereby becomes *undecidable* because they are internally related moments of one and the same process rather than external relations of thematized aspects (factors, functions, dimensions). This relation between thinking and speaking as two irreducible, but constitutive, processes is indicated in the concept of *speaking|thinking*. Here the Sheffer stroke "|," which corresponds to the logical operation "NAND," produces a new process that cannot be reduced to one of its moments, thinking or speaking. I use the Sheffer stroke whenever I denote phenomena that articulate themselves in different forms but the difference of which is undecidable in any practical situations that we might face or analyze.

In this chapter, I provide detailed descriptions of, and explanations for, the fact that there is more to lectures than the talk plus the notes on the chalkboard. This informational *more* consists of forms of communication other than speech (words), including gestures, body positions, body movements with respect to aspects of the setting, and other information in the setting; most importantly, these communicative forms do not simply add up, but interact and mutually constitute each other. When students are sitting in the lecture, they, in fact, participate in an experiential totality—including the lecturer, other students, the room, the university, society, and so on—and in the forms of consciousness that comes with it. There is, therefore, a totality and any individual moment cannot be understood outside this relation to the whole. The informational *more* that I describe here may explain (part of) the gap between understanding students' experiences while sitting in lectures versus that which they experience while studying for an exam from their lecture notes. The first fundamental message of this chapter, therefore, is that to study intelligibility, comprehension, and understanding we need to study communication writ large, not merely language (text) but the irreducible relation between text and context. The second fundamental message is that speaking | thinking is an irreducible and unfolding process rather than an externalization of existing thought into speech.

On meaning as situated process

Vygotsky (1986) proposes *word-meaning* as the *process* that preserves, suppresses, and supersedes the other two distinct but interrelated processes of thinking and speaking.[1] Instead I suggest using the akin processes of *participative thinking, active comprehension,* and *theme* put forward at about the same time by the members of the group around Mikhail Bakhtin. The reason underlying this move is the troublesome nature of the term "meaning," generally used as if it denoted something that students construct and attach to words and the static nature attributed to this thing. *Meaning* as currently used in the scholarly literature is not associated strongly with the processual nature that Vygotsky attributes to it. For the Bakhtin group, the constant evolution of the world is a core issue; and "only active comprehension allows us to seize the theme, for the evolution cannot be apprehended but with the aide of the evolution itself" (Bakhtine [Volochinov] 1977: 146).[2] It is this situated and evolving process of understanding the theme, which, according to Bakhtin and his co-workers, our theories of language-in-use have to capture.

Martin Heidegger (1977b), too, is concerned with coping with understanding in the everyday world in which we find ourselves and that makes sense even before we arrive. Speech is considered to be equi-primordial with attunement/ mood (*Befindlichkeit*) and practical understanding. Attuned intelligibility makes itself known, in and as, speech. From this perspective, therefore, words accrue to, and find their place in, an always already existing intelligibility attuned in and to a texture of significations (*Bedeutungen*), rather than acquiring something like meaning that is attached to them as the outcome of a construction process. New words do not get something like "meaning", and thereby become intelligible— they become intelligible when they find a place in the contexture of a familiar world. More than a century ago, Ferdinand de Saussure (1996) had already suggested that a word could not have something of the kind that Anglophone scholars denote by "meaning" that applies to a determined object—there is never any positive way to determine the sense/signification but only the totality of words constituting difference in the familiar world filled with difference. Late-twentieth-century philosophers of language agree. This world, therefore, constitutes the *con*text of the texts that speakers produce, but this *con*text goes deeper and is more extensive than anything we can possibly articulate. This context constitutes a totality that escapes all systematic thinking (Levinas 1971) and levels out in what is not only subconscious, ready to emerge into consciousness where it is not right now, but rather what is unconscious and, therefore, cannot ever be integrated into consciousness. If talk were not like this, we would always find ourselves in a situation of infinite regress where an explication of what we have said itself requires an explication and so on *ad infinitum* (Rawls 1989).

In familiar worlds, we are attuned, moving into and taking up positions. We orient in this world as a whole person, body and mind being expressed simultaneously. The body as a whole produces and exposes our position on some issue by means of its position in the world, its orientation, gestures, prosody, and so on. This is no clearer than in lectures, which are often thought of only in terms of what lecturers (professors, teachers) say and the notes they put on the chalkboard (overhead projector). But words alone do not explain, for example, why students have a sense of understanding while sitting in lectures, on the one hand, and their experiences of failure to understand while they prepare for an exam with their class notes, on the other hand. In other words, how is it that students have a sense of meaning while partaking in a lecture performance yet experience frustration and incomprehension when looking at the traces of lecture in their notebooks? I suggest that in the lecture, they understand the *theme*, articulated in and through the communicative totality that a lecture provides. In this chapter, I both show that the communicative totality by far exceeds words and diagrams, on the one hand, and the evolving nature of speaking | thinking, on the other hand.

A lecture ends in a cul-de-sac

This episode takes us into a physics lecture on adiabatic demagnetization, a phenomenon that underlies some refrigeration systems.[3] At the end of this first episode, the professor will note that what he has done is not correct but he cannot see where he has gone wrong. This is evidence for the fact that in its evolution, speaking | thinking has ended in a cul-de-sac, which he would not have had any reason to go into if his thought had pre-existed the process of speaking. (Unless he had done so for rhetorical purposes, but there is no evidence anywhere in the lectures that he had done so.)

I take up the episode after the professor has already drawn two axes labeled S (entropy) and T (temperature) and two curves one labeled $B = 0$, the other one $B \neq 0$, where B stands for the magnetic field in which the sample to be refrigerated is placed (Figure 3.1). The professor also has drawn a small vertical line from the upper to the lower curve. This line depicts the events that happen when the magnetic field B is increased (chalk line downwards from $B = 0$ to $B \neq 0$) at constant temperature (verticality of line), which leads to an alignment of the molecule-sized magnets in the sample. This alignment corresponds to a greater degree of order and, therefore, a lower entropy value (i.e., the line goes down with respect to the S axis). The professor now moves to the next step, the first lowering of temperature at constant entropy (same level of S on the graph). The transcription (Fragment 3.1) exhibits the delay in the production of content:

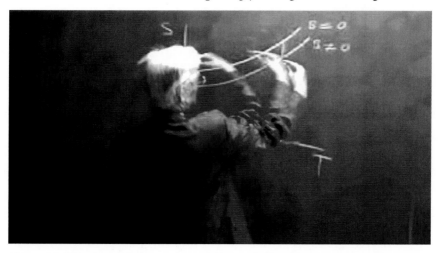

Figure 3.1 This video offprint, constructed by overlaying three images, features a deictic gesture against a graph that the professor is in the course of constructing.

there is a fairly long 0.94 second pause, a drawn out 0.55 second "uh," followed by the threefold utterance of "when you" before the word "adiabatically" emerges from his lips. The transcript shows that in the middle of the sound, there is a considerable jump in the pitch of his voice (from 129 to 184 Hz) after the beginning of the word has already been uttered with an increased pitch in respect to the surrounding talk. While producing part of the sound-word that English speakers hear as "adiabatically," the professor—who is completely turned toward the graph that is in the process of emerging from the lecture—also moves his arm and hand in what scholars have come to call an *iconic* gesture because it provides an image, likeness, or portrait (Gr. *eikon*) of something. The video offprint shows that the hand follows a trajectory approximately parallel to the abscissa to the left at about the height where the little, earlier drawn, vertical line meets with the lower curve ($B \neq 0$). Following the end of the gesture, there is a 0.55 second pause before we hear the words "demagnetize it," which are followed by another pause (0.44 seconds), a drawn out 0.55 second "uh," and more signs of hesitation (0.30 second pause, "uh"). In turn 03, while producing the sound "it uh:::," he draws a horizontal line from the intersection between the vertical line and the curve $B \neq 0$ until it meets with the $B = 0$ curve.

Fragment 3.1

```
01   and when you (0.94) uh::: that when you when you
02   when you 'adia[↑beti↓cally            ]
                  [((gesture in Figure 3.1))]
03   (0.55) demagnetize it (0.44) [it uh:::        ] (0.30) uh its that
                                  [((draws line))]
```

In this situation, the adverb "adiabatically" refers to the fact that the demagnetization of the material (from $B \neq 0 \rightarrow B = 0$) results in an increase in the disorder of the magnetic molecules while holding entropy S constant (horizontal line in the graph means S = constant), which is compensated for by the removal of heat from the sample. In the process, therefore, the temperature is lowered, that is, the system moves to the left on the graph (i.e., lower temperatures).

As in all lectures and lecture episodes I recorded as part of my extensive research agenda, this episode includes talk. This talk stands in some relation to what Mikhail Bakhtin (1993) calls *participative thinking*, that is, the thinking of a conscious human being participating in a societal activity, here teaching at a university and, thereby, reproducing cultural forms of knowledge. More interesting to the present chapter are the modes of communication other than talk that are present in that instant. First, there is a graph, not in its entirety, but in a certain stage of the evolution of a graph, the endpoint of which is not yet known to any of the participants, possibly not even to the professor. In fact, he later abandons the diagram suggesting that there might be something wrong about the picture he has presented.

For the present purposes, this graph constitutes a visual moment of the communicative whole. But it is not the only visual moment available. The hand/arm movement also is part of the communication; and this is so in a very interesting way when we consider the following three aspects. First, when viewed with respect to the graph, the hand moves from the right, showing higher temperatures and a magnetic field larger than zero, to the left where the temperatures are lower and the magnetic field is zero. The gesture is produced *while* the adverb referring to a removal of heat is uttered (corresponding to lowering of temperature) but *prior to* the verb that actually corresponds to the removal of heat as the material is demagnetized when the surrounding magnetic field is lowered and turned off. That is, the effect of the action of decreasing the magnetic field in which the sample is held, the lowering of its temperature, visually is indicated *prior to* being verbally articulated. That is, there is a temporal shift, a *decalage*, between verbal and gestural expressions that denote some abstract idea but that are not co-present at the performative level of communication—which is in contrast to much of the literature on gesticulation that assumes the two expressions to be synchronous (Roth 2002). If what a speaker produces at any one instant is taken as an (even if one-sided) expression of *participative thinking*, then the perceptual moment of his performance is ahead of the verbal moment. The performance, therefore, becomes heterogeneous.

Second, it is significant that my analysis brings out the gesture and, therefore, a visual moment of the entire performance, which constitutes the taking of a position in the lecture hall and the conceptual content simultaneously. Human beings do not attend to all hand/arm movements a speaker produces, especially when they are "grooming gestures," such as when speakers scratch themselves or make other gestures that do not contribute to the sense of what is being communicated. Thus, when this professor talks about liking and disliking making measurements of some variables ("we have our things that turn us on") and about his own interests in moths, he raises both hands, which heretofore have rested on the desk, holds them palms inward at a 45 degree angle for eight seconds before returning them to where they had rested before (Figure 3.2). Whereas some onlookers might be tempted to go as far as suggesting that the open palms are consistent with opening up and confiding preferences to his audience, thereby exposing vulnerability, there is little else to substantiate such an interpretation. Without the taking up of this gesture in the responses of the audience, we do not know its effect. This gesture, therefore, contributes little if anything to the sense of physics.

Here, the significance is a result of the relationship between the chalkboard, the professor's orientation toward it, and the relation of the same or similar perceptual features in the gesture and on the chalkboard. This is so because we see the gesture as relevant with respect to what can be found on the chalkboard, but we find what is relevant on the chalkboard because of the gesture. The relevance of one mode (e.g., gesture) is constituted (motivated) by the other mode (e.g., [ephemeral] line on chalkboard). And here then is the third aspect of interest and significance in this communicative instant: the gesture that moves through a horizontal trajectory precedes the drawing of a horizontal line from the curve further to the right ($B \neq 0$) to the curve further to the left ($B = 0$). Here, each mode motivates the other, each constituting a moment of the communication in process, but each being of a different kind and, therefore, addressing itself to different cognitive processes and abilities.

The recognition of the hand/arm movement as a salient gesture depends, in part, on the orientation of the professor. This is so because if he had not been oriented toward the chalkboard, the sense of the gesture would be different and would have to be established by means of different processes. The professor is turned toward the graph, which, as I will show, has to be taken as significant. Here, it signals among others that attention is to be oriented to the graph and some of the features that any onlooker in the audience can distinguish. This is clear in the context of other instances where the professor walks away from the diagram, about four meters to the right (seen from audience), where he presents himself broadside to the audience.

Figure 3.2 While talking about his appreciation for measuring heat capacities, things that turn people on, and his interests in moths, the professor makes a gesture that does not appear to have cognitive (conceptual) content.

In the episode, there is more of the professor's participative thinking—that is, his position on the subject—expressed. We may experience the pauses, the "uhs," and the repeated utterances of the same words and phrases as hesitations, perhaps even as uncertainty. Such an experience would have been confirmed as soon as the professor reached the left end of the figure after the next iteration of drawing a vertical line down from the $B = 0$ to the $B \neq 0$ curve followed by a horizontal line from the intersection just produced right to the vertical axis. At this point, the professor stops and says, while walking away, "I think there is something wrong with this picture." He goes to his lecture notes and, after inspecting these for a while, indicates that he will return to the issue at some later time. That is, after producing the drawing, the professor announces his uncertainty about the correctness of what he has just produced—both the "I think," which expresses belief rather than certainty, and "there is something wrong" are expressions of this uncertainty. That is, the professor expresses not only content matter but also his uncertainty about its correctness. He does so in his manner of presenting which, therefore, constitutes an integral moment of the communicative action itself—much as is made apparent in Marshall McLuhan's (1995) diction that the medium, here sound and its various modulations (pitch, intensity, rate), *is* the message.

In the next sections, I analyze that part of the lecture in which the professor erases the diagram that appears in Fragment 3.1 and replaces it with another one, this time correct—because implementing the implications of several formulas partially noted on the chalkboard. I begin by accounting for the events between Fragment 3.1 until just prior to the episode of interest; the two points in time are separated by approximately 15 minutes. I then tell the story of the episode in three parts, beginning with the production of a changed graph, an analogical extension to other topics, and ending with a generalization. In the subsequent section, I provide detailed analyses of some significant features observable in this episode.

Noting the source of the error

The introductory Fragment 3.1 ends when the professor expresses the sense that something is not right with his diagram and explanation without being able to say why. He continues to focus on the mathematical aspects of adiabatic demagnetization and writes an equation on the board that he names "Gibbs–Helmholtz relationship" (see Figure 3.3):

$$\Delta H = \Delta G - T\left(\frac{\partial \Delta G}{\partial T}\right)_p$$

He first suggests—incorrectly so as it turns out—that one term of the equation, $(\partial \Delta G/\partial T)_p$ would be zero when the temperature reaches zero. After staring at the equation for a while he writes "$T \to 0$" and "$G \to H$," pointing out that when the temperature of a sample approached absolute zero (0 kelvin), the G (i.e., Gibbs free energy) and H (i.e., enthalpy) become equal (Figure 3.3). He moves on to suggest that this "has a number of consequences," the first one being "$S = 0$ as $T = 0$."[4]

Figure 3.3 The professor looks at what he has written, pausing in his speech, as if considering the consequences of what he has just said.

He then goes on for a couple of minutes elaborating on the fact that $S = 0$, partially sketching several equations because, as he says, he does not remember them in their entirety, and then announces, while turning toward the chalkboard and pointing toward the graph, "another consequence is that." He stops talking, stares at the graph for a while, then walks the 2.5 meters in front of the graph, places his notes on the desk and turns around. He announces, "this is wrong," and erases the graph in silence (Figure 3.4). He quickly sketches a new set of axes, marks the abscissa with the letter "T" (for temperature) and the ordinate with "S" (for entropy).

At the end of Fragment 3.1, the professor expresses uncertainty about the correctness of something he has done without specifying what the exact content is that he has a sense about as being wrong—i.e., whether it is what he has drawn or what he has talked about, or both. The fact is that after having continued the lecture and produced a series of equations, these now have become new resources for action. In fact, they now allow him to recover from what he has considered to be an error: the curves are not in the right place. What he has communicated, thereby, mediates his thinking, which in turn mediates his communicating. He draws the implications of the equation that he has written on the board. In the processes, he communicates to the student audience his orientation. He unmistakably first looks at and then points to the graph (Figure 3.4), thereby rendering evident that "this" is the graph and *it* rather than something else "is wrong." In fact, he thereby provides three indices that point to the graph as the culprit: the verbal "this," his gaze oriented in a particular direction, and the finger pointing in the same direction. The verbal index "this" is not very specific, and there are many entities in the room or in the speech that could be the signifieds. On the other hand, gaze and index finger, themselves physical, point to a particular place in physical space. In fact, "this" generally is used to refer to entities that are proximal (close) with respect to the speaker, whereas "that" is used for entities that are distal (farther away). In the present, there are other signs on the chalkboard closer to the professor. Yet in the context of the gaze and pointing finger, the referent for "this" is more consistent with the graph than with some of the other notations on the chalkboard. The confirmation that the indexical term "this" refers to the graph follows immediately, as soon as the professor has reached that part of the chalkboard after having placed his lecture notes (Figure 3.4, left end). Further evidence that it is this graph that is wrong comes from the fact that the professor erases it rather than something else on the chalkboard.

Here, a pointing gesture, body orientations (gaze, turning of upper body, complete body orientation), and position (walking to be placed right next to the graph) all are integral aspects of communication in this situation: they articulate (physical, ideational) positions and changes therein. The topic of talk, the graph, clearly comes into focus against everything else present in the room and available as a signifying moment in the communication. Thus, there are many other marks on the chalkboard, but these do not stand out. They are not relevant to the present situation, and the various signifiers produced assist the audience in selecting some aspects over others as salient. That is, what the professor does here with his body and with his speech is marking out features, which allow the students in the audience to remark these features as salient, and therefore to re-mark them (first the professor, then the students mark these features). Finally, the graph itself is an integral aspect of the communication: it actually provides the motivation for the gaze and the pointing index finger. The graph provides these signs with a rationale such that the relevance of the gaze and index fingers as pointers derives from the fact that there is something to be pointed to, thereby to be re-marked, and to be remarked by the audience. If the chalkboard had been empty in the area where the professor is gazing at and pointing to, it would have appeared strange; and he would have had to account for the fact that he is suggesting that there is something wrong when in fact nothing could be located where the finger and gaze are pointing to.

With the old graph erased and a new set of axes drawn, the professor is now ready to present another representation of adiabatic demagnetization, which is part of some refrigeration processes (the other part being isothermal magnetization), especially refrigeration processes in physics laboratories that seek to get substances near absolute zero temperature (i.e., near $-273.15\,°C$, $-459.67\,°F$, or $0\,K$).[5]

Figure 3.4 Whereas he has elaborated on his first implications of the equations written previously (Figure 3.3), the professor now points to the graph, then walks to the left and places his notes on the desk, then turns and erases the old graph to begin another episode of doing the cooling by the adiabatic demagnetization process. (Movement from right to left and then to the board.)

Drawing temperature–entropy curves for two magnetizations

Now that the axes exist, the professor appears prepared to draw the graphs themselves, which relate levels of entropy (S), the dependent variable, to levels of temperature (T), the independent variable. He draws two such curves, one for the magnetic field turned off ("$B = 0$") and another for a magnetic field turned on, that is, for a non-zero magnetic field ("$B \neq 0$"). He places the chalk at the origin (intersection of ordinate and abscissa) while uttering, "entropy ... at zero is zero" (line 01). This is the direct consequence he has been talking about for the past 15 minutes: the fact that entropy at absolute zero is *set* to be zero; and this fact is not expressed in his first graph (see Figures 3.1 and 3.4 where the two curves not only do not meet when $T = 0$ but also are different from zero, that is, $S > 0$).

Fragment 3.2

```
01   u:m: entropy: (0.33) at zero is zero [(0.65)
                                          [(((draws
02   so thats what the entropy] looks like (0.33)
     first curve              ))]
03   in a (0.42) in [a zero magnetic field
                    [(((writes "B=0"
04   (0.74)
05   and the entropy (0.51) um <<pp>its not quite zero>
```

06   and [and when the entropy (0.33)
        [((draws second entropy
07   is (.) no] (0.26) when when magnetization [is not zero (1.03)
        curve))]   [((writes B≠0))]
08   over there
        ((chin gestures to right front corner of room, walks to right front
            of room))
09   (3.27)
10   the drawing was not quite [right (.) as you see
                                [((begins walking back to graph))
11   it shoulda been like that
12   (1.30)

The professor, after a brief pause (line 04), then produces the second curve and labels it with the relation $B \neq 0$. In the process, he talks at rather low speech volume, as if he were talking just for himself, about entropy and magnetic field as not being zero. Whereas the drawing of the curve proceeds smoothly after he has found the starting point in the origin, his speech makes offers ("when the entropy") and withdraws ("no") and changes them ("when magnetization is not zero"). He writes "$B \neq 0$" and then, after a brief pause, appears to address a student at the right front end of the classroom, "over there." He walks to that part of the classroom (as in Figure 3.8) and then, while noting "the drawing was not quite right, as you see," walks back to the new drawing.

In this situation, we see examples of two relationships that a holistic analysis of communication in situation needs to appropriately describe and theorize: speech–drawing/writing and hand movement–drawing/gesturing. First, speech and drawing/writing are very different modes and cannot be directly related. They are different parts of a higher-order, integrated communicative unit. They express the unit in a part-whole manner, but, being of different type and with different structure, express *different* moments of the whole. Therefore, speech and writing/drawing should not be taken as equivalent and pertaining to the same, unless this "same" is meant to be the whole. Speaking and writing/drawing, therefore, have some family resemblance with the cinematographic method of voice-over, where there is a plane at which some action unfolds and a second plane at which a voice speaks "over" (more loudly) the continuing movie. The relation of voice-over and film (documentary) is not straightforward, as the movies of the French New Wave cinema in the 1950s to 1970s show. In the limit, image and voice are dissociated completely, as in Marguerite Duras' film *India Song*; and yet, because they are part of the *same* film, they are also part of the same overarching communicative unit. In the psycholinguistic literature, there is, therefore, a debate whether individuals expressing two conceptually very different things have one internally contradictory or two mutually exclusive conceptions.

In the present instance, part of the speech does not refer to the diagram that is in the process of unfolding but can be heard as a meta-commentary spoken in a voice-over mode. Thus, when the professor notes that the "drawing was not quite right, as you see," he invites to be heard as making a commentary comparing the first, now-erased and therefore ephemeral drawing and the present drawing in the same place on the chalkboard. He makes this commentary not while standing directly next to the new drawing but from a distance, a different position where he takes position with respect to two antecedent positions facing different graphs. This distance also has a metaphorical dimension, as it allows him to look at what he has produced and at that which is partially available. By taking distance, he no longer is in the "thickets of things" but speaks from a new position that allows him to look at and compare two different entities, both of which he has produced—not unlike Archimedes asking for a point outside the Earth so that he can lift it with a lever ("Give me a place to stand on and I can move the Earth"). The physical (and temporal) distance to the graphs articulates, both for the audience and for himself, this reflective stance that the distant vantage (leverage) point provides. The nature of his language has changed from being *in* and *for* the production of graphs to one of reflecting *on* the relative appropriateness of the two.

Second, drawing a curve calls attention to the curve in much the same way as a pointing gesture following it when the graph is already there: it makes the entity salient against everything else present in the setting. This "everything else" includes the process of drawing, for we observe the curve unfolding before our eyes rather than the process of its production. The chalk leaves a trace of its trajectory whereas in the case of the gesture over a graph, its trajectory comes to be produced against the existing trace. In both instances, the body produces a similar hand/arm movement that has a corresponding expression in a trace, produced in the former instance, already existing in the latter. The communicative significance arises from the co-presence of trace and movement, each motivating the presence of the other and, therefore, with respect to signification, constituting each other. They are both part of the whole communicative unit. Each in fact is an expression of the whole unit and stands to it in a part–whole relationship where the part, in metonymic manner, refers to the whole of which it is itself a part. But such a referral to, and standing in for, the whole can only be one-sided, as the part inherently cannot equally represent the structures of the other parts. But in the case of iconic gestures and movements that produce some sign, the movement and the signifier (gesture) have great similitude (family resemblance) based on their visual–perceptual properties. Because of this similitude, they are easily seen (perceived) as denoting the same (similar) (aspect of) the concept (idea).

Producing a signifier of refrigeration by means of adiabatic demagnetization

The curves for the temperature–entropy relationships at constant magnetic fields constitute only the theoretical context within which two consecutive processes can be used to decrease the temperature of a sample. The following gloss provides a description of this process. First, a magnetic field around the sample to be cooled is turned on and increased to the desired level (corresponding to the $B \neq 0$ curve). If the temperature of the sample is held constant, which can be achieved by placing the material in a coolant bath, then the magnetic field brings about an alignment of the molecule-sized magnets of the sample. But alignment means more order, and more order means less entropy. Thus, as the surrounding magnetic field increases, the entropy drops, yielding a strictly vertical line of the graph because the temperature T is held constant (see rightmost two images in Figure 3.5). Now the magnetic field is brought back to zero ($B = 0$) without holding the temperature constant. Because the molecular magnets disorient, the entropy associated with the order increases again, which, because the total entropy is constant, is compensated by a drop in the temperature of the sample. In the diagram, the line corresponding to this process of adiabatic demagnetization is a horizontal line from a magnetization unequal to zero ($B \neq 0$) to one of zero ($B = 0$) at constant entropy (S), corresponding to a decrease in temperature (movement of line from right to left). In the current situation, the professor's presentation is captured in Fragment 3.3.

The episode begins with the professor's announcement that they ("let's" = "let *us*") are going to do an adiabatic demagnetization (line 13). He pauses for a long time—the standard maximum silence in (telephone) conversations is about one second—turns to the graph, and, after some mumbling and stumbling, suggests that "first of all we do a isothermal magnetization" (lines 16–17). He produces the "first of all" rapidly, as if trying to make up time and as if formulating what is to come next. However, as if belying his verbal stumbling, the hand already places the chalk at a point on the $B = 0$ line and right after the "first of all," he begins to draw what comes to be a downward line (i.e., T = constant) that stops when meeting with the second ($B \neq 0$) curve (rightmost two images in Figure 3.5). After a brief pause, he then proceeds to produce the line that corresponds to the earlier announced adiabatic demagnetization (line 19, center image in Figure 3.5).

Fragment 3.3

```
13   so now lets do 'adia`batic `demagnetiza'tion
14   [(2.71)
     [((turns to graph))
15   and uh (0.42) i thing
16   [well intr uh well uh <<all>first of all> we [do uh:: (0.28)
     [((first image from right))                 [((draws what will
17   a iso'thermal    ] (0.29) magnetization
     be downward line))]
18   (1.23)
19   then we=ll do: (0.23) an [   adiabatic demagneti    ]zation,
                              [((draws horizontal to left))]
20   (0.54)
21   [and then we=ll do:    ] another one, (0.54) [and another one,]
     [((draws vertical line))]                    [((  horizontal  ))]
```

22 (0.42) <<dim>and another one, (0.30) and another one, (0.27)
23 and another one, (0.17) and another one,
24 and another one, and another one,>
25 (1.05)
26 we done 'we get ↑very very close within but [extre:mely close to
                                                    [₁((walks away from graph
        as shown in Figure 3.6))
27 absolute zero (0.21)
28 but i think you can see [₂from that (0.21) that you=re never
29 actually[₃going to get to absolute zero in a finite <<dim>number
30 of operations.>[₄ (1.72)[₅

The two chalk lines produced so far look like a step down and to the right. After a brief pause, the professor produces a second step, first making the downward line and with only a brief pause intervening, then drawing the horizontal equivalent (Figure 3.5, second and first offprint from the left). The professor proceeds to produce several more such steps, accompanying the drawing of each line by a commentary "and another one" (lines 22–24). He then comments, that in this situation and by means of this process, "we get … extremely close to absolute zero" (lines 26–27) and he invites students to see for themselves that they ("you") "never actually get to absolute zero in a finite number of operations" (lines 28–29). He does not actually explicate the reason for this—which lies in the fact that in this drawing, the two curves meet at the origin (name for the place in the graph where $T = 0$ and $S = 0$). In the previous graph (as can be seen in Figure 3.4), the same two processes would have taken him into negative temperatures. We cannot know whether he actually realizes this while noting that there is something strange in his first attempt at explicating and explaining the cooling process, but he does express his uneasiness and uncertainty about what he has done at that time. As he now completes drawing the steps, he begins turning his body to walk away to the front right corner of the classroom (Figure 3.6), his gaze directed at part of the audience, accompanying his talk by beat gestures that have a scanting effect (center of Figure 3.6), and pausing at what becomes the very end of his trajectory (between the two last positions in Figure 3.6).

As previously, this episode is rich with signifying elements and signification involving words, hand movements (including those that we call *ergotic* [working] and *semiotic* [gesturing])—body orientations, body positions, and, as the transcript shows, minor and major (jumps in) pitch modulations, and changing voice intensities. At any one instant, all of these are expressions—especially when salient in their changes from instant to instant—of the communicative unit as a whole.

This episode begins with a clearly different intentionality expressed in speech and hand movement. Whereas the latter proceeds rather smoothly—if anything, waiting for speech to catch up—the former is full of hesitation and inarticulateness. Speech does not appear to know what it is to say, whereas the hand is ready and enacts what, when all is said and done, will have been essential moments of the

Figure 3.5 As he talks, the professor produces a graphical representation that corresponds to different parts of his narrative:: downward lines correspond to isothermal magnetization and horizontal lines drawn from right to left, correspond to adiabatic (iso-entropic) demagnetization and cooling. (The photo has to be read from right to left corresponding to the professor's movement and to the underlying physics T → 0.)

Figure 3.6 After producing a representation of the cooling process, the professor walks to the right front end of the classroom, pausing lengthily as if to let everything "sink in" prior to continuing the conclusion of this subtopic. (Time unfolds from left to right, the five positions being precisely timed and marked in the transcript.)

communication. The idea is underdeveloped at that instance, in the process of becoming itself, and, because of the intervening formations, expressing itself in different ways consistent with the way in which Vygotsky (1986) describes the evolution of thinking | speaking. It is, in the terms of materialist dialectic philosophy, a very abstract (i.e., very undeveloped) idea that concretizes itself in the speech and manual act, and, in concretizing itself, actually develops into a fully fletched idea, though the same beginning, at another time, might have given rise to different concretizations as well. The hesitations observable in the verbal mode are indicators that the idea is not yet present in its entirety, for otherwise there would not be any reason for the hesitations, stumbles, and mumbles. That is, thinking | speaking does not yet exist in fully fletched form but develops from abstract (undeveloped) to concrete (developed). It is a process that organizes itself in and through concretizing itself. Thinking | speaking becomes as it realizes itself; it becomes something real, whereas before it was only something possible, still ephemeral, a tiny inconspicuous seed that only has the potential to become a majestic pine tree or a crippled dwarf pine depending on the conditions.

As before, we see very different orientations associated with different discourses and topics. The professor takes position with respect to the unfolding idea, and this position is perceptually available in his physical position. While directly in front of the graph and taking it and its development as his topic, the professor's body orientation and hand/arm movements clearly signal to the audience what is the relevant topic at the instant. When he talks about something not clearly perceivable—the uncertainty is signaled by the modifier "I think" to the verb "you can see," which decreases the degree to which a statement can be taken as a fact—he actually has already covered some distance between himself and the graph. This corresponds to the same distance that he has had between himself and the graph in the previous episode, where he compared it with the one he had drawn earlier.

In this episode section, the professor also produces a four-times-repeated up–down hand movement while suggesting that this method never actually allows one to get to absolute zero (i.e., temperature on the Kelvin scale) in a finite amount of time. When the down position is coordinated with sound, we see that they occur precisely when speech intensity and pitch take high values (Figure 3.7). Such gestures neither have figurative content that resembles another visual figure in the setting (i.e., they are not iconic gestures) nor point to some feature in the setting (i.e., they are not pointing gestures). Yet they are gestures with significant communicative—that is, interactive—function, nevertheless, and have been denoted by the terms *batons* or *beat gestures*. (An additional analysis of such beat gestures and its function in social coordination is presented in Chapter 7.) Gestures such as those shown in Figure 3.2 belong to this class of interactive gestures. In the present situation they can be understood as functioning in concert with other signs to underscore the importance of a specific point. Let us take a closer look at the transcription that also features the continuous information on pitch, speech intensity, and speech rate.

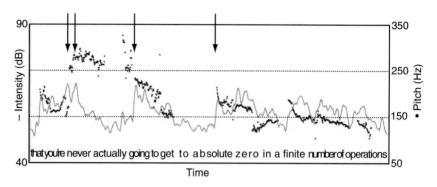

Figure 3.7 Coordination of speech intensity, sound (words), pitch, and down position of beat gesture.

Figure 3.7 shows, in a dramatic fashion, how the down positions of the beats (one of which is indicated in Figure 3.6) fall together with peaks in pitch and speech intensity (volume). Higher pitches and increased speech intensity are generally heard as emphases. That is, two forms of prosodic emphases fall together with the beat gesture, a movement that is usually seen as *scanting* and, therefore, also as emphasizing particular points. In Figure 3.7, two other instances of emphases generated by drawn-out syllables can be observed: "act" (in actually) and "abs" (in "absolute") are heard as emphasized, which is achieved by the drawn-out nature of the sounds corresponding to the syllables. (In line 26, the center of the adverb "extremely," as indicated by the colon, is equally drawn out and thereby heard as being emphasized.) In the present situation, the emphases produced by prosodic and gestural means tell the audience to pay particular attention to the content of the present sentence; here the gestural emphases enhance the more-frequently produced prosodic ones. Emphases are important means that speaking uses to inform the audience how to parse the sound stream and which aspects of the parsed sound stream are more important than others. In this way, speech, above all, teaches the teaching itself (Levinas 1971)—it is teaching how to be heard and understood. It is not that speakers produce these features consciously—gestures, or rather gesticulations, such as those analyzed here are not, in general, produced consciously. Rather, part of a developing idea is its communicative function and the structuring of the produced signs for the benefit of the recipient. These communicative resources are important for the hearing, for it is a process not only about hearing content but also a process that has to organize itself while attending to speech. This self-organization in the process of hearing has to occur, because there are always alternatives to hearing—Derrida (e.g., 1984) invites his audiences explicitly to hear with whichever ear they feel like. This self-organizational moment of hearing responds to the question, "how do I have to listen to hear what the speaker is trying to say?" In this way, hearing can organize and reorganize itself as it attends to the saying, which aids in understanding that which the speaker intends to say. Speaking, oriented to and being for the other, provides resources so that hearing can organize itself to hear precisely that which speaking offers as its content.

It is important here to note that the beat gestures are produced while the professor walks away from the graph rather than while standing in front of and talking over and about it. In the lectures generally, beat and other communicative gestures (such as that in Figure 3.2) are produced when the professor is in the sideways or frontal position with respect to the audience, but not while he is facing the board to draw or gesture toward/along something.

With this, the description of magnetocaloric refrigeration by means of adiabatic demagnetization preceded by a non-temperature-changing isothermal magnetization has come to an end. Moreover, the professor has insistently suggested that absolute zero temperature could not be reached by means of this process. By presenting the graph, the professor has shown how the process is represented graphically and theoretically in terms of a magneto-thermodynamic effect. Is there something else that could be done to assist the audience in learning? Many lectures do not just present materials but also assist audiences in other ways to understand, for example, by performing analogies that elaborate the present topic and connect it to other domains supposed or known to obtain a similar structure in some aspect. In the present situation, the professor produces three analogies within a matter of a few seconds, and the performance of these analogies rests in part on different forms of gestures, changes in position, and changes in body orientation.

Elaborating by means of analogies

Metaphor, whereby the use of the name of one thing comes to be extended by using it for another, is *the* fundamental process that produces the continuous expansion of language and ideas (Derrida 1972). Analogy, the equivalency of likeness or relation, is a special form of metaphor, because one phenomenon comes to be understood in terms of another. Analogy constitutes an important teaching strategy as it allows learners to transfer something they already know onto a new phenomenon that bears general likeness or bears likeness in some respect. This likeness comes to link the two phenomena. Individuals unfamiliar with a domain generally focus on surface (perceptual) features, whereas those very familiar will point to so-called "deep" structures that are common to the two phenomena. For example, in one of my studies, tenth-grade students treated the Foucault pendulum and a magnetic pendulum (an iron bob swinging over magnets) as analogous, because both changed their planes of swing. But for the physicist, the former not only changes the plane continuously but also is based on the gravitational field, whereas the latter is dominated by the magnetic field giving rise to a chaotic and unpredictable movement of the pendulum. A fundamental contradiction in learning by means of analogies, therefore, comes from the particulars of perception: perception is theory-laden but in learning-by-means-of-analogies, the theory is the intended outcome rather than the precondition that guides the perception of the relevant features. It is not surprising, therefore, that students often generate analogies based on surface features that lead them astray from, rather than taking them to, the intended/desired understanding. Teaching by means of analogy may be facilitated if the lecturer not only articulates the source (known) and target (new) phenomena but also points toward the common deep structure that physicists use to establish the relationship between the two phenomena. Such facilitation occurs throughout the recorded lectures generally and in the present instance in particular. Again, the professor produces very different semiotic (sense-making) resources as part of the communicative whole to generate the analogy.

Immediately after the final pause in the previous episode, one can observe what we subsequently recognize as the growth point (seed) for a new idea—the analogical relation between the present cooling process and that which can be produced by other means. Most important among these other means is the one of cooling by adiabatic decompression, which is the process underlying most household refrigerators and freezers.[6] As in other situations, the new idea announces itself in very unfinished and undeveloped form, "that's not going to apply only to adiabatic demagnetization."

As the professor continues talking, his pitch moves into a register (mean = 254 Hz) nearly twice his normal range (mean = 134.7 Hz, SD = 10.3) and there are strong emphases on "that's" and "not only." His hands and arms spread (Figure 3.8, rightmost offprint); but then there are two longer pauses and sounds generally associated with stopping when a speaker cannot articulate him or herself (line 33 of Fragment 3.4). If an idea consisted of verbal components and concepts, these pauses and inarticulateness could not be understood, unless one created some pathological model of the professor in which the pathways between his core thought and his expressions of thought in peripheral means are damaged or blocked. But this is not the theoretical route I take, as I, thereby following Vygotsky, tend to think of ideas in terms of emergent phenomena that evolve and realize themselves over time in the dialogically unfolding thinking|speaking unit. In the present situation, there actually has been the beginning of an idea marked in the hand/arm gesture (line 32): something is extended or expanded. Although in real time, the gesture may not have a unique interpretation at that instant, the audience will retrospectively understand it within a few seconds.

Fragment 3.4

```
31   and <<h>thats going to apply 'not=only to> (.) a:diabatic
32   demagnetization, (0.28) [₁ts going to]
                              [₁((opens arms as in Figure 3.8))
33   (0.95) uh hh (0.98) <<pp>hu uh y>
34   we talked up there bout [₂isothermal compr↑ess↓ion,[₃ followed by
35   an a::[₄diabatic ↑`de[₅compression.]
            [₅((gesture back to position
```

As he begins to talk again, the professor reminds the audience that they ("we") have talked about something before (line 34), which he then articulates to have been isothermal compression and adiabatic decompression. In parallel to the talk, he performs a gesture that begins near the configuration he has taken for some time (since line 32), forms a fist with his right hand, which he then moves like a piston toward his left hand while uttering "isothermal compression" and moves in the reverse direction while producing "adiabatic decompression" (lines 34–35, Figure 3.8). The transcript shows the prosodic emphasis to occur on the "ess" of "compression" and on the "de" of the reverse process. The hand/arm movement is associated with a shift in the body, forward in the case of compression, and backward in the case of the decompression (Figure 3.8), suggestive of the efforts, forces, or energies required—that is, the movement of the whole body is an additional sense-making resource that underscores the importance of the hand/arm gesture. For individuals familiar with car engines or bicycle pumps, there is an easily established relationship between the verbal expressions "compression" and "decompression," on the one hand and the two-part gesture, on the other: a piston moving forward in its chamber, thereby compressing the gas mixtures (air–fuel mix, air) and then moving to the other end, thereby decompressing the gas mixtures. The whole body, in and through the different communicative forms it produces, therefore, becomes an expression of thought, of an analogy. The thinking and its expression, in the body, come to be undecidable, as we cannot tell the difference between thought and its expressions, here vividly and expressively staged before an audience.

The students present in the relevant earlier lecture may remember that the compression and decompression referred to is that of a gas, the classical case generally discussed in physics lectures on the topic of thermodynamics. In the contrast between the gestures featured in Figure 3.1 and Figure 3.8, we clearly see very different positions and orientations associated with the respective (different) gestures. In Figure 3.1, the gesture occurs in a two-dimensional plane, paralleling the surface of the chalkboard. The gesture–diagram relation allows the audience to pick out what is relevant in each, and, therefore, to understand the communicative intent. In the present instance, the professor talks about something that is not directly available on the chalkboard and he produces gestures that use the three dimensions of physical space. Also, he is oriented frontally toward the audience. This is a general and generalizable observation, as I have observed such a correlation between body position (away from the inscription), body orientation with respect to inscription and audience, and type of gesture in very different lectures (seventh-grade environmental science, twelfth-grade biology [physiology], second-year university ecology) with very different conceptual and theoretical contents.

In the light of the performed gestures, the initial hand/arm configuration that the professor produces while pausing and stuttering—in vernacular, such situations frequently are described as "searching for words"—becomes significant. It is, in fact, very near the initial configuration of the subsequent gesture that can be seen as depicting a system that compresses and decompresses a gas. The gesture comes to be the earliest (and most undeveloped) form in which the idea about the compression–decompression turns out to be articulated. It expresses itself over two seconds prior to the verbal articulations begining to say anything that could be associated with the same phenomenon. The open-armed gesture, therefore, constitutes a *growth point*, that is, a seed from which a new idea begins to form and take shape.

Linguistically, there already is a hint of the presence of a common structure that would be part of an analogy linking the two thermodynamic processes articulated so far: in both, there is an isothermal and an adiabatic component. In the phenomenon of interest, the isothermal component occurs together with magnetization, whereas in the analogy, it is compression; the adiabatic component in the magneto-thermodynamic situation occurs during *de*magneti-zation and in the analogy it occurs during *de*compression. That is, the similarity resides not only in the common adjectives "isothermal" and "adiabatic," but also in the parallel structure of a process (magnetization, compression) and its inverse (*de*magnetization, *de*compression). But the professor does even more to assist his students in understanding and comprehending the structural similari-ties that map the two situations onto each other. In their physical expressions, the two phenomena are very dissimilar, one pertaining to the de/compression of gases, the other to the de/magnetization of elementary, molecule-sized magnets. But theoretically, there is an underlying equivalence, which can be expressed in the same diagram.[7]

In the 2.77 second pause, the professor turns around and walks back toward the graph. He produces sounds normally associated with hesitation while gaz-ing toward the graph (Figure 3.9, line 37: [$_2$). He begins at very low volume to utter that this can be followed on a pressure volume diagram (lines 37–38). In the process, he produces another open-handed gesture (Figure 3.9, line 38: [$_3$) before turning around and gesturally following the first (rightmost) step in the diagram (Figure 3.9, line 38: [$_4$–[$_6$). He gesturally follows the next several steps each accompanied by a verbal "like that" (line 39). He then turns around to his left, walks toward the left-hand corner of the classroom, and produces a gesture similar to that in Figure 3.8, but this time as if the right hand held some narrow entity that he was pulling. Simultaneously, he articulates "expanding and con-tracting of a wire, and then elaborates, "anything expanding contracting a wire or a rubber band" (lines 41–42), repeating the previous gesture twice. There is more hesitation noticeable in the production of over two seconds of pauses and the intermittent "uh hm" (line 42). He then utters what, unbeknownst to all, will have been the final and concluding statement: the entropy is zero at abso-lute zero whatever the tension in the wire. As previously, there are deictic–iconic features against graphical detail associated with a full-body orientation to the chalkboard and three-dimensional gestures concerning phenomena not available on the chalkboard away from the inscription and with body orientation toward the audience.

Figure 3.8 Located near the right-hand corner of the seating arrangement, the professor uses iconic gestures seriated into an iconic performance of isothermically compressing, adiabatically decompressing, and refrigerating gas. (To be read from left to right.)

Figure 3.9 The professor walks from the right end of the chalkboard back toward the graph, produces an indescript gesture, turns toward the graph and gestures in a two-dimensional plane parallel to the vertical and horizontal lines corresponding to the cooling process by isothermal magnetization and adiabatic demagnetization but, in the narrative, referring to the corresponding process by isothermal compression and adiabatic decompression. (To be read from right to left.)

Figure 3.10 In the span of less than a minute, the professor covers a lot of physical space from the front to the side of the room, orients his body in different ways (sideways, frontal, back to audience) and uses different forms of gestures. (To be read from left to right.)

Fragment 3.5

    36 (2.77)
    37 u:h um[₂ <<pp>we can>
    38 we can follow that[₃ on a pressure 'volume di:[₄agr[₅am[₆ and
    39 <<p>we go like that and like that and like that>
    40 O::R: (0.51) <<p>or rather> (0.30) with uh (0.53)
    41 [Expanding and contracting of a wire;   ] anything expanding
        [(((gesture similar to Fig. 3.8 but diagonal))]
    42 contracting a wire or a rubber ba::nd, (0.94) uh hm (1.24)
    43 when (.) when the wire the tension be zero or not, (0.16)
    44 at absolute zero its entropy is going to be zero.

In this situation, the professor first maps the compression–decompression case onto the magneto-thermodynamic example by gesturing to and over a graph representing the latter while talking about the former. This directly brings together the two phenomena—at least as long as audience members remember that the graph belongs to the previously articulated phenomenon, whereas the present narrative is about the other, already familiar, one from previous lectures. This repetition is to serve as the analogical source for understanding the analogical target. Moreover, the professor will provide two further analogical cases—a wire and a rubber band—that expand and contract. Here, the link to the previous analog case is produced in several ways. First, both involve processes of some physical expansion and contraction. Second, both accounts involve highly similar gestures, which, in the second case, mainly involve a 45 degree rotation of the gesture, now produced along a diagonal with respect to the horizontal–vertical dimension of the classroom. Third, in all these instances, the body positions and body orientations correspond to that taken in the account of the gas case. All of these points substantiate an idea initially expressed over 60 years ago but, heretofore, neglected in the literature on language, learning, and context: "To be able to express it, the body *has to become*, in the final analysis, the very idea or intention that it signifies to us" (Merleau-Ponty 1945: 230, original emphasis). The body is not separate from the idea (thought) or its articulation in speech. The body is the point where the difference between thinking and speaking is undecidable. But the body also is the only point that gives us access to both simultaneously.

Speaking | thinking in lectures

In the course of this lecture, the professor covers a lot of physical space, orients his body in different ways, writes on and gestures (pointed, outlining) toward the chalkboard, writes whole or abbreviated equations, and draws graphs (Figure 3.10). In these different configurations, the manner of speaking changes, as do the topics (content) of talk and his prosody (pitch, intensity, rate). For example, while he is situated at the right wall of the room (from the students' perspective), his body is oriented sideways to the audience. The speech intensity (volume) is low and almost inaudible, his gaze toward the floor: it is as if he is speaking to himself (Figure 3.10, right). For example, he acts in this manner while formulating for the audience that he is thinking about what they have talked about earlier ("what did we talk about?"). He thereby tells the audience that he is trying to remember something and, therefore, is not talking about and presenting concepts. Simultaneously he provides an explanation for the fact that he is not talking. When he, while standing in the front of the classroom, is talking about issues for which there are not direct equivalents on the chalkboard, he faces the audience broadside so that both of his hands and arms can be seen. In these situations, he stands near the front right desks in the room (fourth position from left in Figure 3.10) looking straight at the students. He is turned sideways when he talks about something on the board, sometimes pointing to a formula or graph. Finally, while writing on the chalkboard or actively gesturing in ways that iconically (visually) resemble some feature on the board, he is facing the board, his back turned to the audience (left two positions in Figure 3.10). All of this is evidence for the different ways in which an idea articulates itself in and through the body of the lecturer, differently in its different moments, which sometimes are aligned and mutually pointing to one another, and, at other times, apparently are contradicting each other.

Associated with the modulations in and of body position, body orientation, chalkboard inscriptions, voice qualities (pitch, intensity, rate), pointing and depicting (iconic) gestures are different contents and meta-communicative (i.e., contextual) aspects, such as certainty/uncertainty about the content of talk or importance/unimportance of what was being said. That is, the conceptual (ideational) content of the lecture expresses itself differently in different modes, and thereby comes to be distributed across these modes, sometimes synchronically, sometimes diachronically, always variegated, and sometimes contradictorily (non-unitary). These contradictions sometimes are the source for conceptual contradictions that may or may not have become salient in the lecturer's consciousness. Thus, strictly speaking and unbeknownst to the students, there are tensions and contradictions that pass during the lectures. This is not a singular phenomenon, but one that I have noted in the course of my research on lectures generally, including at the university level where the professors do have the conceptual and cognitive competencies required to present the scientific facts and theories correctly.[8] In the present instance, the professor walks to the diagram, which spans a graph in a set of temperature–entropy axes, but talks about a pressure–volume diagram, whereas his gesture follows the lines in the *T–S* diagram. Let us take a closer look at the situation.

Isothermal compression and adiabatic expansion are processes involved in the Carnot cycle that underlie refrigeration. A quick search on the Internet shows that the Carnot cycle is presented in a *T–S* (Figure 3.11a) rather than an *S–T* diagram (Figure 3.11b). As the figures show, in the *T–S* diagram, the step-like gesture corresponds to an adiabatic (is[o]entropic) expansion followed by an isothermal compression—the reverse order from that represented in gesture. If the axes are reversed to correspond to the present situation, the Carnot cycle reverses and the isothermal compression followed by an isentropic expansion unfolds opposite to the Carnot cycle underlying refrigeration. Finally, if the diagram were to present the refrigeration in a pressure–volume diagram as the professor articulates verbally, then the two processes would not at all look like the steps shown on the chalkboard and made salient in the gesture (Figure 3.11c). The two change processes present themselves in a counter-clockwise direction and are not orthogonal as in the figure on the chalkboard.

Rather than claiming that there is something wrong in the person's head, I suggest we look at this situation as one of ideas in development. These ideas are unfolded in real time, concretizing themselves in and through the body of the professor as he moves along. Especially when the talk has not been pre-planned in all its details, the idea may never be developed to the point that all contradictions are removed even in a situation where the person has over 30 years of experience teaching. Because of their extensive training in the subject matter, it is likely that professors would catch such contradictions if only they had a little more time and a little more reflection. In some instances, the lecture itself provides the resources to recover from an error, such as it occurs between Fragment 3.1 and the remaining fragments in this chapter. We can think of lectures as the production of resources that not only the audience, but also the lecturer, can use for marking, re-marking, and remarking sense. In the present case, there are repeated instances within the same lecture and within a span of 15 minutes where the professor halts to stare at some inscription on the chalkboard, apparently being stuck or uncertain about what he has said. In each case, he later changes what he has said, drawn, or written, which suggests that what he has done in the meantime provides the resources to detect and recover from some error committed earlier in the lecture. Thus, he first draws his diagram of the refrigeration process by means of adiabatic demagnetiza-tion only to wipe it off the chalkboard later to replace it with another diagram. Moreover, he first interprets one term of the Gibbs–Helmholtz relation as going to zero when he later explains that the chemist Nernst proposed to define the term as zero when the temperature approaches absolute zero because the choice is arbi-trary and changes nothing in the physics of the phenomenon or in the theory.

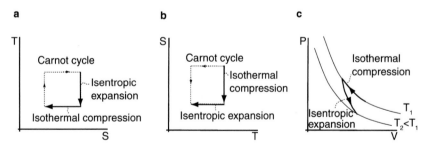

Figure 3.11 Three representations of isothermal compression and adiabatic (is[o]enthropic) expansion.

  a In most (online) resources, cooling is represented using the Carnot cycle in a *T–S* diagram but the two subprocesses are reversed.

  b In a *S–T* diagram, the two processes run against the direction of the Carnot cycle but the step function is maintained.

  c In a *p–V* diagram, the two processes are curves and the direction is reversed.

This case—as my research program concerning lectures generally—supports a theoretical framework in which ideas are not taken as one-dimensional and finished, somehow encoded in the mind, but as unfinished processes continually developing as they concretize themselves in the communicative performance. In the process, they also integrate themselves over, which means, conversations and lectures are entirely historical and historically contingent processes in which earlier instants in time mediate what comes later but do not (causally) determine it. Thus, for example, the second presentation of the isothermal magnetization followed by an adiabatic demagnetization is occasioned, emerging from the contradiction between the implications of one formula verbally articulated and an existing graph on the chalkboard that shows something different. Neither the previous graph nor the equation and the verbally articulated implications *cause* the professor to take up the issue again and to make another drawing and to produce the analogies that follow. If it were a matter of causation, human beings would be entirely predictable, on the one hand, and errors such as the one observed would not have to occur, on the other hand, unless there is pathology in the cognitive mechanism. I instead tend to favor a non-mechanistic dialogical explication in which agency and resources mutually constitute and shape each other (see Chapter 4).

In a dialogical account of (participative) thinking that expresses itself in and across the various communicative modes, an idea (thought) is taken to be an unfinished, unitary process, which articulates itself differently in the different modes. As genes can express themselves differently in different contexts (with other genes) and settings (environments), so the seeds of thoughts do not have to go one way or another. Rather, as thought concretizes itself in speech, it also provides resources for transforming itself. The differences produced in the process are understood as *inner contradictions*. These inner contradictions constitute the "engines" of change in the mind that lead to the mind's development. As an idea unfolds from its initial stages (states), logical contradictions may become apparent within the same mode, for example, the verbal mode, or on the same topic. Thus, in the present instance, the professor indicates at various times that the entropy is non-zero when the temperature is zero (e.g., on the first graph) and that it is zero when the temperature is zero. Such contradictions, which are outer expressions of inner contradictions of thought, also are engines of change, as the mind, once conscious of them, is driven to resolve them.

In such an account, lectures and the participative thinking that goes with them always are unfinished, always in development: each time a lecturer produces some sense-making resource in whatever communicative mode it might be, the ideas, concepts, thoughts actually performed include a new aspect that has expanded what existed before. Such new aspects mediate what is to come, which may be a revision of what has been presented before. For this reason, what the ideas, concepts, and thoughts look like cannot be fully anticipated. Thus, in the present situation, the analogies and generalizations of the sequence of isothermal and adiabatic processes that lead to cooling come to be presented in the second iteration of the graph but are not present in the first.

Toward a holistic understanding of language

Lectures are more than simple texts or verbal phenomena containing information that some professor wants "to get across." They are highly complex phenomena where, if anything, many different forms of information (i.e., semiotic resources) are produced synchronously and diachronically. Moreover, both the ideas presented and the participative thinking that goes with the lecture are unfinished entities continuously in the process of developing as they concretize themselves in real lecture performance. An experience common among teachers generally, and lecturers particularly, suggests that in the course of lecturing on the same content for years, instructors themselves learn and come to better understand the concepts and theories they are in the process of teaching. This would suggest that taken over repeated iterations, the ideas, concepts, and thoughts of lecturers continue to evolve with each concretization, always adding new semiotic resources, which mediate the previously existing configurations of resources for marking, re-marking, and remarking sense. As one chemistry professor once told me, after having taught the same course for 20 years, he now felt ready to begin teaching the course. There is a lot of wisdom in this statement, wisdom that most current theories of knowing and understanding do not and cannot capture. That is, he felt that his own comprehension of the subject matter had sufficiently matured only in the course of 20 years of teaching it. The present model of communication and participative thought during lecturing provides a suitable account that allows us to understand such continuous development of comprehension. It is never a finished product, but always is a process of thinking in the making that grows each time it realizes itself—whether in tutoring, lecturing, or other situations. There is never only one mode articulating ideas but always many, variegatedly and contradictorily articulating an irreducible whole. Moreover, "information" or "concepts" are never presented in the same way but always emerge as situated performances, making use of the resources at hand, continuously transforming the self-transforming participative thought that goes with the activity of lecturing.

Although there are many scholars pointing to the visual nature of Western culture and education, the Greco-Christian *tradition* ("In the beginning was the word") *privileges language* when it comes to knowing and learning, which has led the French philosopher Jacques Derrida (e.g., 1978) to use the nickname and adjective "phallogocentrism" and "phallogocentric" characterizing white, Western, and male-centered philosophy and theories of knowing (metaphysics). At all levels of education, this orientation to linguistic over all other forms of expression can be seen from the ways in which students are examined across academic subjects, where the focus is on "concepts" and textual forms rather than on images, performances, and even emotion. Yet there has been substantial research in a variety of domains but especially in the field of (cognitive) anthropology about the situated, distributed, contingent, emotive, ethico-moral, and performative dimensions of knowing and learning (e.g., Roth 2007, 2008b). When research on learning recognizes that thinking|speaking articulates itself by means other than the verbal mode, two fundamental assumptions generally are made. First, these other aspects influence, determine, or mediate cognition from the outside generally in a negative way, that is, diminishing the quality of thinking (cognizing).

Second, these other aspects can be expressed verbally without loss—thus, if researchers describe the gestures someone uses in their articles, then they do so verbally. Yet there is considerable doubt that such a reduction of gestures to words can be made legitimately. For example, the widely cited Russian psychologist Vygotsky (e.g., 1986) suggested in the early 1930s that speech and gestures cannot be reduced to one another and that thinking generally cannot be reduced to what is expressible in speech. Here "reduction" means that one mode (e.g., gesture) is expressible by the other (e.g., language). How, then, can we think of the speech–gesture and speech–thought relationships if one cannot represent the other and yet is integral to and constitutive of it? This question is very difficult in much of Western thought, but there are nevertheless precedents for thinking these relations, which I explicate in the following analogy.

In physics, the phenomenon of light expresses itself sometimes as a wave (e.g., in reflection and refraction phenomena in camera lenses) and sometimes as a particle (e.g., in light meters and the charge-coupled devices that are used as image sensors in digital cameras). Light *is not* a wave but sometimes expresses itself as such; light *is not* a particle but sometimes expresses itself as such. Because being a wave and being a particle exclude one another, light cannot *be* both particle and wave at the same time. But we can think of light as a superordinate phenomenon that expresses itself sometimes in this and sometimes in that way. How it expresses itself depends on the way we look and on the instruments we use to investigate.

Similarly, we can think of thought as expressing itself sometimes in this (e.g., word, language) and sometimes in that way (e.g., gesture, emotion). In the same way that the wave character of light cannot be used to describe or explain its particle character, we need to think of gestures and words as unable to express the other. Both are *articulations* of thought but they *are not* thought. These expressions are one-sided, which means they capture some aspects of thought without capturing thought as a whole, its essence, and without being able to capture the essence of other modes in which thought expresses itself. Many scholars appear to believe—as shown in their practices of representing research and research findings—that one mode of thought (language, speech, gesture, image) can be translated into another. Authors verbally describe rather than provide photographs or drawings of gestures; and, as I have personally experienced, some editors of social scientific journals ask their authors to eliminate the visual representations of gestures and other perceptual phenomena. But scholars in other fields concerned with the nature of translation know that every translation expresses differently (Ricœur 2004b)—if it were expressing *precisely* the same, translation would be unnecessary—an intuition already captured in the Italian folk saying *traduttore, traditore* (translating is committing treason).

This understanding of the speech–gesture–thought relationship developed in the previous paragraphs undergirds the work of the psycholinguist David McNeill (e.g., 2002), who explicitly grounds his approach in the earlier work of Vygotsky. In my own research group, this approach has been extended to encompass additional modes of knowing, including body orientations, perceptual aspects of the setting, body positions, emotions (as expressed in various prosodic features of the voice), and other properties of the setting. When a phenomenon expresses itself in different ways (modes) to which it cannot be reduced and which do not permit translations into other modes, dialectical philosophers speak of *moments*, which are thought of as constitutive structures of the whole phenomenon, but which cannot be thought in themselves and are independent from the phenomenon because their special nature only comes to the fore in its relation to the whole.

The upshot of these analyses is that language receives a new place. Although still privileged, it is but part of a more encompassing communicative unit. In this unit, there are moments that cannot be reduced to language. These other aspects, drawings, gestures, prosody, positions, and orientations are moments in their own right. Much as we have moved away from Eurocentrism in cultural studies, we have to move away from (phal-) logocentrism and metaphysics in the study of language, learning, and context. This may provide us with inroads to the learning difficulties that differently abled students experience. The research integrating the embodied, distributed, emotive, contingent, and performative moments of thought (cognition) has focused on understanding knowing and learning, much of it in everyday situations outside schools and some of it in school situations including evaluation. For about a decade, work in my laboratory has accumulated research-based evidence that allows us to understand lectures beyond the verbal mode. More specifically, we have come to understand lecturing as an integrated performance of knowledge in action, which is thereby made available to the audience. If this audience writes down only (some of) the words the lecturer speaks, then not only is the verbal mode of the lecture only partially captured but the other modes are not captured at all. This, then, is a possible and plausible explanation for why students understand lectures, where they are provided with the different expressive modes of the lecturer's knowing, and why they may experience a lack of understanding when facing the few lecture notes that they have made.

Throughout this chapter, readers may note one aspect of my description of language heretofore implicit: the author of speech is not entirely in control of the saying and the said. There is some autonomy to language and ideas that the speaker is not entirely in control of—it is not surprising, then, that Heidegger suggests in the introductory quote of Chapter 1 that it is *language* that speaks. This corresponds to the more general experience that we do not always know where our speaking and the ideas it articulates are taking us. Moreover, the language and other communicative modes we employ not only already exist but also are designed for an audience. There is, therefore, a constraint on communicative action that the speaker is not in control. I turn to the relationship of agency and passivity in and of communication in the next chapter.

4 Agency|passivity in/of communication

[B]eing does not resolve itself into empirical events and in thoughts that reflect these events or that aim at them "intentionally."

(Levinas 1971: 126)

Most theoretical discourses concerning language, learning, and context are, at their very heart, agential and "intentionalist." With the adjective intentionalist I denote the fact that the verbs used in theories of knowing, learning, and being are agential, focusing on the subject who *intends* to do something. This is evident, for example, in the theories of learning according to which students "construct" knowledge or "position themselves" in doing identity work. But, as transitive verbs, both to construct and to position oneself, require an object toward which the action is intended and the outcome to be produced. In the case of the two verbs, the products are knowledge and identity. In the opening quote, however, Emanuel Levinas suggests that being does not resolve itself into things that we fully capture in consciousness, empirical events, thoughts, and intentions aiming at the events. Rather, as I point out in Chapter 1, there is a level of passivity in speaking that comes with language, which always already speaks prior to, and despite of, any intentions that I might have. In fact, speaking overflows with intentions, there are always more intentions possible than the one that might consciously or unconsciously generate what I say. This multiplicity of intentions is no more evident than in those everyday situations where a person charged with something responds, "I didn't intend to hurt/insult/… you."

There are many aporias concerning language, learning, and context that are not dealt with in the relevant literatures, but which have already been outlined in, for example, continental (mainly French) philosophy in the course of the second half of the twentieth century. Among the main aporias is a question already prefigured in Chapter 1 about how to think about language—text and *con*text— if our thinking already is irremediably bound up with language, as shown in Chapter 3. How can we approach language without being impeded by language? Or, to put the question in yet another way, "how can any form of thinking, any psychology, sociology, or epistemology be intended and get off the ground given that, at the instant just prior to the beginning of history, no human rationality and language existed?" How could humans—whom Aristotle has called *zōon ekhon* *logon,* the animal having speech (*logos*), and, therefore, reason (*logos*)—and their various forms of culture (knowledge, practices) emerge given that there were no (human forms of) knowledge, no language, and no consciousness, all of which are required in the going epistemologies? Or, relevant to the disciplines we teach in schools, how is it possible for a rationality to have emerged on the grounds of, and as resource for, an essentially non-disciplinary human experience and form of discourse? Most psychologies and philosophies are non-viable in the sense that they require an agential subject conscious of itself and its intentions. But to have intentions means to have a language (Derrida 1972). The question of consciousness is tied to the question of language. But who intentionally constructed the agential subject conscious of itself when there was no language and, therefore, no (self-) consciousness? Who, in individual development, constructs the agential subject conscious of itself in the absence of self-consciousness characteristic of the newl born child that does not yet have the language required for (self-) consciousness?

In this chapter, I outline some of the attendant issues, thereby sketching out some of the theoretical and practical work that needs to be done to arrive at an epistemology that is viable within an evolutionary and cultural–historical perspective. To my knowledge, there is only one group of psychologists who has engaged in the development of psychological constructs that are viable in this way, because they *could have* arisen from competencies that precede those requiring human (forms of) consciousness (e.g., Holzkamp 1983). In philosophy, similar attempts of founding the nature of human beings generally, and that of language, learning, and context more specifically, fall under the auspices of *first philosophy.* Consistent in their critiques with other critical scholars, critical psychologists and first philosophers accept any theory as sound only under the condition that it can explain phenomena—such as language, learning, or context—without presupposing human capacities that only arose as a consequence of, for example, language, including consciousness, self-consciousness, intentionality, and so on.

A second main aporia lies in what I perceive to be a lack of appropriate theories for thinking the relation of the individual and the collective with respect to language, communication, knowledge, subjectivity, emotions, ethics, and so forth. For example, most psychologists investigate emotions as a purely individual phenomenon, caused by various bodily states. Not only are emotions treated as properties of individuals, but also they (usually) are thought to constitute a system separate from and (negatively) affecting cognition (knowing and learning) from the outside and, therefore, the process of speaking | thinking discussed in Chapter 3. Knowing, too, is treated at the individual level so that it virtually is impossible to understand how normal, everyday people pull off—in relations with other people—the production of complex phenomena such as lessons, field trips, or neighborhood schooling. That is, the discussions of learning and context deal with phenomena that have little if anything to do with how people produce the complex social (societal) situations that make epistemological discussions possible in the first place. I begin to articulate issues pertinent to emotions in this chapter and further elaborate on the communication and communicative function of emotion in Chapter 7.

Origin and nature of intentionality: an aporia

The problem is this: language today is theorized inappropriately because one of the essential moments in its use, passivity, is no longer thought, having been covered up by the use of the concepts intentionality and agency. The metaphysical project has covered up the contradiction—deriving from an inner difference—that passivity is involved at multiple levels and in multiple ways when we speak. For example, the speech intention itself is not intended; and when we do speak with a particular intent, others always can impute a different intent underlying and being expressed in our talk. To arrive at a viable theory of speaking, we need to take into account and theorize the missing part: passivity.

All traditional philosophies—i.e., metaphysical projects—begin with some form of statement that posits the "I" (Descartes, Kant, von Glasersfeld), "subject" (Hegel), or "Self [ego]" (Husserl). What human beings can do, including speaking|thinking, is then thought in terms of the intentional activity of this initially posited center of agency. Thus, the Cartesian or (Kantian) constructivist "I" is said to construct its knowledge through engagement with phenomenal and ideal (transcendental) objects. The subject externalizes and thereby objectifies and estranges itself in the object only to return to the subject in a process of synthesis. In its ultimate attempt to establish ontology (science of beings, things) and epistemology (science of knowledge, knowing) of the individual, metaphysics finally failed because philosophers realized that the individual, Self, subject, and I could not exist without the support—the nature of which remains to be specified—of the generalized other, non-Self. Recognizing that in normal everyday activity we are not consciously self-aware, the notion of *Being* changes the former ontologies in the sense that the focus now is on processes (being, after all, *is* a verb), as a result of which the individual emerges.[1] That is, most theories of knowing and language begin with positing the agent of knowing (which for Martin Heidegger is *Dasein*, Being-there, a noun that can be heard as a verb as well). The point is that classical philosophers have failed to provide for mechanisms in which this agent, in whichever form it is thought, constructs itself or becomes at all possible in some form in the first place.

Protesting the classical positing and positioning of the Self, Emmanuel Levinas (1978: 165) writesmost, "the self cannot construct itself, it is already made from absolute passivity." Other philosophers, too, have struggled with the ways in which the human subject possibly could have become conscious of itself, a precondition for doing some form of philosophy for a first time, both from a cultural–historical level during anthropogenesis (i.e., process of becoming human) and during individual development (ontogenesis, literally the creation, generation, origin [Gr. *genesis*] of being [Gr. *ont-*]). Levinas proposes a process in which the subject finds itself as the result of a situation that is *Otherwise than Being*, as his book title suggests, and from *Beyond Essence*. Similarly, Jean-Luc Nancy (2000) offers us an originary and undifferentiated *with* that comes to break up and unfold into Being and beings, Self and Other, and the familiar and strange. For both philosophers, proximity and touch/ being touched are the conditions for an origin of consciousness that is forever without father, which cannot be willed but always already is occurring to us. Today, each person as part of his or her development has this same experience: when we become conscious we always already speak a language.

This situation is (or should be) a serious problem for psychologists, sociologists, and educators who establish theories of language, learning, and context. The theories they use do not contain mechanism by means of which human forms of thinking | speaking and consciousness get or could have gotten off the ground initially, that is, during anthropogenesis or ontogenesis. For precisely the very same reasons, these epistemologies have trouble explaining some important dimensions of individual and cultural development, for example, the exponentially increasing cultural knowledge mobilized in individual actions without a concomitant increase of the biological capacities for thinking and being conscious. Any epistemology requires an ontology, for without a discourse (Gr. *logos*, word, discourse) of/about beings, that is, of the things that are to be known, we cannot establish an epistemology, a discourse *about* knowledge (Gr. *epistēmē]*) of these thing-beings.

The proposals made by philosophers of difference—including, for example, Jean-Luc Nancy, Jacques Derrida, and Emmanuel Levinas—for dealing with the fatherless origin of consciousness, and therefore language, lead us to a situation where we always already find ourselves in a dialogic situation at the very instant in human development when we become conscious of Self and Other, of Being. At the very instant that a first person—who in the process becomes *the* first person—utters the first word, he or she already presupposes its intelligibility: it had not been his or her word (discourse) but always already a word (discourse) that (or the possibility for which) was shared. That is: "Language *presupposes* interlocutors, a plurality" (Levinas 1971: 45, emphasis added). We do not "construct" intersubjectivity; intersubjectivity always already exists in and with language. The first word did not have a single author, a father, but already was a collective possibility—and the collective possibilities that exist in, and emerge from, language give rise to interesting phenomena that learning theorists do not currently capture (e.g., the persistence of "misconceptions") and, in fact, ignore when they talk about attempting to "eradicate student misconceptions" (see Chapter 5). The intersubjectivity that talking is said to establish is presupposed at the very instant that someone has spoken the first word (and therefore a condition of/ for the act of speaking). Similarly at the level of individual development in today's culture: at the very instant that a child becomes conscious, it is already caught up in a dialogic situation that presupposes the very intersubjectivity that its language is said to develop and support. Prior to being a self-conscious being, the child always already is subjected to intersubjectivity—although it is not yet a subject (of consciousness) proper. When the child becomes conscious, mediated by its immersion in and use of sound-words (i.e., language), it already finds itself caught up in a world shot through with significations (i.e., context).

In Chapter 3, it may appear that thinking | speaking is an individual phenomenon. This is far from the case—because language presupposes interlocutors, it is always marked by plurality even if in the case of a monologue or individuals talking to themselves (Bakhtin 1984a). To articulate the irreducible dialogical nature of everyday situations and the collective (participative) forms of thinking | speaking that characterize them, I draw on an episode from an outdoor environmental education program that an environmentalist group has designed to teach science in more meaningful ways. A class of elementary students has come to a saltwater lagoon where, at the dock station of a three-part program, they get to take measurements of pH, dissolved oxygen, temperature, turbidity, and salinity to assess water quality.

Mundane conversation at the dock

I begin with a gloss of the episode, which necessarily gives us a third-person perspective rather than exhibiting the actual, lived work that allows the participants not only to pull off the situation but also to understand who is talking to whom and what speakers intend with their talk (e.g., ask a question, make a statement, give a response). Nina, the environmentalist, is orienting toward some next activity, which, as we find out, is taking up something that will turn out to be a thermometer. But Lisa, standing behind her and facing the other way (Figure 4.1a), has already begun to speak, "do we do it again?" (turn 01, Fragment 4.1). Both the use of "do" and the rising pitch toward the end mark the utterance, for culturally competent speakers, as the beginning of a question–response pair. Whether it is realized as such has yet to be seen. After Nina completes her utterance, there is a brief pause and Lisa repeats what she has said, "do we do it again," but this time the pitch does not rise toward the end, as it normally would be in an utterance where a question is posed (see the prosody marker in turn 04). While she speaks, Lisa moves around the back and toward the right side of Nina (Figure 4.1b). There is a pause before Nina begins to speak, "you find, if you want or you can go find out what the bridges should do" (turn 06).

Fragment 4.1

```
      01  L:  do [we [do it again?    ]
                  [((Figure 4.1a))
      02  N:      [you dont think we] couldnt do that take up?
      03          (0.32)
  →   04  L:  do [we ((b)) do it ⁻again
                  [((Figure 4.1b))
  →   05          (0.65)
  →   06  N:  you find [if you ˈwant or you can go find ˋout what
                         [((Figure 4.1c))
                  <<dim>ˋthe bridges should do.>
      07          (0.92)
      08          ^learn from them.
      09          (1.21)
      10  L:  <<all>we can do it [again [if we want, we are
                                  [((Figure 4.1d))
                  allowed to]>
      11  N:                          <<len>[this=is a::
                  sample>   ]
```

While talking, Nina lays her arms around Lisa's shoulders (Figure 4.1c), clearly oriented toward the latter and addressing her, that is, in her turn Nina provides the sought-for answer to the question, or rather, she completes a question–response pair. There is a pause; and then Nina speaks again, "learn from them," before another pause develops. Lisa walks away toward another girl (Figure 4.1d) saying, "we can do it again if we want, we are allowed to," while Nina, now having Daniel standing right next to her, begins to speak about sampling temperature at the dockside.

Any culturally competent person, including the fourth-grade student Lisa and the environmentalist Nina, understands this situation generally and the instant between the beginning of turn 04 and the end of turn 06 as a question and its associated response. From an individualist (constructivist) perspective, Lisa is heard to ask a question and Nina as responding, which would be the result of her interpreting what has been said, figuring out some response, and then sharing the response by realizing it in a language intelligible to the child. But conversation and speech act analysts suggest that we cannot understand conversations in this way. Whether an utterance is a question or something else is a function of a turn pair, including the turn in which a question has been produced and the one that becomes the response follows. For example, if Nina in her turn 06 had said, "don't insult me or you go back to the school," then she would have expressed in and with her utterance that the previous utterance had been heard as an insult. It would not have been a question at all but an insult, even if Lisa had intended the utterance as a question. From the perspective of conversation analysis, then, turn 01 is not a question, has no effect; it is not a *con*versation but more a soliloquy. The utterance in and of itself is nothing, it becomes salient only as part of an *adjacency pair*. Such a pair is achieved *after* the utterance has been repeated. From this perspective, therefore, there is no question as such. To understand the dynamics of *this* conversation, we need to look at and theorize the turns rather than prying out individual locutions and imposing extraneous sense ("meaning") onto them. What matters in the analysis of language is its function in situation rather than what it may do, say, mean, and so forth in other situations. Focusing on a single turn is a one-sided way of considering the turn pair that constitutes the utterance *as* question. At the same time, the answer is an answer only because it responds to a question. It is the second speaker who makes the call on the utterance which, therefore, is nothing until it is "called," that is, made to be something (a question, insult, invitation) in and by the next turn.

This analysis is consistent with speech act theory (Austin 1962), where each speech act is understood as comprising three components: performance (locutionary act), intent (illocutionary act), and effect (perlocutionary act). In producing an utterance, a speaker constitutes the performance. As with acts in general, the performance (locutionary act) realizes a particular intent (goal, illocutionary dimension of the speech act). Finally, as all acts, the speech act has an outcome or effect (perlocutionary dimension of the speech act); this effect completes the speech act. That is, participants in communication do not know what the outcome of an utterance is until it comes to be known through the response of another person in the situation who, because of the human capacity

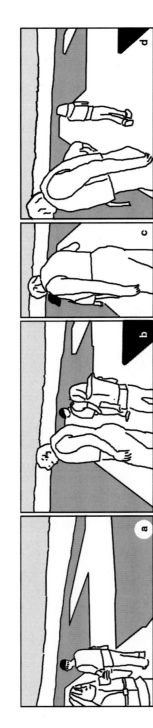

Figure 4.1 Scene at the dockside station of an environmental program for elementary school students.

   a Lisa asks a question facing away from the instructor (Nina).

   b Lisa walks around the back of the instructor.

   c Nina actively orients and attends to the student, placing her arm around the child and leaning toward her.

   d Lisa walks toward her classmate to whom she calls out the result of the question–answer exchange with Nina.

to possibility, *is affected* by the preceding performance. Because of its effect on other participants in the situation, any speech act, therefore, implies a responsibility that the speaker has with respect to the other, who has been affected in the action.

This first, necessarily brief analysis shows that we do not know the nature of an utterance in and by itself because what it does in and for the conversation can be found out only by looking at the following turn. But because we are trying to understand *this* conversation, what matters is not any interpretation we can give to a single utterance, but the internal dynamic of the *con*versation, which requires us, at a minimum, to study turn pairs. The term conversation comes from Latin (*convertēre*, to turn about), where it was a deponent verb, that is, had passive form but active sense and turned to an entirely active form only in late Latin. Speech act theorists conceptualize the codependence of turn pairs by proposing that a speech act consists of three irreducible moments: the *locutionary* moment concretely realizes the utterance, the *illocutionary* moment embodies the intent (plan) to be realized by speaking, and the *perlocutionary* moment constitutes the effect of the speech act. As exhibited in the previous paragraph, this effect is available only in and from the subsequent turn so that conversation analysts propose the turn pair as the *irreducible* unit of analysis. By analyzing conversations, we therefore find adjacency pairs such as question–answer, greeting–return greeting, invitation–acceptance/rejection, and so forth. But if turn pairs cannot be reduced then the contents of a conversation cannot be attributed to individuals.

Presenting the situation in this way, the speech act not only is a diachronic process, happening *in* time but also is *distended* across time, spread across turns; and it also is distended synchronously in its distribution across speakers. The speech event is understood and theorized in terms of *sequential* pairs, constituted by two locutions. The second turn becomes the first turn in the subsequent unit, as it not only constitutes, in revealing the effect, the second part of the previous unit (turn pair) but also, because it has an effect: sets up the next turn pair. Each turn, therefore, is interlaced with the preceding turn, which it completes, and the subsequent turn, which it sets up.

Viewed in this way, we already have a conceptualization of how communicative situations are pulled off. There is an inner connection whereby each turn is a chain *link* connecting two other turns, the one it completes and the one that it sets up. Although we can identify the turn as a link, it is a link only when it connects the preceding and the succeeding turn—in and by itself, a turn is nothing. This has serious consequences for making attributions to individuals, whose talk is taken out of context and used as if it were representing something characteristic of them (see Chapters 5 and 6). Thus, all conceptions and conceptual change research makes this abstraction when it uses interview or classroom data to attribute misconceptions to some *individuals* (usually students) and not to others (usually researchers themselves and natural scientists) or to language. When a conversation is viewed as an interaction chain, where individual speech acts reach across three turns, then the production of a conversation and its results (recording, transcription) always are collective—i.e., social and societal—in nature. The knowledge required for pulling off an interview is shared; and the knowledge that the analyst, who intends to understand a student, has to have is to be precisely the same knowledge that the student exhibits in the process of participating in the socially shared event—here the dockside lesson on the environment.

Passivity

Most social analysts drawing on such forms of analysis as those provided in the preceding section concentrate on the *agential* aspects of a communicative situation, considering individuals in terms of their intentions. In this way, analysts focus on the locutionary and illocutionary moments of the speech act, pushing into the background—or altogether suppressing—the essentially pre-essential passivity involved in the speech act. We have already noted the complex interrelation of speaker and listener, both of whom communicate to the other, while analyzing the conversation between the second-grade teacher and her student Connor in Chapter 1. In the present instance, too, Lisa is not just producing an effect in/on Nina, whose utterance completes the turn 04–06 sequence as a question–answer adjacency pair. To be able to respond at all, Nina has to open up, actively attend to what Lisa is saying *while* the latter is saying it. But opening up—an essentially agential moment of Being—to something, the nature of which I cannot anticipate, also means exposing myself to something that I cannot intend: something unknown literally will af-fect (Lat., *ad-*, to + *facere*, to do), do something to me and *subject* me to something unknown. In this exposure, I am absolutely passive: my "face is exposed, menaced as if inviting [others] to an act of violence" (Levinas 1982: 80). In actively attending and listening to Lisa, Nina, as part of the same turn 04, has opened herself to being affected, exposing herself and thereby becoming vulnerable. (To be insulted by another person, I need, at a minimum, to listen to what he or she says.) Similarly, while Nina is speaking and producing the second part of what will have been realized as a question–answer adjacency pair, Lisa not only actively attends and listens to (agential moment) Nina, but also exposes herself to be affected.

The exposure that comes with hearing is an existential. Hearing is constitutive of speaking, because speaking would have never gotten off the ground without there being listeners at the same time—in a fortunate accident of phonetic development of English, the difference between oral and aural is undecidable. It is because human ancestors had the capability of hearing that they would develop the capabilities for speech. Deaf-dumb children—who do not hear in addition to being blind—have, for centuries, existed in mere vegetative states, unable to become human. For such children, educating/training by means that circumvent the predominant senses of hearing and seeing constitutes a process well captured in the title of a book on the issue: *Awakening to Life* (Meshcheryakov 1979). It is not surprising, therefore, that the ear has been used as a key metaphor for understanding the concept of understanding (e.g., Derrida 1984; Nietzsche 1954a).

This analysis suggests that we must not only attend to the agential moments of speaking and listening but also to the essentially and radically passive moments of the same event. This form of passivity is radical in the sense that I do not decide to do or not do something, but rather, the passivity comes together with the decision of doing something. The very spontaneity that comes with speaking is conceivable only on the condition of this passivity (Derrida 1972). The difference between agency and passivity thereby becomes undecidable. Radical passivity adds another layer to turn-taking, and thereby further intertwines the contributions (locutions) of the two speakers and makes them irreducible to the sequential arrangement. This added moment introduces synchronicity into the inherently diachronic nature of talk, which is at the heart (and constitutive) of the conversation analytic program. For there to be anything such as language, it has to be operative simultaneously in the speaker and listener. "Surely, one can conceive of language as an act, as a behavioral gesture. But then one omits the essence of language: the coincidence of the revealer and the revealed in the face" (Levinas 1971: 38). If we only consider the locution, the physical act of speaking anchoring the said in the speaker, and the intent, the illocution, then we miss the effect speaking and hearing has on the interlocutor.

Speech act theorists were right in pointing out that we need to account for the effect on the Other, the perlocutionary moment of the (distended, distributed) speech act. But this perlocutionary dimension of the speech act becomes available only in the subsequent turn. This subsequent turn is only one moment of the perlocutionary event, the other moment of which is pathos, a term denoting that we are or have been affected by something in a way such that the *what-by* cannot be grounded in an a priori (forgoing) *what* nor in an a posteriori achieved *what-for* (Waldenfels 2006). That is, I cannot know the something (what) that will affect me when it begins, and cannot explain what the being-affected was for (i.e., there is no telos for an experience that I have not intended). As a way of articulating these relations, I use Figure 4.2, which maps the different forms of experiencing, agency and passivity, onto the sequence of talk from turn 04 to turn 06.

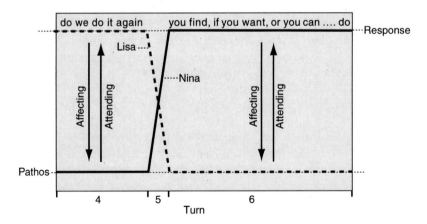

Figure 4.2 The unit of analysis for a conversation involving two speakers/listeners, exemplified with data from the dockside station of an environmental science unit for elementary students.

While Lisa (broken line) is speaking, Nina is attending and listening, opening herself up to be affected. That is, if Nina were not attending and listening, Lisa's utterance would not bring about an effect; it would not have an effect, such as would happen if she had uttered "do we do it again" to and for herself. It would be an instant of soliloquy. This is, in fact, how we can understand her preceding turn 01, which did not at all appear to have an effect—not on this conversation as far as bystanders do or analysts can note. Competent members of culture—lay as well as professional sociologists and psychologists—might explain this in terms of Nina attending to something or someone else and, therefore, not attending to and hearing (understanding, comprehending) Lisa. When the interchange is underway, however, the perlocutionary moment begins to be realized in and through Nina's attending to Lisa. Nina is affected, an essentially passive moment of human experience, *because* she actively attends to someone else; and Lisa's utterance has an effect not in itself but because Nina attends to her. Nina is now actively attending to and concerned with Lisa and can be seen from the fact that she places her arm around the child while continuing to articulate choices for what the latter might do next.

The second part of Nina's contribution comes in and with her utterance, the *response*. In her speaking and in Lisa's listening, the roles have been reversed, and thereby the ways in which loci where locution, illocution, and perlocution are concretely realized. Lisa cannot know what Nina will have said once the turn has ended, and therefore exposes herself to being affected; and to be affected requires Nina to speak (act).

Figure 4.2 graphically makes salient that the speech act not only is sequentially (diachronically) spread across two speakers but also contributes a synchronous aspect to the perlocutionary moment because it necessarily is both pathic and responsive. The perlocutionary moment is not merely sequentially distributed over different participants but, because of its temporal diastases, also is synchronous with the locutionary and illocutionary moments of the speech act (realized by Lisa). Here it is important to keep in mind that pathos and response cannot be thought separately, they are two ways in which the same experience (here Nina's) is expressed and expresses itself. Pathos/passion and response are not two events that follow one another; they constitute *one* experience that is heterochronous and temporally diastatic (Waldenfels 2006). They have to be thought together and as expressions of the same experience, despite the never-ending and necessary gap between them (Derrida 1993). In other words, the difference between them is undecidable.

From an epistemological perspective, therefore, knowing cannot be reduced to persons: speaking to someone for some purpose presupposes the understanding on the part of the recipient. It makes no sense to speak if I know that the listener cannot (cognitively, reflexively) understand (except speaking with infants, for whom this is part of the life trajectory). Conversely, listening presupposes the intelligibility of the spoken, even in moments when the intelligibility of a communicative act is not immediately evident. The presupposed nature of the intelligibility of the spoken was exhibited nicely in experiments involving randomly generated responses to questions, which the questioners—who did not see the "counselor" or "psychologist" responding—always heard in intelligible and meaningful ways (i.e., with respect to their "questions") even though the response was not designed in this way. Interested readers may read up on the ELIZA program that mimicked a psychiatrist, an experiment in which the research participants were told that they were communicating with a "psychiatrist," and, therefore, acted as if in a particular situation—i.e., amidst (under) a "group"—that renders particular ways of acting (talking) inherently meaningful (e.g., Weizenbaum 1995). The upshot of this story is that in communicative situations, knowing is a collective characteristic, in simultaneously synchronous and diachronous ways, irreducible to individuals (who *do* produce utterances) or the collective (who is the source and recipient of utterances).

My language is not mine

Passivity has another dimension in everyday conversation where I, as everyone else, use language and/to express myself: this language is not mine. In most everyday situations, I do not even think about what I am going to say, but speak, in the same way that I do not think about where to place my feet, but walk. But if this is the case, then what I say is not conscious prior to having been articulated so that I am passive with respect to my own utterances—"the timbre of my voice, the style of my writing, this is what for (a) me will not ever have been present" (Derrida 1972: 352). My thoughts and my ideas concretely realize themselves *in the process* of (rather than prior to) speaking—as we see in the lecture (Chapter 3) where the professor speaks for a while only to realize afterward that he has produced something that does not make sense. Moreover, because my talk is *for the Other*, I (have to) presuppose that what I say inherently is intelligible: I cannot say anything I want but have to say what I can presuppose the Other to understand already. This does not mean that I have to be conscious of this orientation to the listener: I inherently take up different positions and talk differently when I face a child, my partners, a colleague, an audience of strangers, and so on. That is, in talking I am constrained to realizing cultural possibilities of talking and using language—and the passive voice in "I am constrained" points us to the role of passivity in conceptualizing my talking. What the participants in Fragment 4.1 are saying and how they are saying it is constrained by the possibilities of language itself. It is as if language makes use of the participants to realize itself in this as in other everyday settings—as if language speaks through me, its mouthpiece.

In Fragment 4.1, Nina and Lisa orient to and away from one another, exhibited in the ways they move their bodies in the situation. They speak spontaneously, and they do not have to stop to select their words. But the words they do use *in any case* have come from the generalized other, the Other. Each word in the sequence "you don't think we couldn't do that take up?" (turn 02) has existed prior to Nina's arrival in this world, even though she now is a woman in her fifties. At this instant, in the here and now of this outdoor workshop for children, she reproduces these words not just for herself, not to articulate herself in a solipsistic manner about something—as this has been theorized in radical constructivism—but *in order to* speak to Lisa. In her speaking, the words, which have come *from* the Other now are *for* the Other and return *to* the Other. In being for the Other, the language has to be comprehensible to the relevant Other, here Lisa. The words specifically, and the utterance as a whole, have to be such that they already are intelligible to the Other, they have to already exist as a general possibility of intelligible talk.

There are, therefore, at least two reasons why the language is both Nina's language and not Nina's language. First, if the utterance is already understandable to Lisa, if the utterance already realizes a cultural possibility of communication, then the intelligibility of what Nina says *precedes* her. As general possibility, it is available to all, and although Nina realizes a possibility of the English language in *this* rather than in another way, it is nevertheless a general possibility and, therefore, already one that is available to others as well. It is simultaneously her English, her utterance, and not her English, not her utterance. Second, the utterance is for the other, to which the English thereby returns so that in the very production it is already English for the Other rather than for herself. This is why Mikhail Bakhtin and the members of his circle theorize the word as straddling the speaker and the listener, the author and the reader (e.g., Bakhtine [Volochinov] 1977). Lev S. Vygotsky (1986), too, suggests that the problem of consciousness is tied to the nature of the word, and then emphasizes that consciousness always is consciousness *for* the Other as it is consciousness for the Self. As far as the listener, audience, or recipient is concerned, such as Lisa in this situation, in being spoken to she is already presupposed to be a welcoming host to an English phrase that is both hers and not hers.

There is, of course, something singular in the act of speaking itself, and this aspect, that breaks the symmetry that apparently exists when language is both one's own and not one's own. In the instant of speaking, those repeatable aspects of language that can be found in the dictionary are iterated and reiterated. But there is something singular, pertinent to this instant and in this instant: as a once-occurrent event, the utterance has an effect on the world that cannot be undone (Bakhtin 1993). Thus, in another interaction at the dockside, Nina talks to a boy, who becomes upset over having forgotten the units in which a thermometer measures the temperature—degrees Celsius. The boy becomes upset at the very instant that Nina poses the question. Of course, she does everything to console him, but she cannot take back or undo the fact that there is at least an instant that he is upset, marking the departure for a new way in which they interact—she places her arm around his shoulder saying that he does not have to worry.

Although there is a certain degree of agency in the performative dimension of the production of the utterance, the type of action we are in the process of observing is not clear until we have available the next turn. What is the effect of the utterance "you don't think we couldn't do that take up?" (turn 02), which, because it rises toward the end, we can hear as a question? (The fact that there is a question mark in the original transcription shows that the graduate student who had produced it heard a question rather than something else like a statement or an order.) The effect of the utterance on *this* interaction and on *this* situation is available from the events that follow: Lisa's take up of the words or utterance, Lisa's actions if the utterance is heard as a request, her response indicating the utterance has to be treated as a question in the description and explanation of the event as it has happened. Here, Lisa utters what grammatically sounds like a question, "do we do it again?" (turn 04), but which intonationally is not marked as a question. In any event, it is only from this next utterance, or from something else she sees Lisa doing, that Nina comes to know about the effect of her utterance. That is, each participant is both actively producing sound-words and passive with respect to their effects. We do know this to be the case from our everyday experience—even if we have not yet acknowledged it as such—each time that we say something only to find out that the other person is ascribing to us a different intent than the one we might have had. If I articulate something in jest and the recipient of my utterance tells me that she or he is hurt, then I have found out about the effect of my utterance only after the fact. The point is that we cannot theorize intent and effect as the same, even when in many or most cases they may fall together. The more general case is that they are not the same and so the more comprehensive theory includes them as different entities that frequently come to be the same. Or rather, we may theorize the two concepts as the same, but this same, as seen in Chapter 10, is different within itself, it is a heterogeneity, a mêlée.

A second level of passivity can be observed at the level of the content and structure of the utterances: conversations unfold so quickly in real time that there is not time to take time-out and reflect, think up a next turn privately, and then copying the pre-thought into speech. A better way of thinking about conversations unfolding in real time is that speakers are the means by which language realizes itself in concrete ways even when speakers never have thought about some topic or phenomenon before. The concept of *participative thinking* (Bakhtin 1993) may assist us here in furthering our understanding. I already show in the preceding chapters how sense is distributed across different material aspects of the situation and that sound-words are but one of the means of marking sense. Being in a world always already shared with others gives me a sense of what is going on; my consciousness of what is happening goes together with my participative thinking. This is one of the reasons why I can hear people respond even before a preceding speaker has completed his or her utterance. Lisa starts, "do we" and then, while she utters, "do it again?" (turn 01), Nina already begins her response, "you don't think we," which she then completes speaking on her own, "couldn't do that take up?" (turn 02). In fact, one can already hear her respond to the question that is in the process of producing itself, that is, she responds to a question that has not even been articulated.

Emotion

Discussions concerning the epistemology of science or the epistemologies students, teachers, or scientists espouse rarely, if ever, concern themselves with the emotional and emotive aspects of Being, knowing, learning, and so forth. Yet emotion, too, needs to be understood as an integral aspect of any situation we study so that speaking and emoting no longer are treated as separate entities of research. The question of knowing generally tends to be treated independently of emotions, though the latter are an integral part of our daily lives, both at the individual and collective levels. Vygotsky (1986) notes a major shortcoming of psychology, even in the beginning of the twentieth century, that it did not attempt to understand thinking|speaking without also considering affect. Vygotsky considers the major weakness of psychology to be the separation of theories of knowledge from theories of emotion. Emoting is theorized as something external to thinking. But, thereby realizing an idea that Georg W.F. Hegel (1979a) first articulates at the beginning of the nineteenth century, Vygotsky holds that externalities *cannot* influence each other. If emotions are external to thought, then thoughts would appear to be "thinking themselves, segregated from the fullness of life" (Vygotsky 1986: 10). That is, without emotion we cannot understand thinking let alone the continually unfolding speaking|thinking unit. Why do we speak|think?

In the approach I advocate here, emotion comes to take the place it deserves in the study of communication, which includes both the production of the particular situation as such and the reproduction of this type of situation according to the society in its current cultural–historical state and condition. Emoting and thinking|speaking interpenetrate each other; they are, in fact, two moments of the same phenomenon. Thus, affect, as mood and attunement, make themselves known in speaking by means of "intonation, modulation, in the tempo of talk, 'in the way of speaking'" (Heidegger 1977b: 162). This will be especially clear in Chapter 7, where I analyze an argument between a student and her chemistry teacher. The difference between emoting and thinking|speaking is undecidable—only in this way can they mutually effect each other in the way Vygotsky suggests. Let us take another look at the present episode.

Lisa and Nina, as other interlocutors, communicate affect to others through speech parameters such as pitch, intensity (volume, loudness), and rate; they also communicate emotions (and empathy) through their orientation toward each other, for example, placing their hands on, or arms around, another person's shoulder. These are the ways in which children, prior to having developed self-consciousness, come to know and know about emotions. These speech parameters are indicators of emotions and mood/attunement (*Befindlichkeit*). Thus, for example, research shows that conversation participants who are in agreement with one another (unconsciously) tend to align their pitch levels and they tend to diverge in pitch levels in the case of conflict (see Chapter 7). Figure 4.3 shows that when Lisa asks her question ("do we do it again?" [turn 01]) for the first time, Nina is speaking at a pitch level that is far above—at times twice as high as—that of Lisa's speech. She also speaks much faster than Lisa, as shown in the spacing in the words (Figure 4.3). From the physical placement and orientations as well as from the topic of the talk, any culturally competent speaker understands that the two are not in alignment. We may gloss Nina as attending to her next task, which, as the unfolding episode not represented here shows, leads her to work with Daniel. In fact, as she is speaking, Daniel walks around until he stands next to Nina: this *is* the response that completes turn 02 as an invitation to what comes next for Daniel. Lisa is behind her and bodily oriented toward her group mate (Figure 4.1a). The drawing shows that when Nina does respond to Lisa, she begins in the listener's pitch range and slows down in her speech rate (panel 2, Figure 4.3), just as I have observed in many other studies where conversationalists are in tune with each other or attempt to align one another (e.g., Roth and Middleton 2006).

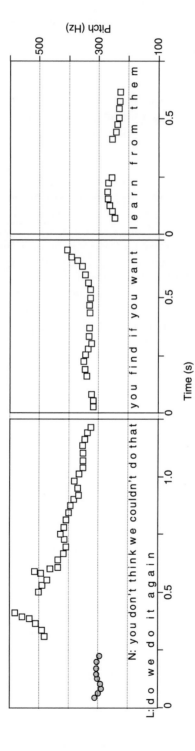

Figure 4.3 Nina, who initially spoke with a very high pitch (out of synchrony with Lisa), moved into and slightly below the pitch range of Lisa and slowed down the rate of her speech while she put her arm around Lisa.

Being in synchrony and harmony is an important condition and outcome of interactions and interaction ritual chains (Collins 2004). Synchrony tends to positively affect current affective states and has a positive valence, whereas being out of synchrony has negative valence, that is, it is experienced as discordance and otherness. Speech parameters, therefore, are an important way in which orientation toward another is made available to this Other; and, because of the situation of pathos involved while attending and listening, these parameters are part of the way in which listeners literally are *affect*-ed. In opening up while actively listening, Nina creates the opportunity to become attuned to Lisa, and this tuning has occurred—like a pendulum mounted closely to another on the same wall that has become entrained to the other—in her opening up to be affected. The attunement to Lisa is observable (and, therefore, objectively available) in the alignments of both pitch and speech rate (and the rhythms that the two lead to).

There is another important emotional element that is more elusive and never appears to figure in social analyses: Nina and Lisa are not just talking, not just participating in a lesson. As Connor and his teacher (Chapter 1), Nina and Lisa are reproducing and transforming a form of societal activity, schooling in the form of a field trip, which constitutes an essential way in which the collective reproduces itself. There is a motive embedded and embodied in such activities, which, in and through the participants' work (labor), also comes to be reproduced and transformed. Collective motives serve to orient need satisfaction of society. At the level of the individual, need satisfaction is regulated by emotions such that we act to achieve goals that have positive valence (need satisfaction) and avoid threats to our well-being, which have negative valence. The participation (actions) of both Nina and Lisa has to be understood in terms of their personal long-term goals, which always are oriented toward anticipated outcomes that have positive emotional valence—even at the cost of actions with negative valence in the short-term—and toward the avoidance of outcomes that have negative emotional valence. This participation has to be understood not as a phenomenon *sui generis* but as an event by means of which a part of society is reproduced and transformed. Getting in synch and harmonizing prepares the present (local) affective conditions and context that will support the positive valence in the anticipated outcomes. In Chapter 7, I return to these issues in greater depth.

Ethics

Ethics has become an important topic of interest in education (e.g., Noddings 1984). Ethics is not something that differs from discourse but is co-extensive with language and emotion (Derrida 1972): the difference between language, emotion, and ethics is undecidable. In the preceding section, I work out how speaking has an affect on listening; and in listening and responding, we have an effect on the speaker. There is, therefore, an important ethical moment in each communicative situation, which, as any moment, cannot be reduced to Lisa or Nina as individuals or to their singular (solipsistic) (rational) decisions to act according to a particular ethico-moral principle (e.g., the Kantian imperative).

Without the orientation to the other, attending and listening to her, no *conversa-*tion (Lat. *conversāre*, turning-to) and *com*munication (Lat. *commūnicāre*, sharing with) would be possible between Lisa and Nina, the collective nature of the event indicated by the *com-* (*con-*), the prefix indicating that which is common to a group, the *essential "with"* that founds all humanity *beyond essence*.

Lisa turns to her partner and together they go to the bridges—she *has Nina's word* that this is what she can do. Nina *does not renege on her word*. The two statements from the present corpus show that language not only makes statements but simultaneously promises: "You cannot read without speaking, speak without promising, promise without writing, writing without reading what you already promised even before commencing to speak" (Derrida 1988b: 103–4). Being in language means being in an ethical relation.

There is, then, a double ethical relation in the mutual orientation in face-to-face encounters with the Other. As a speaker, Lisa *is* in an ethical relation: in speaking, her words affect Nina, who, in attending and listening to Lisa, is affected (Figure 4.2). Nina is in an ethical relation because only by offering herself up to be affected can she hear and understand what Lisa says. She has to offer herself so that Lisa's utterance can become part of a speech act rather than remaining an act of soliloquy. Both are responsible to and for each other, and this responsibility precedes them and is realized despite them, as long as they *co*-participate and *com*municate to produce *con*versation. This ethical relation precedes them, is a prerequisite and antecedent of any intended (i.e., classroom talk) or unintended communication (as when I am asked for the time by a stranger in the street). Nina, therefore, is responsible prior to speaking or rather, prior to responding. And, because pathos/response is *one*, though temporally diastatic, experience that realizes the perlocutionary moment of the speech act, she is responsible despite the radical passivity that comes in and with pathos. It is not surprising, therefore, that Jacques Derrida, commenting on the work of Emanuel Levinas, said that

> [i]f someone tells you from the start "do not return to me what I give you," you are at fault even before he finishes talking. It suffices that you hear him, that you begin to understand and acknowledge. You have begun to receive his injunction, to submit to what he says, and the more you obey him in restituting nothing, the better you will disobey him and become deaf to what he addresses to you.
>
> (Derrida 2007a: 147)

Ethics and the responsibilities that arise in and from talking to another person can be observed at work in the conventions continually enacted in conversations. These "conventions" are relative to the relevancies arising from turn-taking. "Sequence relevancies, therefore, turn out to be moral relevancies in a much deeper sense than vocabularies of motive because they are not specific to a particular social structure" (Rawls 1989: 165). For example, if something can be heard as a question, then a response is required or an explication why the apparently sought-for response is not forthcoming; but this is a requirement itself, subject to the permissibility of a non-response, a condition from which arise both the contingency and ethics of social situations. When an invitation is made, the generally expected response is an acceptance and non-acceptance generally is explained (perhaps with an excuse)—otherwise the interlocutor can be said to be rude. That is, what conversation analysts theorize as turn pairs *enact* the ethical responsibilities that come with the phenomenon of language, itself resting on the presupposition of a multiplicity (two or more interlocutors). It is not, therefore, that we intentionally take responsibility but we are always already responsible and, therefore, can only accept or betray it.

Rethinking agency

In this chapter, I take a mundane conversational situation between an environmentalist offering field-trip experiences to schools and a fifth-grade student participating in one such experience as a paradigmatic situation to articulate epistemological and ontological issues. Without communication generally and without using language specifically, there simply would not be any ontology or epistemology: this *is* the concern of first philosophy. Communication is a good paradigm because it is a requirement for any philosophical talk about ontology and epistemology to have become possible: that is, communication constitutes a suitable paradigm for thinking about how humans have pulled off the challenge of creating ontologies and epistemologies in the first place *without having to presuppose all the conditions that enable talk about such topics*. Communication also is a good paradigm for thinking about how children come to know, for they participate in communicative situations prior to any consciousness and self-consciousness. Thus, communicative situations in which children participate prior to being conscious of themselves as independent Selves, constitute the ground from which subjectivity emerges: subjectivity literally means being subjected (Lat. *sub-*, under + *jacēre*, to throw, to cast) to the other. In the perspective developed here, therefore, subjectivity "is the breakdown of the difference between Same and Other, the breakdown of intersubjectivity, and a proximity to the Other" (Wall 1999: 47). The sharing in and of the *with*, which precedes the being-with required in communication, has to exist from before and beyond Being, because it is the condition for the first sound-word not only to be spoken but also to be understood: language always already presupposes interlocutors. This epistemology is one acceptable on evolutionary and cultural–historical grounds. It allows conversations to emerge, and with it consciousness and knowing as we know them today, including communication about epistemology and ontology. Simultaneously with consciousness emerges ontology in everyday human praxis, our attention to things as things; and this praxis provides the ground for language to turn upon itself and, therefore, for epistemologies (metaphysics) to emerge and evolve in the way we articulate them today.

The analyses I provide in this chapter exhibit the centrality of passivity with respect to being in the world (e.g., having a conversation), learning, and the making of context. This passivity, however, has neither been theorized nor been addressed in educational theorizing. Current learning theories of all sorts of ilk are aspect blind to this dimension of language, learning, and context and, thereby, fail to understand the fundamental constraints that learners are subject to. A similar absence makes it impossible for us to understand the difference between the planned and enacted curriculum: if agency were to be the only dimension responsible, then there ought not be a difference between the two dimensions. However, students and teachers are both agential and passive with respect to the ways in which they talk the enacted curriculum into being (see also Chapter 2): it is a collective process and product so that teachers also are subject to their conditions as much as they bring these about (and changes therein). The relation between teachers and students is built on language; but the "relationship of language presupposes transcendence, radical separation, the strangeness of the interlocutors, the revelation of the Other to me" (Levinas 1971: 45). This has some implications in the way that dialectical theories of language, learning, and context used in cultural studies are best articulated.

The most frequently cited cultural sociological theory links *agency* and *structure*, where structure itself consists of the dialectical relation of (material, social) *resources* and (personal) *schema* (Sewell 1992). That is, in acting (e.g., speaking) we employ resources (e.g., sound-words) and in the process form new schema; and our schema mediate what we can perceive as resources and how we perceive them. But without schema and resources, there cannot be anything like agency—there cannot be action without a (material) subject and a (material) object involved in the transaction. This theory, therefore, can be expressed as

agency || resources | schema

But seeing the world as populated by individual agency "and social structures leads inevitably to the assumption that structures at one end or the other are responsible for social order" (Rawls 1989: 165). Rather than understanding these terms as dialectically related, that is, as negations of each other (as in Hegelian dialectics), I understand the relation as dialogical in the sense that there is always cross talk. This relation, however, is asymmetrical in the above expression in the sense that agency is by itself in relation ("||") to another relation (resources | schema). I show in this chapter that agency inherently stands in an irreducible and constitutive relationship with passivity. An improved theory, therefore, may be expressed as

agency | passivity || resources | schema

In this expression, agency and passivity presuppose each other just as resources and schema do in existing dialectical theories. It is not an opposition of two terms; rather, the two terms are but poles of an equivocal passage that Jacques Derrida, in various places (e.g., 1972), ever so obliquely, refers to as *différance*, but also as *khôra* or *trace* or *margin*. If Bakhtin had been familiar with Derrida, he might have added "word" to this list. The concepts denote the delay between presence (*Sein, Être,* Being) and the presence of the present (*Seiendes, étant,* beings) (Heidegger 1977a). This expression—in whichever form—is consistent with other phenomenological works that deal with the first appearance of something in our perception that we could not anticipate because we did not know of its existence: the existence of an essential passivity in the welcoming of the unknown, the radically new, the absolutely foreign. The order arising from interactions, therefore, is self-organizing because neither individuals nor existing structures can be its master.

In the social sciences generally, and in science education specifically, theories that build on an agency|structure relation have come to have considerable currency. The present chapter shows that there is more to social situations than agency generally and to speaking (language use) specifically; there is also more to social situation than simple passivity, a form of action where someone *decides* to enact non-action. The foregoing analyses show that with speaking comes *radical passivity*: to listen, hear, and understand what Lisa is saying, Nina has to open up and expose herself to be affected by something that she cannot anticipate. It is precisely this capacity to be outside of myself in the world where I am open to be affected and modified that makes the world comprehensible and immediately endowed with sense (Bourdieu 1997). Conversely, to find out the answer to her intended question (which turns out to be realized in and by Nina's response), Lisa has to abandon and expose herself in the same way. That is, to produce this social and societal situation as it unfolds (diachronic moments) and in its totality (synchronous moments), we require radical passivity as an integral part on the yonder side, of and as the complement to, structure, expanding agency to become an agency|passivity dialectic that complements the schema|resources dialectic that constitutes structure.

Thinking about language, learning, and context in education in terms of agency|passivity||resources|schema comes with tremendous potential for understanding what happens in our classrooms and what the particular constraints are in attempting to achieve specific learning outcomes. Future research has to work out how curriculum planning, teaching, and research on language, learning, and context have to be reconfigured to address and accommodate the essential passivity that is presupposed in, and makes possible, the already-theorized agency. Most importantly, passivity as articulated here does not refer to situations where someone decides not to speak—e.g., because someone else "silences" them, or because the person feels, as students from First Nations often feel in Western-style schools, that there is no space to get into the conversation. In such a situation, there is an intent that orients a particular form of agency: not doing something that others in the situation already do, which is a derived form of passivity. Rather, as I show here, I am concerned with theorizing passivity that comes with speaking and hearing that is at the very heart of agency, the intentional moment realized in and by speaking. That is, I am concerned with what Levinas might call a passivity more radical than any conceivable passivity.

5   Cultured conceptions

In Chapter 4, I suggest that with language there comes a radical passivity: my language never is mine as it is both mine and not mine simultaneously. This leads to the fact that "an utterance finds language basically already prepared for use. It is the material for the utterance and it sets constraints on the utterance's possibilities" (Vološinov 1976: 79). This has consequences for how we understand language (said to express knowing), learning, and context. Yet much existing research continues to attribute—in the way psychology has generally done—"facts" that they extract from the language of research participants *to these participants* rather than to the language. This research, especially when it is based on interview techniques, "*projects* the entire dynamic of the interrelationship between two people into the individual psyche" (Vološinov 1976: 80, original emphasis). Thus, for example, the literature in science education has accumulated over the past three decades a tremendous amount of research on people's "conceptions"—one bibliography currently lists 7,000 entries concerning students' and teachers' conceptions and science education. Adherents to the theory understand conceptions as mental frameworks that are subsequently imaged in language—much like Aristotle believed that the words are the signs of the soul.[1] Yet despite all of the research on conceptions and despite all the advances in the associated conceptual change theory, there is evidence that students' talk about concepts remains virtually unchanged by instruction even under the best of conditions. In this chapter, I describe and exemplify a theoretical alternative to knowing and its expression in language, which ultimately allows me to understand the stable nature of student talk about scientific phenomena; and it allows me to understand why instruction faces such challenges in bringing about conceptual change. To exemplify the presentation of the theory, I draw on videotaped interviews that covered ground similar to the one featured in a widely distributed documentary *A Private Universe*.[2] The theoretical alternative to language, learning, and context presented in this book questions some of the fundamental presuppositions and assumptions made in the documentary and in the constructivist and conceptual change literatures. These include the locus of the misconceptions, the relation of individual and collective, and the situated and constitutive nature of the talk eliciting (mis-, alternative, pre-, naïve) conceptions. I conclude with some sobering suggestions and recommendations for the praxis of teaching and the possibility to bring about formal knowledge for and in *all* students any time in the near future.

Why we should rethink knowledge

There is a considerable literature on the ways in which people all along the life span are seeing, articulating, and explaining the world. This literature shows that students come to school with ways of talking about natural phenomena that differ from the ways scientists talk. These different ways of talking are evident in the following brief excerpt from an interview with a seven-year-old child who already features in Chapter 2. The interview intends to solicit explanations of the origins of day and night, the phases of the moon, and the seasons.

Fragment 5.1 (excerpt from Fragment 2.1)

01 I: so the question is very simple. (0.24) .hhh could you explain me:?
          'why:: (0.55) 'why: we have day and why we have night;
02   (1.28)
03 AJ: kay (2.06) ((licks lips with smack)) be (0.16) cause .hhhh (0.84) we
          need 'day to pla:y: anweneed night to sleep. (0.69) .hhh and then
          if we dont have 'day we dont have (lunch?) light and we can bump
          to <<dim>something or something> (0.47) .hh=yea (1.04) we can
          bump to something

In this situation, the child explains the existence of day and night in terms of human needs generally and those of a child in particular—playing, sleeping, and not getting hurt. This explanation, as ample research shows, is likely to be different from that astronomers would provide in a professional context (unless, of course, they are joking over a glass of beer), according to which the Earth rotates thereby changing the parts that are exposed to the Sun; the parts lit by the Sun experience day, the others night, and those in between are in transition. Educators, educational psychologists, and learning scientists have come to infer—as part of a "first wave of a cognitive approach"—what have variously been called (mis-, alternative, pre-, pre-instructional, prior, naïve) conceptions from such talk. These conceptions tend to be ascribed to individual students, who are said to hold, construct, or appropriate them. Thus, conceptions researchers would (a) interpret the *stretch of talk* to be the result of misconceptions or naïve conceptions, that is, structures *in the mind*, (b) attribute these conceptions to the child and perhaps her lack of appropriate school training, and (c) may characterize the talk as "quite uninformed and uncommitted discussion of phenomena" (as suggested by a reviewer of a paper on the topic at the heart of this chapter).

To assist students in getting their science right, researchers from a variety of fields frequently recommend challenging students' conceptions, confronting children or students with experiences, and leading them to be dissatisfied with their existing "mental frameworks" (conceptions). Despite numerous approaches that employ various forms of discrepant events to undermine entrenched beliefs, most students apparently "resist change." Presupposed in the recommendations for conceptual change and in theorizing any change observed is, once again, the attribution of (mis-, alternative, pre-, pre-instructional, prior, naïve, canonical, non-standard) conceptions not merely to the individual person but to his or her mental structure. This research discussed so far falls into a cognitive (metaphysical) approach to conceptual change; another approach with a different ontology and epistemology exists in a sociocultural approach. Thus, some researchers draw on the work of Lev S. Vygotsky (1978) to suggest that conceptions are not entirely one's own; thus, children first encounter or construct conceptions interpsychologically, that is, in the public domain that they share with others, before "constructing" them intrapsychologically leading them to reorganize their own understanding, as if common, mundane talk about phenomena could be reduced to individuals. Others suggest approaches grounded in a theory of situated cognition.

In this chapter, I continue to elaborate the different theoretical perspective taken in this book. The perspective presented here is "radical" not only because it breaks with cognitive approaches of all brands, but also because it distinguishes itself from other social and sociocultural approaches to cognition, including critical discourse analysis, sociolinguistics, ethnomethodology, and conversation analysis. Like an increasing number of researchers in philosophy, social studies of science, social psychology, cognitive science, and education, the perspective outlined here theorizes the content and function of talk and language rather than the inaccessible mind. Throughout this book I am concerned with talk, how people concretize the commonly available resources of language rather than theorizing the forever-inaccessible contents of the mind, conceptions, or mental constructs or the situated or embodied aspects of cognition offered as alternatives. I thereby do not say that there is nothing happening in the brain—of course there is a lot happening there. But what is relevant to understand conversations as unfolding processes, we need to theorize how people mobilize the resources at hand, the ones they make available to each other and anyone else overhearing the situation. And precisely these resources are not to be looked for in the brain but in the public space of the situation and in the language available to any participating conversationalist. We can conclude that "language gives us to think but also *it steals* [elle vole], *it* [elle] whispers to us, it withdraws the responsibility that it appears to inaugurate, it carries off the property of our thoughts even before we appropriated them" (Derrida 1991: 106, original emphasis).[3]

Some researchers already suggest that what students bring to school are not conceptions as individual properties, but are ways of seeing and speaking about the world that are characteristic of the communities in which people participate. The forms and contents of these discourses are, like other human practices, functions of the particular contexts in which these are used to expose, describe, and explain relevant phenomena at hand. If texts and contexts are treated as sense-making phenomena, then systematic relations can be established between the structures of the social setting and the functional organization of language. Thus, even a cosmologist can marvel over the beauty of an autumn sunrise; it would be precisely the talk of a rotating Earth that would or might dispel the aesthetic of the instant.

That there is more than the child concerned in the production of conceptions can be gleaned from the following considerations. Taking another look at the brief exchange between interviewer and child (Fragment 5.1), we see that the interviewer is doing more than just posing a question. He is *formulating* what he is going to do rather than just doing it. That is, by saying "this question is very simple," the interviewer announces that a question is forthcoming and he foreshadows it to be an easy one. He also formulates what he expects the child to provide, an explanation rather than just any response ("could you explain me"). This talk then becomes a resource for the next performance—which indicates the collective production of the situation *as* an interview. (It becomes a resource with and despite all of its ingrammaticisms, which I leave in the transcript because *this* is what people say and what others are dealing with pragmatically rather than with something they have purportedly wanted to say, and which other analysts *routinely* add to transcripts.) Here, the child uses the conjunctive "because," which frames and denotes the subsequent talk as a reason: "we need day to play and we need night to sleep." That is, in both instances, the interviewer and the child have done more than just posed and answered a question: they also have accounted for, formulated, and framed *what* they are doing *while* doing it. That is, they have done so for practical purposes and in embodied and situated ways. Moreover, they have talked to and for the benefit of the Other and they have monitored the effects of their talk by attending to what the interlocutor makes available to them.

As shown in Chapter 2, in the process of doing (displaying) practical, accountable, situated, and embodied talk, they have produced an event that viewers of the videotape and readers of the transcript can recognize as a typical interview generally, and a conceptual change interview specifically. They have reproduced a particular societal activity and, in the course of it, they have achieved the production of text of the type used in conceptual change interviews to make inferences about conceptual structures attributed to an individual child's mind. Because the two collude and thereby achieve the interview collaboratively, one has to question whether it is legitimate to extract the child's locutions and attribute it to *her* mind. An alternative would be to do choose a unit of analysis that includes interviewer and child situated in culture, therefore making the (mis-, alternative, pre-, pre-instructional, prior, naïve) conception a collaborative production made possible by the particularities of the English language that they share.

The purpose of this book as a whole, and of this chapter in particular, is to argue for a "fairly radical theoretical rethinking," not unlike that which Edwards and Potter (1992) propose in their announcement of discursive psychology, through a reformulation of talk-in-interaction as process and topic, a rethinking that abandons all ideas of talk as a pipeline between a person's understanding and the world. The language of talk is the phenomenon of interest and, I suggest, simultaneously is shared by an individual person and culture so that conceptions, ideas, beliefs, or attitudes always already are *general* possibilities that inherently belong to the collective other. Moreover, language-in-interaction is the very medium that produces and reproduces the form of societal activity—it is a form of institutional talk—during which the (mis-, alternative, pre-, pre-instructional, prior, naïve) conceptions are elicited. This talk is designed for recipients and therefore *for* the researcher or teacher, who inherently is assumed to understand what the talk is about. That is, the ultimate purpose of this chapter is to provide a coherent theoretical frame for the relationship between interviews and interview data, on the one hand, and the interpretive reductions that lead researchers to the identification of knowledge.

A received way of thinking about knowledge and language

Received approaches to knowledge and language are Aristotelian, taking the former to be an inner structure and the latter as a system of signs standing in for and pointing to the latter. The analysis in Chapter 3 embodies a different approach according to which the difference between thinking and speaking is undecidable. To articulate how my approach differs from received approaches, I begin by outlining just enough of the principles underlying the research on existing ways of thinking about knowledge and language. I do not provide this outline to set up a straw-person but rather to provide an inherently incomplete sketch that allows my readers to understand my choice of a different model. Throughout this chapter it is evident that the steps from the interview contexts to the descriptions and explanations of interview texts and their topics require many assumptions and presuppositions before one can speak of conceptions that individuals are said to hold in their minds. In the subsequent section, I then show how my approach leads to a different way of understanding and theorizing talk about phenomena that are of interest to scientists and science educators (e.g., models of the universe, Earth, Sun, day, and night).

Conceptions are theorized as cognitive entities, furniture of the conscious mind, but they are unlike signs. Conceptions are human inventions that "once labeled become communicable through the use of language" (Pines 1985: 108); that is, conceptions are different from language, which is but the vehicle that makes them available to others. Conceptions are said to be mental/cognitive regularities that are labeled with words and, by means of these, can be "employed in thought and communication" (Pines 1985: 108). "A word is like a conceptual handle, enabling one to hold on to the concept and to manipulate it" (Pines 1985: 108). These definitions are consistent with a recent statement of leading conceptual change theorists and researchers, who describe conceptions as "learners'" "mental models," or as the "learner's" "internal representations," constructed from external representations of entities constructed by other people such as teachers, textbook authors, or software. The essence of the cognitive perspective on conceptual change is characterized by "knowing as having structures of information and processes that recognize and construct patterns of symbols to understand concepts and exhibit general abilities such as reasoning, solving problems, and using and understanding language" (Greeno et al. 1996: 18). The mainstream approach to conceptions also is captured by stating that "[c]ognitive approaches provide analyses about the ways in which knowledge *must be structured* and about the *structures* of knowledge *in learners' minds* that will be available to support task performance and to transfer to new situations" (Anderson et al. 2000: 12, emphasis added).

Conceptions are organized into networks of relations, which often are represented in node-link diagrams or ontological category trees; conceptions themselves can be thought of as theoretical nodes where a multitude of meaningful relations cross. Researchers have come to denote *misconception* as the use of conceptual relations in inappropriate contexts. Concept map, semantic network, or node-link diagram are some of the diagrammatic forms that illustrate concepts and the conceptual relations in which they are involved. These relations are expressed in propositions that may be communicated in the form of sentences. Thus, for example, node-link diagrams (concept maps) have been used to show the differences between radical and non-radical (simple, slight) conceptual change, corresponding to conceptual change across and within ontological categories (Chi 1992). Depending on the study, conceptual change may refer to the process of change or outcome of the change process; recent conceptual change theories integrate affective components that are said to mediate the mind such that there may be no change, superficial change/assimilation, or true conceptual change/accommodation.

Conceptual frameworks (conceptions, misconceptions, alternative and naïve conceptions) generally are inferred from interviews, clinical interviews, or tasks in which persons are asked to demonstrate/predict, observe, and explain some physical phenomenon. There is an (implicit) assumption that the (interview, task) situation itself does not mediate the conceptual organization but that the situation simply allows reading out—like a computer printout that shows the results of a calculation or the contents of computer memory—an at least temporarily stable mental organization. Strong arguments have been made on sociocultural grounds contesting the "reading off" of conceptions from interview texts. However, the fact that conceptions are very resistant even to intensive instruction gives legitimacy to the reasonable nature of the assumption that conceptions and mental models are independent of the environment in which they are elicited. The resources in the setting have been treated as transparent. Thus, the method of identifying a conception is to excerpt statements interviewees make irrespective of anything else in the setting or the nature of the setting itself. This can be seen in the following excerpt from the seminal article on the nature of conceptual change:

(I)... it seems these are strange results. What attitude do you take of these results?
(CP) I say they don't really mean all that much; it just depends on what your frame is. It's sort of like potential energy depends on the way you define zero to be?
[...]

CP's reference to potential energy is significant in pinpointing a conception which enables her to regard the values given to a variable as arbitrary, being dependent solely on the observer's point of view. She attempts to resolve some counterintuitive results of Einstein's view of time by drawing an analogy between time and potential energy. No matter that the analogy might break down with further analysis—it serves her belief in absolute time.

(Posner et al. 1982: 219)

In this quote, the authors derive from the quoted interview excerpt that the subject CP has a conception that "enables her to regard the given to a variable as arbitrary, being dependent on the observer's point of view." There is no reference to the fact that CP has responded to a query on the part of the interviewer (I) and for the purpose of answering this query, rather than primarily developing relativity theory—which is done as a matter of course *in* and *through* the interview. The authors attribute an intention to resolve "counterintuitive results," when in fact the event shows us that the interviewer denotes the results as "strange." Asked what she makes of these "*strange* results" (emphasis added), CP then makes statements that complete the interviewer's utterance as a question, which means she has to address the strangeness. There is no indication or evidence that she would have noted or talked about anything strange: it is the interviewer who contextualizes and occasions the response. As a result, the cognitive approach often focuses on what people (students) do *not* do, how they misconstrue, misconceive, or alternatively conceive some phenomenon. Thus, "the constructivist approach to cognition has emphasized forgetting—the distortions, confabulations and general unreliability which results when memories are schematically assembled in some kind of cognitive processor" (Edwards and Potter 1992: 36). I show below that interview participants talk about scientific phenomena even when they have never talked or thought about them before, in which case, what they say *cannot* be driven by or be the result of a conception.

Talking (about) phenomena

Until now, most researchers have deemed conceptions to belong to the minds of individuals. The content and structure of these conceptions are thought to be available through a person's talk during interviews or their answers to questionnaires. My analyses exhibit the nature of conceptions as something distilled from practical, accountable, situated, and embodied language-in-interaction. Given that talk generally is quite variegated, researchers have to "distil" or "abstract" conceptions from widely ranging and varied participants' responses and simultaneously assume (presuppose) that the variations in talk constitute (error) variance of otherwise different but equivalent forms of talk. In Chapter 2, we see how a person, such as the child AJ, does not just talk, spilling the contents of her mind for some interviewer. Rather, she talks for the benefit of the interviewer in a language that has come to her from others which thereby returns to the Other, *in order to* produce the interview as a societally recognizable phenomenon *even though this is the first time that she participates in an interview*. In the following sections, I articulate how the interlocutors accountably talk about scientific phenomena and I explicate that talk within a non-rationalist framework. Here, I limit myself mostly to words, though, as seen in Chapter 3, communication by far exceeds the use of verbal language.

First-time talk about a topic

Researchers interested in knowledge generally assume that it takes a "mental structure" to produce talk. Each suitable instance of talk is used as a piece of evidence for an underlying conception. Researchers tend to discard all those stretches of talk from an interview that do not map onto an existing mental structure that they have formulated.[4] But we do know that in everyday life, including in interviews, human beings participate in conversations on topics that they have not talked (thought) about before, and about which they *cannot* already have a conception because, so goes the theory, the latter is the result of a construction. That is, if people talk about a topic that they have not talked about before, then this means that a conception is not a requirement for intelligible talk. In fact, the position taken in this book is more parsimonious, as it only assumes that people participate in interactions and they do so in ways that maintain the activity (conversation among friends, school talk, interview), including the reproduction and transformation of conversational topics and contexts of talk (see Chapter 2). When necessary, conversation participants provide advance warnings (e.g., "I have not thought about this before," or "this may sound stupid but …") or retrospective evaluations (e.g., "I may be wrong," or "I may not have answered your question") for the potential inadequacies of what they have said. This is apparent in the following interview fragments.

Mary is a female adult graduate student at a Canadian university who speaks English as a second language. During an interview, to which she has been invited by her friend Penny, another graduate student, and, prior to Fragment 5.1, Mary talks about the movement of the Sun. Penny picks up on her statement and asks for clarification (turn 08). Mary says in her turn, "in the morning it should be in the east" (turn 10). Again, the interviewer asks for an elaboration in the form of a reason for what was said (turn 12), upon which Mary responds that she never has thought about that, yet immediately continues to elaborate a response (turn 14).

Fragment 5.2

```
    08  P:  yea (0.86) a:nd which? direction. (0.30) maybe east? or north? o:r-
    09      (0.33)
→   10  M:  `o:h:: ((hand moves up to the chin, eyes move upward gaze toward
            ceiling, "pensive")) (0.26) in the morning it should be in the east.
    11      (0.17)
    12  P:  yea:. why?
    13      (1.06)
→   14  M:  <<pp>uh> why::? (1.70) <<p>uh: i never think about that.> i
            ^thi:nk (0.33) i:ts=a becau:se (0.24) of the movement of the ↑`sun.
```

In this fragment, Mary repeatedly produces markers for the fact that she has not thought about *this* topic before. First, when asked about the direction of the Sun, she initially moves her eyes toward the ceiling, and brings her hand to the mouth in what a culturally competent person might see as a "pensive instant." Second, she then suggests, in the conditional, that the Sun "should be in the east." In this, Mary articulates that she is not certain about the content of the statement but that, for whatever reason, the Sun *should* be in the east. Third, when asked to articulate a reason for the sky position—an indicative of insufficiency from the interviewer's part that requires further clarification—Mary produces the interjection "uh" and an interrogative ("why") with a sharply rising pitch, features that together are heard (by any competent speaker of English) as surprise. Finally, Mary explicitly states that she has never thought about the topic of the question. She then formulates what she is doing, "I think," and, in doing so aloud, makes available what she now thinks for the first time. But if she thinks this for the first time, she cannot have a conceptual framework that is at the origin of, and therefore causally determines the utterance. Such frameworks are, in conceptual change theory, the *outcome* of intentional constructive processes so it is likely that Mary would have remembered building the conception previously. Her thinking develops in this situation much in the same way that we see the thinking of the professor lecturing physics develop as he speaks (see Chapter 3). The poet Novalis (2001) writes—in a text entitled "Monologue"—that those who have a fine sense for the fingering, the tact, the musical spirit of language, who sense within themselves the tender forces of its inner nature and move their tongue and hand accordingly will be called prophets. Here, Mary does precisely that: even without having thought about the topic before, she allows language to play itself out in and through her tongue.

There are other indicators, often subtle, that participants use to mark the fact that they have not thought/talked about a topic before. Requested by the interviewer (Fragment 5.3, turn 64), Mary begins by producing an explication for not having sunshine with a conjunctive ("because") that introduces the reason for something that preceded it, but then slows down to produce an interjection. Then there is a pause, before she marks that she has heard before what she is going to say. Here, she formulates deferring to someone else, and then appropriates what she reports to have heard to make it an instance of her own thinking (turn 66). This reporting of things someone else has said is an important aspect of the reproduction and transformation of language, a topic I deal with in Chapter 8.

Fragment 5.3

61   I: so do you think 'why we have day an:: night.
62   (0.42)
63   M: because of t-the movement of the sen (0.68) and uh in the evening
          we couldnt a get ta ta the sunshine <<dim>so thats the reason we
          have that.>

64 I: yea: but ↑`why we didnt have the sunshine.
65   (1.18)
→ 66 M: because we are at ah (0.22) i heard (0.14) i think because of (0.62)
          the other half of the earth (0.14) have the sunshine
67   (0.72)
68 I: the other (0.33) half of the earth

By flagging the content of future speech as the speech of someone else, Mary defers to that other, the agency, for having figured out the reasons for the absence of sunshine. She then takes ownership by formulating the instance as one of her thinking. In this instance, in the absence of further evidence, saying that she is thinking for the purpose of this conversation—which may be thinking for the first time—requires fewer presuppositions than saying that she has a conceptual framework, for the existence of which there is more negative rather than positive evidence. In the last turn (68), the interviewer acknowledges Mary's answer as sufficient for that part of the discussion: she not only repeats Mary's statement, but also does not require any more elaboration from her.

A similar situation, where a new topic enters the conversation and to which apparently the interviewee has not given consideration before, occurs during the interview with the seven-year-old AJ (see also Chapter 2). In the following fragment, the interviewer has asked AJ previously whether she has studied the Earth, Sun, and planets. The interviewer then requests her to answer the questions of an online test in the children's version. AJ has already responded to the question about the nature of the orbiting body with "moon" and "planet," both with rising intonation, which flags the words as possible answers presented in the form of questions or possible responses rather than as affirmative statements. In Fragment 5.4, there are three additional pointers to the fact that AJ has not thought (talked) about the attendant issues before and, therefore, that she cannot have a corresponding mental framework constructed on some previous occasion. Yet, she participates in the interview and produces answers that some might be tempted to interpret as evidence for underlying conceptions.

Fragment 5.4

01 I: so which one you think (0.93) uh p mo show (0.61) the shape of
          the orbit?
→ 02   (2.29)
03   if you dont know its fine. you just say i dont know- (0.72) o:r- uh;
04   (0.18)
→ 05 AJ: <<pp>i> <<p>think this one.
06   (0.27)
07 I: thisoneletter,
08   (0.45)
09 AJ: <<dim>be::.>

10 I: letter <u>be</u>. (0.20) okay, just write (.) be for me there. (0.63) or make
          an ex next to it. (0.19) okay. (1.08) oh, okay. .hh (.) ↑why (0.22)
          ↑why do you think be is the right answer. (0.69) s:there a reason for
          that?
→ 11 AJ: .h um no h .Hh i dont know, ↑i dont think so.
   12   (1.21)
   13 I: ^okay.

After the interviewer's question about the shape of the orbit of the Earth around
the Sun, there is a long pause (turn 02). The interviewer than says that it is fine
not to know and to indicate so (turn 03). That is, the interviewer treats (for all of
us to see in the transcript) the pause to mean that AJ might not have a response
and does not know the answer to his question. Modifying her answer with an "I
think," AJ then points to one of the drawings (turn 05) and, following the interviewer's invitation, articulates the answer in terms of the letter "b" that denotes
one of the answer choices. Here again, uncertainty is made available in the modifying formulation of what she does as "I think," which makes what comes thereafter
less than certain and possibly makes it an instance of thinking-aloud rather than a
recall from memory or a read-out from/of an existing structure. This uncertainty
is further evidenced when AJ is asked about a reason for the particular drawing to
be the right answer for the question about the orbit. AJ responds that she does
not know and that she does not think so (turn 11). Here again, the child participates in the interview, responds to the forced-choice item, and has her responses
taken into account in the online survey, although there is a lot of evidence that
she does not know (i.e., does not have a conceptual framework) and has not
talked/thought about the topic previously or before she actually speaks. In any
case, AJ's response proves to be satisfactory to the interviewer, who marks the
end of that part of the interaction with a simple agreement to what he heard from
AJ ("okay" [turn 13]).

Conceptual language: from the other, for the other

In fields where real-time talk is of interest, *recipient design* and similar notions are
used to theorize the fact that speakers do not just produce solipsistic utterances
(i.e., they do not "speak in tongues"), nor choose any possible way of articulating
a topic. Rather, speakers *design* their talk for the intended recipient—they do not
even have to cogitate about telling something appropriately, and therefore differently, to different people. Thus, a professor returning from work talks differently
about her day to her husband (who is not in the field) than she talks to her
seven-year-old daughter; and to both she talks differently than she would if she
talks to a fellow professor who has come over for a dinner party. In the same way,
interviewer and interviewee (consciously and unconsciously) *design* their talk *for*
the other and *for* the purposes of *this* activity, here interviews. They do so with
a language that is not their own, which they have received from the other, and
which they are using to address the other. The contents of an interview transcript,

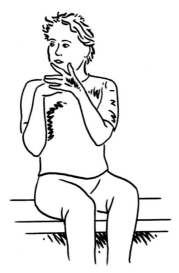

Figure 5.1 Mary produces a gesture simultaneously with her utterances in which the left-hand gesture is aligned with "Earth" and the right-hand gesture with "sunshine"; the backside of the left hand literally is facing away from the window and is dark.

therefore, cannot be thought in terms of the result of a singular person, but the content, form, and function of the said is thoroughly social, ideological, inherently general, and singular simultaneously (Bakhtine [Volochinov] 1977). In contrast, the Harvard-Smithsonian documentary on the way Harvard graduates think about the universe suggests that their ideas are not scientific and therefore private. But, given the present considerations, the universe(s) that the graduates talked about cannot be so private after all, but constitute possible universes that each of them shares with all of us. In fact, the statement that the graduates have private universes acknowledges these universes as universes, and therefore as general and collective possibilities. At a minimum, the Harvard graduates would have found a considerable number of peers talking about the universe in their way; and if the graduates talked to the filmmakers in their way, they must have presupposed that what they said was both culturally possible and intelligible. Consider Fragment 5.5, for instance, which I extracted from the interview with Mary. Previously, Mary and Penny had been talking about day and night.

Fragment 5.5

```
88  P:  okay; (0.13) then why:- (0.14) why there (.) there is a (0.42) you
        know this kind of; (0.75) uh ^phenomena;
89      (1.58)
90  M:  u:m::: (0.39) (aday?) (0.38) i think because uh (0.68) when
        therisa (0.72) the earth and sun move together?
91      (0.24)
```

```
     92  P:   uh hm=
→    93  M:   ((Looks emptily into the room rather than at interviewer,)) =there
                is the ↑point h that=uh (1.53) that=u::h (0.17) the s:::::
                (0.34) the earth ((faces interviewer)) will face the 'sunshine
                (0.25) the sun:
     94         (0.22)
     95  P:   uh [hm:::   ]
→    96  M:       [and then] again the sunshine a[n the  ] other half
     97  P:                                        [uh hm]
     98         (0.18)
     99  P:   uh hm=
→   100  M:   =isa not facing the sunshine
    101  P:   [uh hm   ]
→   102  M:   [an is not] facing the sun;
    103  P:   uh hm=
→   104  M:   =so they <<dim>couldnt get the sunlight> (0.25)
                thats [the reason.]
```

A few seconds prior to the fragment, Mary tells Penny that she has not previously thought about the issues that they currently are talking about. Penny nevertheless asks her about the reasons for having day and night (turn 88). Mary formulates that she is thinking aloud (turn 90) and then, in a stop-and-go fashion, hypothesizes that the joint movement of Earth and Sun may produce it. Here, the "I think" and the rising pitch at the end, which signals a question, and the slow production, all can be taken as evidence that she is thinking aloud, for the first time. Mary then describes the Earth as "facing the sunshine" while holding her left hand, to which her right hand approaches forming an arrow configuration. Subsequently, she uses her right hand to point in the reverse direction while saying "the other half" (like the back of her left hand) and describes it as "not facing the sun(shine)" (turns 100, 102). She then draws a conclusion: "they couldn't get the sunlight" (turn 104). There is a lot of tentativeness in Mary's talk which can be ascertained from the fact that Penny subsequently goes over the same conversational terrain to make sure she has understood what the interviewee has said.

Even though she has not thought about the issues before, Mary produces an answer. The English language she uses provides her with resources from which to draw inferences in the then and there of this interview. The possibility space constituted by the known expressions of language and the inferences that can be drawn from them probably is not unlimited, which does not make it surprising that researchers find only a limited number of "cognitive models," though there is a lot of reduction of variation going on to squeeze a complex interview protocol into any one of these models. Here, from the expression "facing the Sun," anyone can infer that there is another side not facing the Sun without ever having thought about this before. The left hand exhibits precisely those features (Figure 5.1). Held up, the palm is pointed toward the window and light falls on it, whereas the backhand side is darker, "not facing the Sun." The situation itself, brightly lit palm and darker backside of the hand, exposes a model even though Mary has not thought about it before. Similarly, from the expression "one half," anyone can conclude that there is "another half." What we see here, therefore, is the realization of a number of tropes, which are resources that can be used to make further inferences.

Mary realizes in a concrete way possibilities afforded to her by the English language she speaks—and of which she does not even have to know explicitly any syntactic or semantic rules. In fact, children make such inferences without knowing any formal grammar whatsoever. Why then do some researchers make attributions about the mind when, in fact, participants such as Mary and AJ merely realize the possibilities of a language and culture that they have received from others. The language Mary uses is not hers; in a sense, she borrows it from the Anglo-Saxon culture in the same way that Anglo-Saxon children borrow it from their own culture. Moreover, Mary does not merely use a language that has come to her from the other, but she also uses it *for the other* and she does so in a way (implicitly) deemed suitable for the occasion at hand—an interview about Sun, Earth, day, and night. That is, when Mary speaks, she concretely realizes *cultural* possibilities of talk, and she speaks in a way that presupposes the intelligibility of the said, not only to *this* interlocutor but also to the generalized others who constitute the community of which Penny is part. In Mary's talk, we hear language speak, using Mary as a means to achieve concretization. If this were not such, no researcher would be able to analyze conversations, because the analysis presupposes precisely the same kind of discursive competence from the analyst that the two interview participants exhibit to each other and which they require to be able to pull off the interview in the first place. If researchers understand what Mary and Penny are talking about, then they ascertain the possibility of talking in this way and its intelligibility; if researchers did not understand, they could not analyze the conversation to say that Mary has a misconception.

I conclude, therefore, that what Mary and AJ produce are not just singular (solipsist, private) utterances, but, in addition to being bound to the contextual particulars of the conversation, these are texts that through and through are framed and mediated by a language that neither is their language nor is it a language just *in itself* and *for themselves*. Language, as language, presupposes interlocutors and, *ipso facto*, is shared rather than private as the makers of the Harvard-Smithsonian institute suggest in the title of their documentary. What is being said—in addition to how it is said—inherently is *from* the other (i.e., culture) and *for* the other, realizing possibilities, which by their very nature exceed the singularity of (in each case and each time) *this* speaker. If language and the societally mediated text, context, and content are *cultural* possibilities, then the latter cannot be ascribed and reduced to characteristics of individuals. Interview participants reproduce cultural possibilities for language and conversational topics, so that the "misconceptions"—if we want to use this term—are not their own but are misconceptions that exist in the culture and are understood by non-scientists and scientists alike. Educators interested in "eradicating" misconceptions about the Sun, Earth, day, and night, therefore, tell us that they want to remove culturally enabled ways of talking. It is precisely because these ways of talking are cultural possibilities that even astronomers can marvel at a "beautiful sunrise"; and, in so doing, they concretely realize and reproduce (i.e., keep alive) the cultural possibility to talk about the Sun as the agent of movement. In a sense, then, it is language that exposes itself (rather than people) and its sense in and through interactions, and individual speakers are but the means by which language realizes its own possibilities in concrete ways.

Individually owned conceptions deconstructed

In this book generally, and in this chapter particularly, I propose a language-based perspective on forms of talk that educators have taken as evidence for underlying, "individually held" conceptual frameworks. Language is a cultural phenomenon through and through so that, in a strong sense, "conceptions" and "misconceptions" are cultured—forms of language-in-use that are cultured, that is, cultivated, propagated, grown, developed, refined, and improved. The cognitive functions on which (mis-) conceptions are based therefore reside in the text rather than in the subject. Even when such a process occurs in the confines of the most intimate self-awareness, it constitutes an "attempt to translate oneself into the common code, to take stock of another's point of view, and, consequently, entails orientation toward a possible listener" (Vološinov 1976: 114). The very notion of a "(mis-) conception" therefore implies its cultural rather than individual origin. The individual not only receives the language for realizing (mis-) conceptions from culture but, in and through participating in culture, reproduces and transforms these (mis-) conceptions as well. Consciousness generally, and any conception specifically, therfore, is not merely a psychological phenomenon but especially a sociological phenomenon. This has a consequence that we can talk about and understand everything without having appropriated beforehand that which is signified by the words and language we use.

The present perspective distinguishes itself from socio*linguistics*, for example, in that it takes discourse and its pragmatic realization for the purpose at hand as topics rather than language and linguistic structure per se. Concepts are not "out there," in the ideal, purified world of pure thought as Plato conceives of it, a perspective that the Daedalus of the logos, Immanuel Kant, has developed to its pinnacle. Past research from the sociolinguistic perspective has overlooked the fact that there are possibilities in language that frame what and how people can engage in discourse, and, in this sense, concrete discursive acts realize *real, concretely existing* possibilities and therefore possible concepts. Furthermore, from the perspective outlined here, grammar and other features of talk are themselves practical and interactive achievements for the purpose of making the current activity what it is rather than—as other linguistic analyses appear to suggest—something that can be taken *a priori* as determinant of talk. I return to the contingent achievement of grammatical features in Chapter 8.

From the fragments presented as illustrative examples and also from the analysis of these fragments of interviews, educators and other learning scientists can take that human beings do not depend on an original cognitive framework *inside* their minds to speak their thoughts, but their talk and explanations are spontaneous and contextualized within interviews and for the interviewers, both reproducing and transforming cultural forms with the use of a certain language, and also realizing the activity per se, that is, the interview. Language is pure exteriority, and it is precisely through this exteriority that the world becomes objective: "objectivity results from language … The thing becomes theme. To thematize is to offer the world to the Other in speech" (Levinas 1971: 184). We, therefore, need to abandon the idea of individually owned "conceptions," the solipsistic ways of understanding the world, always already thematized in and with the sound-word; and we need to abandon the idea that students learn by having their misconception eradicated in and through instruction. This exteriority that comes with language, the relation with the Other, precedes anything that we exteriorize with language, such as ideas (in an interview), knowledge (on a test, exam), opinions, attitudes, and so on, because the objective exteriority of anything phenomenal is already situated in the world established by language. That is, once again, we cannot separate out the production of text and the production of *con*text, both depending on the nature of language.

One of the main aporias for the conceptual change approach has been the resilience of (mis-, alternative, pre-, pre-instructional, prior, naïve, canonical, non-standard) conceptions to instructions. Thus, even students who have taken several high school courses in physics do not change their ways of talking. This has lead researchers to suggest that the (mis-, alternative, pre-, pre-instructional, prior, naïve, canonical, non-standard) conceptions have persisted. This resistance has proven to exist even when extraordinary efforts have gone into the construction of curricula based on analogies involving leading advocates of the approach in the design. (See Chapter 3 for the use of analogies in teaching.) That is, *because* students use their *everyday* language and experiences as sources and resources for building analogies—which includes theories and logic implicit in everyday language—the latter are inconsistent with the scientific canon. That is, a language-based approach explains *why* the analogy-based approach to conceptual change does not work. This makes immediate sense when we think of language as providing the very resources (the tools) with which to conduct societal forms, including interviews about scientific phenomena and concepts. Language is always considered to be both that of the person and that of the culture: from my, the speaker's perspective, the language I speak is always both mine and not mine, always from the other and for the other. At the very instant I express myself, I draw on a language that is not mine, which must be the language of the other so that he or she can understand. Even if I cogitate in the privacy of my home, pursuing my own most private conversations with myself, I peruse a language that is not mine—because of the nature of language, even private cogitation exteriorizes. It is therefore not surprising when French poet Arthur Rimbaud (1951: 254) says, "I participate in the unfolding of my own thought: I watch it, I listen to it … the symphony stirs in the depths, or it surges onto the scene." Ways of talking, however, constitute cultural possibilities: they are inherently collective phenomena that cannot be eradicated by instructing this or that child. These ways of talking could be eradicated only when the cultural possibilities themselves were to be eradicated, that is, when a part of the discursive possibilities available in a culture were to be cut off from discourse. This is as unlikely to happen in the same way that swearing does not disappear because school rules interdict swearing.

The perspective on language, learning, and context outlined in this book has considerable consequences for teaching. As educators, we no longer can expect students to restructure something in their minds—which may happen more or less suddenly—but have to put up with the painstaking reconfiguration of ways of talking to make it appropriate to different kinds of situations. This is shown in my own past research where I have followed students in real time, from one second to the next, over periods that range from several weeks to several months and in different content domains. Thus, saying that the Sun rises in the morning, moves across the sky, and sets in the evening is appropriate in many settings, social situations, and textual productions (novels, poetry, sitting with a loved one on a beach facing west), but it is inappropriate in others, including science classrooms and interviews about scientific conceptions. Educators involved in language learning know that it takes years to become even a rudimentary speaker of a foreign language. This, too, is the case, as my own research shows, even when students have spent eight years in immersion classrooms where the language of instruction *is* the foreign language (Roth 2005b). From this perspective, then, why would educators expect students to fluently talk about science, mathematics, or history concerning some phenomena within the days, weeks, or months allotted to a topic? Moreover, my language perspective renders evident that talk has specific, pragmatic purposes. This dimension of language heretofore has not been taken into account both in research using interviews and in the teaching of disciplinary-specific ways of talking—in both situations, conceptions are thought to exist in the head and independent of the sociocultural and cultural-historical setting. The present perspective, on the other hand, predisposes us to instructional forms in which students get to talk, not just about certain topics, but about science, mathematics, or history for the purposes of successfully realizing the ongoing activity, satisfactorily and completely discussing the topic at hand, and using scientifically appropriate forms of talk.

Beyond individualism

To identify conceptions and conceptual change in any talk, many assumptions have to be made about the nature of talk (individual production rather than collective phenomenon), the methodical question of the unit of analysis, the manner of abstracting content from the talk and attribute it to an individual, and about an underlying conceptual framework that generates this talk. A pragmatic approach to language is a useful method because it does not have to make such assumptions (though it makes others). I consider an important aspect of the pragmatic approach to be its reflexive orientation. It can be used, in the same way as discursive psychology, as a method to analyze itself: it treats psychology generally and the study of cognition particularly "as an object *in and for interaction*" (Potter 2005: 739, original emphasis). That is, it is a method that can be used in two ways. First, it can be used to describe and explain how educators (cognitive, developmental, educational psychologists) construct versions of what it is to know concepts and how conceptual change is proposed and produced. It is a method that ultimately can be used on this text I have produced, which proposes something like a phenomenological approach to language as a theory and method for studying how people know and learn. Second, it is an approach to understanding language, learning, and context from the position of participants, considering *their* practical and situation constructions, terms, orientations, and displays. Because the fundamental dividing line between individual and collective consciousness is undecidable in any conceivable practical situation, language, learning, and context become practical, accountable, situated, embodied, and displayed phenomena; and they thereby become something that professional and lay participants (researchers and everyday folk alike) can take as constituting their objective reality.

In articulating a phenomenological language perspective on conceptions and conceptual change, in focusing on how these are constituted in talk and how these are expressions inherent in language, which is not the language of the speaker (alone), I inevitably raise issues about how the learning sciences construct their truths about conceptions and conceptual change. That is, to arrive at the identification of conceptions and conceptual change, researchers have to enact multiple levels of reductions. First, the text about phenomena and conceptions has to be uncoupled from the reproduction of the interview as cultural–historical form of activity, a phenomenon described in Chapter 2. Second, performances have to be uncoupled from the turn-sequences described in Chapters 4 and 5; and these have to be ascribed to individuals who independently (without being confounded) produce the utterances. Third, the now individual utterances involving particular concept words and concept word constellations are flattened to *one* mental structure—as any competent user of statistical methods such as multidimensional scaling knows, this comes at a great cost of stress, a measure of the force required to squeeze a rich semantic field into a very small number of dimensions. Fourth, language is reduced to a tool that serves the articulation of an underlying structure rather than being the relevant phenomenon itself—language as the background, contested terrain (e.g., concepts), and tool for the articulation of relevant topics (e.g., phenomena). Fifth, the inherently situated features of talk, the mumbles, stumbles, quirks, pauses, hesitations, and so on, have to be suppressed even though, as we see in Chapter 2, they may be interactional resources that people actively deploy in making sense (e.g., about whether AJ knows or does not know the answer to a question or whether she might be afraid to give the wrong answer). Sixth, thought is reduced to a structure rather than a process so that it becomes difficult to theorize how thought may change. Whether the reductions enacted and presuppositions made are valid and useful is, in part, itself a paradigmatic issue and that, therefore, cannot be resolved across paradigms. It is also an empirical issue the possibility of which ought to be demonstrated rather than taken for granted. I have described cases that provide evidence that the reductions and presuppositions lead to insurmountable aporias—ascribing a conception to an individual who has never thought or talked about a phenomenon is scientifically unsound, as is attributing to individuals what inherently and irreducible is the product of a collective effort.

In this chapter, I am concerned with the phenomenon of conceptions, in particular with raising issues that run counter to the idea that knowledge in the head is the relevant phenomenon and theories for scientists concerned with language, learning, and context. However, similar issues can be raised concerning beliefs, attitudes, or identity (see Chapter 6), which, from the presented perspective, also are phenomena that are discursively and pragmatically constituted in talk, mostly interviews and questionnaires. As such, they are subject to the same constraints elaborated here, which do not permit ascription of these phenomena to individuals but require us to see and theorize them as sociocultural and cultural–historical phenomena through and through. There are cultural–historical ways and possibilities of talking about beliefs, attitudes, and identity; and these ways and possibilities are concretely realized, recognizably reproduced and transformed in societal formations (lessons, interviews) as resources for others. Once learning, scientists adopt a phenomenological approach to language, new, fruitful agendas open up for researching many of the difficult and unanswered questions and aporias that face our disciplines today. In conceptual change speak, this approach not only provides an "intelligible" alternative that addresses some of the obstinate and persistent problems but also promises to be "fruitful" by opening up new areas and topics for the social scientists concerned with language, learning, and context. For me, this is so because teachers and students make talk available to one another. Whereas there are numerous reasons (intentions) and formal frameworks that might explain what people say and why they say it, I am more concerned with the phenomenon that interaction participants themselves encounter: language in interaction is practical, accountable, situated, embodied, and displayed. By making psychology relevant, language-in-interaction is itself theorized as a phenomenon, which has a greater potential than traditional approaches to lead to knowledge useful to language users themselves.

The relevance question has both practical and theoretical dimensions. For conceptual change researchers, the present approach offers new ways of understanding, for example, the production of "(mis-, alternative, pre-, pre-instructional, prior, naïve, canonical, non-standard) conceptions" from and with the *very same linguistic resources* that in some later stage allow the person to produce scientific conceptions. Teachers may find the approach more useful because they do not have to think about and infer hidden frameworks and intentions, but are provided with a theory of the phenomenon as they encounter it—in and through language. The approach may also be useful in other school contexts, for example, in a school counseling session designed to mediate between students who have gotten into a fight, it may turn out more productive to assist the involved students in understanding how discourse is used to create effects rather than reflecting on hidden intentions and understandings.

6   Talking identity

It is wrong to say: I think. One should say: someone thinks me ... I am an other.

(Rimbaud 1951: 252)

What is identity, this concept of which the transparent identity to itself is always dogmatically presupposed by so many debates on monoculturalism or on multiculturalism, nationality, citizenship, and belonging generally? And before the identity of the subject, what is *ipseity*? The latter is not reducible to an abstract capacity to say "I," which it will always have preceded.

(Derrida 1996: 30–31, original emphasis)

In Chapter 5, we observe how interlocutors, while presupposing language, draw on language to talk about certain phenomena. In the process, they contribute to producing texts that researchers subsequently transcribe and then analyze in their entirety to make attributions about the knowledge (conceptions, misconceptions, conceptual framework) that a person is said to "have" on the day of the interview. Knowing, and, in an educational context therefore, learning, is not the only phenomenon of interest to educators. Motivation, interests, attitudes, locus of control, aspirations, perceptions, and the likes are also thought to be important dimensions that mediate the teaching–learning process. The concept of identity, who someone is, may be thought of as integrating all of these dimensions. But because one has to talk to a person to find out anything about who he or she is (wants to be) we may anticipate that identity, too, will be marked by characteristics of shared language and therefore by culture. It is impossible to solve the question of selfhood—of whom one speaks in designating person as distinct from things, and who speaks by designating him/herself—apart of a philosophy of language (Ricœur 1990). Precisely because language presupposes the interlocutor and is iterable, thereby describing multiple instances, the talk of identity cannot reveal what is *singular* about the experience of a person.

In recent years, identity has become an important research topic in its own right. Some hold that it is something fractured, changing with the situation in which a person finds him/herself. Others treat it as if it were something that individuals "construct" and that is attached to them, something they carry around or enact in relevant situations. But much of the debate, from whichever side it is approached, does not deal with the very identity of the identity concept itself—as Jacques Derrida suggests in the introductory quote to this chapter. For Derrida, identity not only involves trouble in the sense of disorder (Fr. *trouble*), but also confusion (Fr. *trouble*) and tender emotion (Fr. *le trouble de*). He wonders whether this "*trouble de l'identité*" assists or inhibits the recollection of past events necessary for the construct of identity. Does it heighten the desire for memory or does it drive the genealogical fantasy to despair, does it suppress, repress, or liberate? All of these questions are tied to a triple quandary of language that emerges from two laws that are contradictory both within and between themselves, contradictions heightened by the fact that in the French version, the two laws differ only by the trace "*qu*":

1. *On ne parle jamais qu'une seule langue* [One only ever speaks one language].
2. *On ne parle jamais une seule langue* [One never speaks only one language].

(Derrida 1996: 21)

Identity (from Lat. *idem*, same), who we are for ourselves and who we are in relation to others, is a mysterious phenomenon for at least two reasons. First, I, the author of these lines, can point to a picture taken in 1958 (Figure 6.1a) and say: "This is me when I was five, my parents, and my four-year-old brother." In this case, although there are substantial differences between myself today (Figure 6.1b) and the child in the picture with respect to the physique and particulars of the body, including size, hair color, and so on, I am making an assertion about the sameness of whoever is depicted and that "I," Wolff-Michael Roth, can indexically (point to and) refer to as "I." I can make the assertion even though I do not remember the moment in which the photograph was taken. I can make such an assertion despite recognizing that I was more aggressive at that time in my life, continuously fighting with other kids. The change also is available to others, who recognize that "Michael has mellowed in his later years." Thus, who I am and who I was is part of an auto/biography, a narrative featuring the same person (character) with both constant and changing character traits through the course of his life (a plot). Much like we talk about English as a language continuing through time despite the considerable difference between its instantiation during the sixteenth century and today—as modeled in one of the chapters of *Ulysses*—we speak of the identity of persons despite the observable and lived differences in the courses of their lives.

a    b

Figure 6.1 a Photograph of author at age five (front left).
   b Photograph of author at age 55.

I can make this statement about myself at the age of five without sounding unintelligible even though, as I am moving from situation to situation and instant to instant in my daily life, I am someone different with respect to the others surrounding me—my partner, colleagues, graduate students, friends, or family. In each case, what I do depends on the situation—my friend Bob is also the head of the department with which I am associated—so what we talk about and how we talk is a function of context. Others observing me might say, "Michael is a very different person on Bob's farm than in the department meeting"; and they might say the same thing about Bob. That is, separated by a few hours or days, Bob and I are *said to* act and talk in very different ways, which observers might take as evidence to say that I (we) are very different persons on the farm and in the department. Who I am with respect to friends and colleagues is inherently frail so that a stable identity in interaction with others is the outcome of continuous reproduction, which, in dialectical logic, also implies change and transformation.

There are, therefore, at least two aspects to identity. On the one hand, a person appears to have a core identity, which undergoes developments that are articulated in autobiographical narratives of self. In this perspective, events in our lives may provide us with resources to understand ourselves differently, leading to changes in our biographies. This aspect has been articulated in terms of the narrative construction and reconstruction of Self, which is a function of the particular collective with which we identify. But this core Self itself is problematic, "the source of all presence, reducing itself to an abstract point, a pure form stripped of all thickness" (Derrida 1972: 335). Second, in contrast to the contention of identity as a (relatively) stable phenomenon that is constructed in biographical narratives, the experience of the different ways in which we relate to others in the varying contexts of everyday life has led postmodern scholars to conceive of self in society as something frail, brittle, fractured, and fragmented (Giddens 1991). The Self is the result of interactions which themselves use identity as resource. We have to ask, "how can our identities simultaneously be continuous and discontinuous, context-independent and situated, stable and frail, or adaptive and brittle?" and "why are there differences between the self in narratives and in ongoing, concrete daily life?"

This makes it appealing to construct a theoretical account in which distinct forms of identity are the *effects* of different forms of practical and discursive actions.

Identity work, working identity

In previous chapters, we see how forms of talk ("knowledge," "conceptions") themselves come to be the topic of talk—e.g., when Connor asks his teacher, "what do you mean like?" or when the interviewer asks AJ which one of several images shows the Earth and the Sun—or a resource that people mobilize for the matters at hand—e.g., the sound-word "cube" to denote a group of objects. These forms of talk, constitutive of emerging and emergent texts—and the *con*texts that they produce and with which they are irreducibly interwoven—therefore constitute the presupposed ground, the resources and tools, and the topics at the same time. Thus, for example, in Chapter 2, the interviewer articulates the context by formulating for the seven-year-old girl, AJ, what he is going to do, namely "asking an easy question," before asking a question about how day and night come about. The question itself concerns a topic that knowledgeable science educators would immediately attribute to a kind of research that has become synonymous with the terms conceptions and conceptual change. Here, I am concerned not with identity as it is inferred from someone's actions but with identity talk, both as topic—i.e., talking identity—and as resource—i.e., identity in talking. That is, at issue is the question of who someone is and identifies with when identity is brought into and talked about in conversations with others. Based on the preceding chapters, my readers may already anticipate that something similar is at work based on the nature of language that must inherently be intelligible and shared to serve as the ground, tool and resource, and topic for a conversation. Identity is not something that is internal to ourselves but, in and through language, any interiority always already is exteriorized. In this chapter, I use excerpts from conversations about knowing and learning that I had some time ago with students while being a high school teacher and department head of science interested in improving instruction.[1]

Identification: the making of identity

> The mind ... has to recognize itself as itself, that is to say, as I. But how are we to recognize what will necessarily be erased and forgotten, since "I" is, per definition, what *I* can never say?
>
> (de Man 1982: 720, original emphasis)

Identity concerns essence—how someone *is*. But essence means constancy rather than flux and change. When the *I* says "I," what does it mean? Which self-identical entity is pointed at/to by the *I* of the "I"? In this subsection, I focus on the making of identity through the process of *identification*. In identi*ficat*ion, the *I* of identity, now properly identified, is *made* (from Lat. verb-producing suffix—*ficāre*, to make, produce, bring into a certain state, cause) to have an identity. We see identification at work in the first of the fragments mobilized here.

Fragment 6.1 begins when I orient Preston to "the first statement" on the questionnaire ("Scientific knowledge is artificial"). In fact, more is happening: the full statement is broken into two, as I already orient Preston to respond in view of the second part ("the next thing") of the questionnaire item ("whether it shows nature as it really is"). The turn ends with an explicit solicitation of Preston to articulate what he thinks about when he reads that sentence.

Fragment 6.1

01 T: All I want to know from you is what your ideas are about these questions and if you change your view just let me know what sort of caused that change … Why don't you tell me about, what you think about that first statement, "Scientific knowledge is artificial," and then the next one is— and the next thing will be, we'll look at is whether it shows nature as it really is. What do you think about, you know, when you read that sentence?

02 P: Well, you know, I mean, first of all, I am a very religious person and that sort of, kind of rearranges my knowledge about science. I think about different things. When I think back of all the things I have been taught such as how the Earth was made, how the things are (growing?), it makes me really think about what is true and what isn't and what is real and what isn't. And sometimes the facts, what I have learned in science and religion, can't be compared to each other.

03 T: Which religion are you talking about?

04 P: I am a Presbyterian Christian. So, you know, they say, "God says 'Boom, let there be light and let the Earth be'," whereas science says that there was dust collected out of space. I, like, it is very hard for me to say that. But in a way I do think that science is not artificial because it explains a lot more about the world rather than what religion does. And that's why I think that more people can be drawn towards science as it really is, because it is easier to believe, rather than religion.

Through his turn 02, Preston completes a question–response sequence. But he does not just respond. He actually begins by making a statement about himself, who and what he is: "I am a very religious person." Here, Preston, the speaker, begins with the reflexive pronoun "I" to point to himself, who becomes the subject of the statement. This *I* "is" the subject of the predicate "very religious person," and therefore has a place among all those individuals specified by the quality "very religious person." The speaking subject, Preston, thereby comes to be the subject of the uttered statement resulting in a self-attribution to a group of people with a particular kind of attribute or quality. This identity, being a very religious person, is a resource for and textually mediates ("rearranges") his "knowledge about science." Here, therefore, Preston uses identity, his identity, as a resource for creating a context within which any further statements (text) he makes about science and scientific knowledge are to be heard (and read), and which, therefore, come to constitute the *con*text within which his text is lodged, intelligible, and plausible.

That is, by talking Preston not only contributes to creating the interview context but within the interview he produces other contexts to allow his interlocutor to understand the real response, which is what and how he thinks about science.

It appears as if identity is the result of the statement of an identity—similar to the mathematical identity "=" in 2 + 3 = 5—in which the person denoted by the reflexive pronoun *I* comes to be (as a form of the verb "to be," which in its third person singular inflects as "is," from Latin *esse*, to be, itself an imitation of the Greek *ousia*, being, from the stem of the present participle *ont-* of the verb *einai*, to be. Identity (from Lat. *idem*, the same, + the noun-forming *-tās, -tātem* that functions equivalently to the English *-ty*) here takes its sense from its etymological roots to become identity in the sense of *idem*, the same, *idem-identity* (Ricœur 1990). But the situation is more complex in that there is not a simple statement of identity, a fact (*-ty*) of *idem* in the mathematical sense valid outside of any spatiotemporal situation. There is some work at work producing the very factuality of the fact. In this instance, we can see an interesting process that leads a person to be someone. Preston does not simply state an identity. Rather, we observe a form of identification consistent with the philosophical analysis of the concept, which comes to the conclusion that an "identity is never given, received or attained, no, only the interminable and indefinitely phantasmatic process of identification endures" (Derrida 1996: 53). Thus, there can be no auto/biography, no memory, reminiscence, and recollection (technically, anamnesis) of self without identification, and precisely *not* identity.

The matter of identification, however, is not settled in and with the predication that makes Preston a "very religious person." As soon as there is an opportunity, and rather than continuing with the last statements made, I ask Preston to specify the particular religion he is talking about (turn 03). He completes what I have begun as a query–response sequence by naming one Christian denomination, Presbyterian, before continuing with his elaboration of the issue started before. Here again, identity is the product of a process of identification with a particular religious group (movement) and Church.

In responding, Preston does not immediately provide an answer to the question, which asks him what he thinks when reading a statement such as "scientific knowledge is artificial." Rather, he formulates remembering, thinking back about "the things" that he has been taught, "how the Earth was made," and "how the things are (growing?)." He articulates that it is these things that make him "think about what is true and what isn't and what is real and what isn't." He then draws again on religion to state that what he has heard in its context cannot be compared to science, which is the marked topic of the conversation. It is marked not only because the conversation is in the context of physics, his interlocutor being his physics teacher, but also marked because the written statement about he has been asked to talk is one in which the subject, scientific knowledge, comes to be specified as artificial.

Preston responds just as he has been asked in the question "what do you think …?" He repeatedly formulates *that* he is thinking (i.e., process, noesis) and *what* he is thinking (i.e., content, noema). By means of the personal pronoun *I*, reflexively pointing to the present speaker, the process of thinking (noesis) and its contents (noema) come to be resources for constituting who Preston is in addition to the stated identification with the Presbyterian Church. The identity work continues when he states that "it is hard for [him] to say," as he attributes to science the statement that "the Earth was made" when "dust collected out of space." He sets this against what "they" say, which is that "God says 'Boom, let there be light and let the Earth be.'" Here "they" may be Presbyterian Christians, but it may also be the generalized others who have taught him. In both instances, he clearly frames the positions as received, something he "ha[s] been taught" about "how the Earth was made." In one instance, the source of the statement is "they," which, because of topical collocation, can be heard to be believers in the (Presbyterian) Christian faith in one instant and science in the other instant.

Preston then commits to a statement prefaced by the formulation "I think," thereby articulating something about who he is: "science is not artificial because it explains a lot more about the world than what religion does" (turn 04). Equally, he formulates himself to think "that more people can be drawn to science as it really is, because it is easier to believe … than religion."

From the perspective of the questions about language, learning, and context raised in this book, it is interesting to note the tension between the reflexive self-reference using the pronoun *I*, the *autonomous* subject of action, and instances where the *I* becomes the indirect object. This allows the speaker to be in the recipient position of an action; it produces a passive orientation of the person subject to *heteronomy*. This tension between autonomy and heteronomy of the subject is a core contradiction in the question of identity and Self (Ricœur 1990). Thus, Preston actively "thinks back of all the things," but then appears in the recipient position when the things remembered "make [him] think about what is true and what isn't and what is real and what isn't." Also, rather than stating something like "I find it hard to say that," he actually refers to himself in the dative form of interest, "it is *for me* to say that." This form of referring to himself parallels the passive voice, such as when he says "I have been taught," and thereby articulates his identity in terms of what happened or came to him. He thereby constitutes the locus of control outside of himself, heteronomy, the patient and recipient rather than the agent of action. This tension between autonomy and heteronomy is evident throughout the account Preston establishes for and together with me. Here, then, the content of talk and the grammar of language interact in the sense that the latter produces specific effects in the former.

Contradictions, repertoires, and devices

Contradictions are central to life, both those of logical type and those that come from the very nature of life. The former arise when a person makes statements that do not appear to fit into the same frame, which sometimes arises when a different frame is used for hearing an utterance than was used in the production of the statement. Such contradictions may also arise when a speaker, in a new immediate conversational context, says something inconsistent with a former statement. The first of the two logical contradictions is quickly settled, as soon as it is discovered, when the interlocutors repair the "misunderstanding." The second of the logical contradictions is frequently accounted for, when pointed out to the speaker, by some discursive device that makes the contradiction disappear in one form or another. Thus, for example, scientists—when asked for how they can simultaneously claim that science produces truth and that social forces influence scientists—tend to invoke the *truth-will-out-device* (Gilbert and Mulkay 1984). Therefore, although there are (some, many) scientists influenced by politics and economy, tending to bias their research and findings, truth will eventually come out because of the objective nature of science. The device, therefore, makes the contradiction—between statements that science is objective and that scientists are influenced by social contexts—disappear.

In contrast to the logical contradictions, inner contradictions cannot be resolved. Thus, for example, although our entire body changes completely, both at an atomic level as well as at a biological, physiological, medical, neuropsychological, or psychological level, we tend to say that the core person remains the same—a core that therefore must constitute a singularity. Inner contradictions also exist in concepts such as *thinking|speaking* where the two moments cannot be reduced to the same but, as irreducibly different, exist in and constitute the very concept.

Contradictions are not just theoretical concepts but are topics and resources for conversation. One speaker can ask another to account for such contradictions, leading to further talk. This can go on for a while until there is no further recourse. The contradiction therefore becomes one that is embedded in, and arises from, life itself generally, and language particularly, which has no further recourse to locate itself than in the non-locatable experience of language specifically and life generally. Thus, in Fragment 6.2, I ask Preston "but how is religion not artificial?" raising the topic of talk to a contradiction between what the student has said and the apparent state of affairs.

In the preceding fragment, Preston introduces his religion; and the conversation is, in part, about the specific religion he belongs to. His discourse constitutes a way of *con*textualizing the text proffered in response to the request to articulate his position on some questionnaire item. This current position on knowledge specifically and life more generally, however, is one that is lodged between the past and the future, what he has been and the experiences that he has had, on the one hand, and what he wants to be and will be in the future, on the other hand. The very resources of language that constitute identity in the past also project identity into the future, ahead of itself (Bakhtine 1984). Identity thereby comes to be lodged between the past and the future, what we have done and experienced and what we want and will be. Here language plays a major role, as there is no remembering without it, the forms and genres it gives rise to especially with respect to (personal, collective) memory, history, or (personal, collective) identity (Ricœur 2004a). And "memory, as an inversion of historical time," made possible by language that also creates the separation of the One into Self and Other, "is the essence of interiority" (Levinas 1971: 27). The Self, therefore, is impossible without language, but, because of the exteriority of language, the Self is itself inherently exteriority (Other). I, any I, therefore understands itself as another. This, therefore, is an inner contradiction of identity and Self that we cannot ever understand other than through that which Self is not, the generalized other.

A first indication of the past and its role in shaping who Preston is arises at the instant when I ask the student to deal with an apparently perceived contradiction between science, denoted as artificial, and religion, denoted as not artificial. As the interview unfolds, the contradiction is navigated, attenuated if not temporarily resolved, in the recourse to a form of influence that has no further explication: Preston's upbringing, and, therefore, the influence anybody's upbringing has on knowing and identity.

Fragment 6.2

01 T: See, because if something is out there, then we could eventually find a way, may be a way of describing how it really is.

02 P: See, see, you look at things completely different than I do, because I am religious, that's why. Whereas, are you religious at all?

03 T: I mean, not in any organized …

04 P: Yea, I mean, like, you can obviously say that you cannot … I cannot say that I do not see nature as it really is. I think that science knowledge is artificial because I would think that religion is completely by the book of God, is not artificial, because I have grown up that way, and therefore I can't say that … Newton, I can say that Newton is artificial that all the things that he has said is artificial, that is my way of thinking, right.

05 T: But how is religion not artificial? I mean, you have to make a basic commitment, or belief …

06 P: And that's the only argument I have is because that's the way I've grown up, that is why.

07 T: But you have to make that—you have to make that basic commitment.

08 P: That's right.

09 T: See, question three actually asked you, "Do scientists have to make similar commitments? Do they have to believe that what they come up with?"

The end of this part of the conversation, as well as the end of the fragment, comes (about) when I formulate what the third question asks of Preston. By moving on from the current topic related to the second question, I not only change the topic but also indicate at the same time that, at least for the present instance, the second question has been addressed satisfactorily. This also means that whatever Preston has said could not be interrogated any further because the student has drawn on something that constitutes the very foundation of intelligibility, always already shared. What he has said, therefore, may serve as sufficient support for an argument or explanation. Such forms of talk are denoted by the term *interpretative repertoires* (Roth and Alexander 1997). These repertoires constitute the very grounds of being so that questioning their contents, for example, by asking "why?" would constitute an irrational act (Rawls 1989).

   In the present instance, we see how the conversation comes to be such that further questioning does not move the issue along. Preston already mobilizes in turn 04 the influences to which he had been subjected during the time that he grew up ("because I have grown up that way"). With this form of talk he shores up the claim that "religion is completely by the book of God," that it therefore "is not artificial." He contrasts this with Newton, who, as Preston suggests, has made artificial statements (which in a strong and etymological sense it is, the result of craft, from Latin *ars, artis*, art, craft + *facēre*, to make). I follow up asking about the apparent non-artificial nature of religion, offering "basic commitment" and "belief" as resources for thinking this nature differently (turn 05). In return, Preston mobilizes the same argument again, "because that's the way I've grown up, that's why" (turn 06). There is no use attempting to interrogate this issue any further, as "that's the only argument" he has (turn 06). I articulate again the issue of the "basic commitment" that one has to make (turn 07), which Preston acknowledges (turn 08).

Characters and plots

Biography, including autobiography, constitutes a genre. As a genre, it makes use of recognizable, culturally specific characters and plots. There is a "Law of the genre," as a chapter title of *Parages* (Derrida 1986) states, which interlocutors, as part of the *social contract* implicit in language, hardly ever break. Thus, the narrating voice belongs to a subject who tells something, remembering an (auto/biographical) event, knowing who s/he is and what it precisely is that s/he talks about. The narrating voice "responds to a 'police', a controlling force or law enforcement ('what are you talking «about»': correspondence truth). In this sense all organized narration is a police matter, even before it determines itself as genre (thriller)" (Derrida 1986: 150). In this way, the autobiographical narrative constitutes its subject ("I") in a second way: as a knowledgeable narrator of a particular content that the narrator is thought/held to be particularly knowledgeable about. But we need to be on the alert and suspect concerning this constitution of the autobiography, because we are dealing with "the interpretation of the past from the point of view of the present" (Vološinov 1976: 81).

Who I am and can be in narratives of myself, therefore, is always already a cultural possibility. This is so, as the poet Arthur Rimbaud (1951: 254) suggests, "because I is another." He also says, as the opening quote states, "on me pense [I am thought]," but he follows this sentence stating that it contains a play of words. We, therefore, can hear him say: "on me panse [I am taken care off/I receive bandages." Here, the poet clearly recognizes the heteronomous aspects of identity, the Self which is another, already thought by the other. Derrida (1984) describes the same heteronomy in an essay entitled "Otobiographies," where autobiography is articulated as the *différance*, the undecidability, of allography (i.e., writing of the other) and thanatography (i.e., writing of death). The *living* Self dies in the account that inherently is Other, in the language of the other. Every autobiography, therefore, is already an allobiography (Lacoue-Labarthe 1975), the writing of the Self as other.

Having grown up in a particular way constitutes a powerful influence, influences that apparently, as treated here in this conversation, cannot be interrogated further. The family constitutes a context and an influence in which consciousness is formed prior to all consciousness. Having grown up in a certain way allows us to think consistently with these ways, corresponding to significations that are not any further accessible and questionable by Preston himself (or any other person in such a situation). Here, then, what a person thinks or believes narratively is folded back into a time when children are subject to the influences of their parents, prior to the development of a self-consciousness of their own. This aspect of identity therefore derives from a time when the person has not been a self-conscious agent actively constructing identity and a time when the other was very much at work. It is the source and part of the production of the tension between autonomy and heteronomy of the agent. Thought and beliefs thereby become the result of influences that any culturally competent member can understand. It is part of a familiar narrative form: growing up in a family, being a child (*character*), whose character generally, and whose thoughts and believes specifically, are shaped during a particular instant in a *plot* that constitutes life, here childhood. But all of these facets, traditionally ascribed to persons and their families, really constitute effects of language, for it is "here that motives of behavior, arguments, goals, evaluations are composed and given external expression. It is here, too, that arise the conflicts among them" (Vološinov 1976: 81). That is, what researchers have thought about in the past as constituting the singularity of identities, in fact, are moments of erasing this singularity in service of subjecting a life to the intelligibility that comes with language and the generality it brings about.

Childhood influences, enacted by parents, siblings, and by members of the wider family (uncles, aunts, grandparents) and (family) friends are part of stories of life, biographies and autobiographies. In my interviews with scientists and students alike, the questions about why someone becomes a scientist or plans to study science at university invariably include references to childhood experiences (e.g., Roth and Hsu 2008).[2] These experiences are mobilized in support of the plot positively or negatively, that is, to support the argument about why a person has become what he or she is at a later stage in life. This is a realization of the teleological possibilities arising from the constraints that come with emplotment—my later life prefigured and made visible in early events. In a positive manner, the influences are *said* to be the causal antecedence; in a negative way, the person has become a famous scientist despite some negative influences, thereby supporting suggestions of a strong character able to deal with hardship and difficult circumstances. This is so whether someone writes a biography of a scientist—we only need to think about the proverbial stories and myths about Albert Einstein as a child and student doing poorly or failing— or whether someone tells, or participates in, the production of an autobiography, such as happens in this and further conversations with Preston. Because of these commonalities, we may use the term *auto/biography*, especially because of the disjunction between author (narrator) and hero and the requirements that genre places on narrative independent of the nature of the author (Bakhtine 1984). Moreover, the autobiographer does not simply tell a story from his or her perspective, it is the narrative of a life that takes into account context and the way in which the Other may see him or her figuring before this context-producing ground (Roth 2005a).

In turn 04, Preston mobilizes an interesting possibility of language when he says, "this is my way of thinking." The turn, in fact, singularizes what he has said before ("religion is completely by the book of God, is not artificial" and "Newton is artificial") and attributes this way of thinking to himself, making it a characteristic of who he is, a feature of his personality, identity. But in saying what he does, it turns out that he is not so singular at all—he loses absolute ipseity (from Lat. *ipse*, self + noun-forming -*ity*) or selfhood. All the while he talks he remains—he has to remain—intelligible; and he achieves this precisely in this talk (*logos*) and the forms of reason (*logos*) that talking embodies. This intelligibility derives from the very possibility of talking in this way, semantically speaking. Precisely because it is a general possibility, what he says and how he says it *cannot be so singular* after all; what he realizes are general and generalized possibilities available to other culturally competent speakers and hearers of this language. That is, the very fact that the utterance "that is my way of thinking" is part of a communicative act also presupposes this way of thinking as a general feature of culture, enabled by the very language in which the statement is expressed.

Concerning the contradiction, at issue for understanding *this* conversation is not whether what Preston says is, in fact, the official position of the particular religious group that he identifies with in and for the purpose of this conversation. He does not, in fact, if we compare what he says with the official position of the Presbyterian Church. Thus, elsewhere in this and other conversations, Preston makes statements about the age of the universe that are consistent with the creationist discourse of some Southern Baptist congregations, which articulate beliefs in intelligent design and the ready-made creation of human being in contrast to evolutionary theory. However, the position of the Presbyterian Church is actually in non-contradiction with the theory of evolution, as can be seen in an official statement on its website.[3] Elsewhere in our conversation, Preston denies the usefulness of the theory of evolution, attributing to the universe an age of about 50,000 years. Yet unless the position is challenged in and for the conversation, other positions do not matter for understanding the development and evolution of the topic at hand. In this conversation, he is not challenged so these contradictions do not matter to its history.

The many voices of identity

We never have but one voice, a fact that Fyodor Dostoevsky has employed for artistic purposes in stories and novels. The multiple voices within a person produce a tension that is the very condition of development of ideas and personalities (Bakhtin 1984a). The multiplicity of voices that constitutes a tension within a person is also at work in the present interview as seen in Fragment 6.3. It begins with a reference to "committed scientists," "who believe in Big Bang and evolution," but who also "still see a place for God, in a personal relationship" (turn 01). In this, the utterance constitutes a comment upon a tension Preston has articulated before between science and religion in the context of a conversation about the nature of science and scientific knowledge. This comment articulates the possibility to integrate science and religion, especially for Preston, who has to wrestle with the uneasy relation between the two domains that he has articulated so far. In fact, he articulates an acknowledgment of the fact that "that's something that [he has] wrestled with for a long time" (turn 02) and therefore concretizes the preceding utterance as a comment. Over the next two turns, we accomplish a question together, as Preston finishes what turns out to be the first part of a question about his way of thinking about science. This nature of the collectively *achieved* question then is both affirmed ("yea") in turn 05 and then translated and specified in terms of "what [he] can do in science." This sets up—without us being able to know at that very instant—what, after the fact, will have been an account of and explanation for the difficulties Preston experiences at the time in his two science courses, physics and chemistry.

Fragment 6.3

01 T: They still see a place for God in a personal relationship although they are committed scientists and although they believe in Big Bang and evolution and I guess that's something you have to wrestle with.

02 P: That's something that I have wrestled with for a long time.

03 T: But doesn't that affect your overall, the way …

04 P: I think about science?

05 T: You can, yea, what you can do in science.

06 P: Why do you think I, why do you think it is hard for me to grasp the concepts in class, hearing you lecture in class about the way, the way light comes in and how it diffracts into an electron? It's hard for me to grasp that knowledge. Whereas he is not, he who is a complete atheist, they grab it and say, "I can agree with you Doc, I can say that, because I … "I was thinking in my … how can you actually say that when you know other things, like about what religion has to offer or something like that and although in my words, because I am not a very full Christian, I cannot say "well, God has created life," you can't, "that's the way life is," I can't say that because I don't know much about what the Bible is to other people, right. But, and there has been times where it has affected me, that's why it sort of is reflected in my marks as well, because I never really told anyone, because they wouldn't actually believe me. If I was to say, "well I can't take chemistry because that's … I don't believe in that," I don't, it's hard, "I just, I just do the chemistry you know to get the marks" and … but I feel guilty in the other way, because that's not what I believe in.

07 T: Right. How come you selected the sciences?

08 P: Because I always have wanted to become a doctor, ever since I was five years old, I always have seen so many, the media really changes you, you see so many (injured?) people and a person fainted in my store, I didn't know what to do. I didn't know how to do CPR or something like that, and I have always wanted, always wanted to save lives. And that's why, my parents had that perfect image of me you know, oriental families want their son to be the best, and H, his parents probably, Ferdinand, Patrick and they always want their sons to be the best and it … my parents sort of pushed me to take science OAC ((Ontario Academic Credit)) courses and that OAC courses. So I followed their advice, I, I thought they knew what they were doing, so I took those courses, regardless of my opinion because I thought they were doing the right thing. And so I wanted to be a doctor, so I decided to pursue it, and then I tried to take that advantage and now they are taking that dream away from me that I can't become a doctor because, now they are coming back to reality that I don't have the

marks for it but its too late I am already in the middle of the OAC year, and, and the dream is gone, now I don't want to be a doctor anymore, my parents took that away from me. So that's why it is hard for me to believe. Its hard for me to distinguish between religion and science, it really is.

09   T: So when when you think about the, ah … the number four; "Scientific laws and theories exist independent of human existence, and scientists merely discover them"; would you say that is true, or …

Immediately following the articulation of the struggle arising from the relation of science and religion and the question about what he can do in science, Preston frames his difficulties of understanding science concepts in terms of a rhetorical question, "why do you think it is hard for me to grasp the concepts in class?" (turn 06). He then contrasts these difficulties with the experience of "he who is a complete atheist," who "grabs" science. This connection between the atheist—he names particular students and teachers—and science repeatedly returns in this and other recorded conversations between the two of us. In Fragment 6.2, Preston has already opposed his religiosity ("because I am religious") to what he articulates to my (his teacher's) different way of looking at the pertinent issue, although, immediately following, he raises as a question whether I am religious rather than attributing atheism to me as he does in another conversation. These students can agree with the teacher ("Doc"), though Preston does not tell us why these atheist students actually can agree. He also mobilizes this feature when saying that all those whom he knows to be atheists also get the best marks to the point that there is a sort of collusion between atheist students and atheist teachers. This link, because of the apparent logical consistency between being religious (Preston elsewhere refers to a similar situation of another student) and doing poorly in science, on the one hand, and being an atheist (which he knows from discussions in his dorm) and doing very well in the sciences, on the other hand, provides an explanatory resource for his not doing well. This link is further elaborated in terms of the knowledge that comes with being Christian, knowledge that competes with science, and knowledge that an atheist would not have. Thus, he asks, "how can you say that?"—leaving aside what the "that" actually refers to—"when you know other things, like what religion has to offer" (turn 06).

This account and explanation is very rich in terms of the different voices that come together in one and the same (here Preston's) utterance. He uses direct speech—here transcribed with the quotes to mark relevant instances off—that real or hypothetical people have or could have uttered. Elsewhere in the interview, Preston notes that he has had many debates with peers in his dorm concerning the question of religion; he also suggests that he is an avid debater and a member of the debating club. In our conversation, Preston recreates these debates—much like Dostoevsky allows ideas to emerge from debates of different voices in the theater of a protagonist's mind (Bakhtin 1984a). In the ephemeral theater articulated here, Preston tells us what he thinks; he also tells us what he can or cannot say (e.g., "well, God created life," "that's the way life is"). In this way, Preston himself doubles, appearing both directly and indirectly, which he achieves by formulating, and therefore framing, what is coming next or what has preceded the talk. He also allows others, both specific and generalized others, to enter this theater, presenting their ideas or using them to personify ideas (the atheist). They enter both by means of direct speech ("I can agree with you Doc, I can say that") and by means of indirect speech, generally marked when a speaker uses a construction such as "X says *that* ..." followed by indirect speech ("how can you actually say *that*").

In turn 08, Preston mobilizes a common conception (description) of oriental parents (families) and the relations they have to their sons: "they want their son to be perfect image ... and they always want their sons to be the best." He then lists the names of three classmates (H, Ferdinand, Patrick), all of oriental (Chinese, Korean) origin. He is the author of an auto/biographical account that places himself in a context that is familiar to those who work with or are Orientals. To have their sons be the best, oriental parents "push" them in the way that Preston's parents pushed him to take the college-level courses in science (Ontario Academic Credit [OAC]). Like many of his oriental peers, he "followed [his parents'] advice," especially because, as he formulates, he thought "they knew what they were doing." As a consequence, he took these courses "regardless of [his] opinion" and because he thought "they were doing the right thing." There are interesting tensions, however, between his autonomy—here expressed by his own desire "to become a doctor, ever since [he] was five years old"—and his heteronomy—here expressed by the fact that his parents want him "to be the best," the fact that his parents encouraged him to take the prerequisite OAC courses for getting into the sciences and pre-medical programs, and his claim that *they* are taking this dream away from him. He lists a variety of influences, the media and the experience of a person who had fainted in his [parents'] store. He did not know what to do, especially not how to do CPR. In this account, Preston uses these experiences from his early life to render intelligible the long-standing nature of his interests and how his parents supported these by suggesting that he take the courses that would allow him to get into pre-med programs.

Like the influence that parents have on their children, early experiences are a familiar part of the plots that constitute a life and the life narratives that we can intelligible tell. Moreover, mobilizing experiences from early life underscores the long-standing nature of this particular interest. Wanting to be a doctor nearly goes as far back as he can remember. But now, given his lacking grades in the OAC science courses ("I don't have the marks for it"), this dream of becoming a doctor has come to an end, it is gone. Now he no longer "wants to be a doctor anymore." Along the way, his parents have had very mediational roles. On the one hand, they advised him to enroll in the science courses prerequisite for getting into the pre-medical science programs of the province. On the other hand, he states that his parents took that "away from [him]" as they "are coming back to reality" in stating "that [he does]n't have the marks for it."

Auto/biography and narrative

The reality of the genre and the reality accessible to the genre are organically interrelated ... [g]enre is the aggregate of the means of collective orientation in reality, with the orientation toward finalization.

(Bakhtin [Medvedev] 1978: 135)

In the foregoing analyses, we see how identity is a resource (e.g., for explaining why Preston thinks differently from his teacher and other students about the relation of science and religion) and a topic (e.g., when the conversation is about who Preston is or how, being an Asian male, he has been influenced by parents during his childhood who always "want their sons to be the best"). As we talk about identity or mobilize identity talk as a resource, Preston and I also produce the very context, so that the genre (auto/biography) and the requirements for reproducing the interview/conversation format come to be intertwined. By talking, resources are produced for making out who Preston is, that is, identity is produced together with talk (e.g., some may think that he *is* inconsistent from one minute to the next or that he *is* unknowledgeable about the real commitment of his Church). In each of these cases, language is the (unfathomable) ground that allows any two persons to actually have a conversation without explaining every term; and language always comes with excess, says more than it literally says in any given instant of the interview. Language is a resource and tool that provides possibilities for telling who someone is or for providing supporting statements that shore up a particular, more tenuous claim or argument. Language may also be a topic in its own right, for example, when Preston says, "I never want to talk physics as a language, because I never knew how to talk, and I never want, I didn't know how to speak to my parents like that, because they were gone, they are out, I used to always think my way." Even ways of talking, the genres in which we deploy language, may become the topic, such as when Preston talks about his debates with peers (generally in the evenings in the dorm), for example, Fragment 6.4.

Fragment 6.4

01   P: I am very very stubborn at that when it comes to debatable topics such as that and I attempt to accuse, I attempt to attack their weak spots of what they think and I, I have this sort of advantage of manipulating people, 'cause I have a way of talking, and I, there was a couple of people who where completely atheists who thought about that they were really good science; they wanna be scientists; and I said, "what about religion. Have you ever thought about what you actually want to believe? Have you ever thought about what your destiny is? Science can't provide you that." All they can say is what you are made of. They can't say what you are going to be, where you are gonna go.

In this fragment, Preston talks about being a "stubborn" debater, someone who "attacks [the] weak spots" of his peers, someone who, in debating, "manipulates" others, and what forms of argument he deploys in these debates. In addition, aspects of identity are revealed in and by the description.

When (an aspect of) identity is the topic, then, to constitute intelligible talk, the content is cast in terms of more or less familiar characters and plots. This is so both on the part of the person asking questions, here the teacher, and on the part of the person whose identity and life is the topic. Biography and autobiography, therefore, take on the same characteristic features making them indistinguishable—from a linguistic and structural perspective—with respect to the composition of the content. For example, what Preston thinks and does today is an outcome of the influences that he has been subject to during early childhood. The most important influence is his family, which, being an oriental family, has particular (perhaps stereotypical) ideas about their son having to be/become "the best." The character here is that of an oriental boy, growing up in a family with traditional oriental values, eventually sending him to this private school that is to prepare him for entry to a pre-med program (plot). In this casting of the identity and life, Preston, in his utter singularity, is not so singular at all. This itself, as we see, becomes the topic of the conversation when Preston lists other oriental students in his class who, from his perspective and in his understanding, have had similar experiences (e.g., the pressures that come with being a son in an oriental family).

Identity and the means of capturing it, auto/biography, is not singular but is always told using an always-and-already-shared language, which provides certain linguistic resources and genre (character, plot). There is reason in language. And when the "I is identified with reason—as the power of thematization and objectification—[it] loses its very ipseity. To represent oneself is to empty oneself of one's subjective substance" (Levinas 1971: 92). As such, identity and auto/biography become intelligible precisely in the loss of singularity, absolute selfhood (ipseity), and pure subjectivity. Rather than constituting an utterly singular phenomenon, auto/biography is told in the form of recognizable, always already available language and the possibilities and constraints it provides for such telling; auto/biography is designed for the ear of the other, is oto/biography. Talking identity and telling auto/biography, therefore, are subject to compositional constraints; these constraints are stronger than those coming from the relationship between the narrative and the real life of a person (Bakhtine 1984).

One may think that the narrative of a person's life told by the person is more authentic, closer to the life as it really happened. But, because of the properties of language, autobiographies are no truer than biographies. Both are subject to narrative (literary) constraints rather than to any constraints between narrative and the world to which it refers. Similar to what Maurice Blanchot (1959: 14) says about the story, we may say that the auto/biography is not the relating of a real event or series of events that the interlocutors try to constitute. Rather, the narrative is this event itself, the coming of the event, the place where this event is called to produce itself, an event still to come, in the course of which the narrative realizes itself. These constraints are the same as those for the autobiographical novel, in which, for example, "relationships of family, of life-story and biography, of social status and social class are the stable all-determining basis for all plot connections; contingency has no place here" (Bakhtin 1984a: 104). The plot constitutes a particular relation of time and space, a particular *chronotope* (from Greek *chronos*, time + *topos*, space) that names "the intrinsic connectedness of temporal and spatial relationships that are artistically expressed in literature" (Bakhtin 1981: 84). Chronotope is not only a constitutive category of literature but of other areas of culture as well, here the telling of an identity as the result of a particular constellation of culture (Asian), family relation (influence), and time (childhood). The importance of the auto/biographical chronotope in talk lies not so much in its role as organizing feature of the narrative internally but—much like auto/biography in the agora of classical Greece (Athens), and pre-eminently so—as the exterior real-life chronotope in which the representation of one's own or someone else's life is realized as part of the life itself, for the purposes of the activity at hand. Thus, in the present instance, the topic was the nature of science and scientific knowledge, and both inter-locutors draw on the auto/biographical chronotope to produce accounts that make Preston's current position on knowledge and science intelligible.

Chronotope and the auto/biographical form of narrative constitute rhetorical resources for verbal presentation and representation for the emplotment of a life. Language—the forms and contents it affords—does not constitute a neutral, transparent medium that presents and represents the world in a mirror-like fashion (*mimesis* in Aristotle's poetics). There is, therefore, always a (dialectical) tension between the facts of an emergent and contingent life, on the one hand, and the plot requirements of an intelligible narrative (*mūthos* in Aristotle's poetics). Auto/biography, as a form of the narrative report of identity, "transforms facts into stories. But these stories bring with them their plot types, tropes, and typologies" (Ricœur 2004a: 256). This, then, leads to the situation in which "the principle of a distinction between interpretation and fact is thereby undermined, and the boundary between 'true' and 'false,' 'imaginary' and 'factual,' 'figurative' and 'literal' story falls" (Ricœur 2004a: 256).

Identity and auto/biography are resources and topics of talk, drawing on and mobilizing particular possibilities and constraints of the language and culture. Talking identity and identity in talking—drawing on specific chronotopes and auto/biographical forms—therefore constitute poetics of the everyday. In contrast to Aristotle's *Poetics*, "which is silent about the relationship between poetic activity and temporal experience" (Ricœur 1984: 31), the poetics of everyday identity and auto/biography actively lodges itself in life, produces life (e.g., the conversation between Preston and me), and accounts for life at the same time. It also projects our lives forward, "in the language of our consciousness ... without breaking the unity of our life projected ahead of itself, into the event to come ... and which never coincides with its own given actuality" (Bakhtine 1984: 37). Today's situ-ation becomes intelligible as the intersection of the life in the past, accounted for in auto/biography, and life in the future, aspirations and anticipated life forms, accounted for in possible auto/biographies. The very grammar of the sentence "I always have wanted to become a doctor ..." bridges the present perfect tense ("I always have wanted") with the future ("I want to become"), embodies this projec-tion of identity from the past to the future. Here, grammar, a structural feature of language, and content, a semantic feature, are irreducible moments of the same utterance (more on grammar as achievement in Chapter 8).

Identity, language, passivity

> Man, determined first and above all as a subject, as being—subject, *finds himself*
> *interpreted* through and through according to the structure of representation.
> (Derrida 2007a: 111, original emphasis)

In the preceding section, we see how the particular requirements of the narrative provide resources and constraints for the telling of an auto/biography. Without such narrative resources, we cannot tell auto/biography so that *precisely* when I use the most personal reference "I," which excludes *everyone* else, "*what* I say really is everyone" (Hegel 1979b: 74, my emphasis). These resources, there-fore, not only constitute possibilities but also the constraints for establishing an identity. This leads to the fact that the drama of identity plays itself out in the tension between the real life in its once-occurrent, never-repeatable form, on the one hand, and the intelligible accounting of who someone (I, the other) is in narrative, which, drawing on language—its semantics, genres, and syntax—that inherently casts life in terms of repeatable instants. This aspect of who someone is, can be, and can become, therefore, with a considerable degree of passivity— as Derrida writes in the quote that introduces this section, as subject, I always already *find myself interpreted,* through and through, according to the structure of representation. Everyday language is a passion, interwoven with everything else not properly language of everyday life. In any account of my life, I simultane-ously denote an utterly singular, never-repeatable individual, and a certain type of individual, always already intelligible as such. Although I have considerable autonomy and agency to mobilize language and its resources to represent myself, this language is that of the Other, so that I am subject to this Other in a state of heteronomy. And, leading to a passivity more passive than passivity, the "essence of representation is not a representation, it is not representable, there is no repre-sentation of representation" (Derrida 2007a: 111), deepening the fundamental condition of Being to always already find itself thrown into this world, as being-there (Heidegger's *Dasein*). Speaking is like a temple that imposes upon us a certain number of usages, an implicit religion, a rumor that changes in advance of anything we might want to, and can, say that charges our speaking with more intentions than we can ever admit to have had in and prior to uttering.

Derrida articulates another important aporia of identity and passivity in an essay on the poet and philosopher Paul Valéry entitled "*Qual Quelle*" in both French and English versions (Derrida 1972). Accordingly, the most telling fea-ture about the individual person is her/his timbre with respect to which the content of talk is of little importance. But, in speaking, the timbre of my voice is that which I do not hear: I am deaf to the most spontaneous of my voice, and therefore, by extension, I am deaf to myself. I can be, in the final analysis, spontaneous only under the condition of inconceivable and irremediable passivity with respect to my self-representation in and during the event. Thus, "[t]o hear oneself is the most normal and the most impossible experience," which leads to the "[w]hen I speak (to myself) without moving tongue and lips, I believe that I hear myself although the source is other; or I believe that we are two, although everything is happening 'in me'" (Derrida 1972: 353–4).

In the scholarly discourses concerning identity, the term is often lodged within an intentional discourse, as if the person in question actively *constructed* or *positioned* himself or herself in this or that way. What such discourse fails to acknowledge is the passive dimension that comes with language use, which is always a language that has come *from* the Other, is produced *for* the Other, and, in so doing, *returns to* the Other. At the very instant where the speaking subject first becomes conscious of him/herself *as a speaking* subject, he or she already is a more-or-less fluent speaker. When the person discovers him/herself as a person—becomes self-conscious—with a particular identity, the whole machinery that enables the production and co-production of identification and consciousness is already in place. Who I am, therefore, is always already in the image of the Other, from whom this linguistic machinery has come to me. Not only language itself comes from the Other but also the kinds of texts people produce, the genres, their constituents and structures (e.g., narrative, plot, character), the living or dead metaphors, and so forth. The agency of the *I* always already is grounded in the passivity of the *me-I*, which finds itself thrown into a world full of significance pre-dating all signification.

> [N]o matter what an Odyssey or Bildungsroman it might be, in what whatever manner the story of a constitution of the *self*, the *autos*, the *ipse*, organizes itself, one always *imagines* that he or she who writes should know how to say *I*. In any case, the *identificatory modality* already or henceforth has to be assured: assured of language and in its language.
>
> (Derrida 1996: 53, original emphasis)

In the culture where the speaking subject is a member, the forms of telling one's life already exist. In fact, as the intelligibility of any life narrative precedes the telling, any autobiography always already realizes existing biographical forms and contents, characters, and plots. Any presentation of the self always already is a re-presentation. This interconnection between auto-presentation and re-presentation therefore marks the impossibility of pure presentation, or, in other words, it marks "the presence of the alter ego at the very heart of the ego" (Franck 1981: 157). Language, which has come to me from the Other, provides precisely the required means to take the perspective of the Other on my emotions, the stirring within myself, thereby making possible empathy, transference, and countertransference. This arises from the fact that I cannot ever recognize and describe someone else's behavior as choleric unless I first take an exterior, the Other's, perspective over my own affect. In using language, I unavoidably and inherently take precisely the perspective of the Other onto myself.

There is some level of agency, too, but this agency itself grounds out in the passivity of givenness, the experience of a world and language always already preceding myself. Even in the case where the *I* were to have formed itself, it would have to have situated itself in a non-situatable experience of language:

> The *I* in question *formed* itself without a doubt, as one can believe, if it managed to do at least that, and if the trouble/confusion of identity [*trouble d'identité*] of which we were speaking a while ago does not, precisely, affect the very constitution of the *I*, the formation of the *speak-I*, the *me-I*, or the appearance, as such, of a pre-egological ipseity. It would have *formed* itself,

this *I*, at the site of an unfindable *situation*, always referring elsewhere, to another thing, to another language, to the other in general. It would have *situated* itself in a non-situatable experience of *language*, that is, language in the broad sense of this word.

(Derrida 1996: 55, original emphasis)

The phenomena of identity, identification and dis-identification, or the experience of who I am and with whom I affiliate all have to be theorized in terms of the experience of language available to the speaking subject who is subjected to language it uses. This language, by the very act of communication, presupposes its possibilities as preceding my speaking and the listener's hearing. The upshot of this is that the highly agential theories of and presuppositions about identity currently in vogue need to be revised—as suggested in Chapter 4—to take into account the inherent passivity that comes when we speak a language that never is our own, and which therefore constrains me in my telling/constitution of myself, who I am with respect to myself and to the Other. Thus, it is not merely the case that a student who agentially "positions" herself does some form of identity work when, "unsatisfied with her progress in mathematical discourse[, she] is likely to call herself a 'terrible mathematician' or a 'slow thinker'" (Sfard 2008: 290). Rather, the very designations "terrible mathematician" and "slow thinker" are inherently intelligible ways of accounting for and denoting certain experiences that have come from the Other. The student therefore *is given*, by using language, as much as she *gives herself*, a particular form of identity. This passivity, which I have called radical—because it is inherent and unavoidable in and with language-in-use—is an aspect of language, learning, and context *completely* unattended to in current scholarly endeavors.

Ultimately, then, we might say with Martin Heidegger, Maurice Blanchot, or Jacques Derrida that language speaks (Gr. *Die Sprache spricht*). Paraphrasing Blanchot (1959: 286), we might say that language is not deprived of sense but deprived of a center, does not begin or end, never stops; it is something which we suffer only if it stops, at which point we would find out that it continues to speak when it stops, that it perseveres. Human beings, then, speak primarily and only in as far as they correspond to language, when they listen to its appeal (Heidegger 1990). Language perseveres but is not silent, because in it silence speaks to itself eternally. This does not resolve the problem of the experience of the *I* in its utter singularity, its once-occurrent nature. Here, emotion plays an important role, because it is precisely affectivity that constitutes the ipseity—self-hood—of the "I." As a consequence, "the ipseity of the I consists in staying outside of the distinction between the individual and the general" (Levinas 1971: 90). Affect therefore preserves, suppresses, and supersedes the individual and the general, a topic to which I turn in Chapter 7.

7 Culturing emotional *con*texts

> To present inhabitation as the becoming conscious of a certain conjuncture
> of human bodies and buildings is to leave aside, is to forget the overflow of
> consciousness in things, which does not consist, for consciousness, in a repre-
> sentation of things, but in a specific intentionality of concretization.
>
> (Levinas 1971: 126)

In Chapter 4 I point out the integral relation between speaking and emotion.
According to Lev Vygotsky, we cannot understand an instance of thinking|speaking
if we treat affect as something *external* to thought. To really understand the mutual
constitution of thinking|speaking and emoting, these processes have to be thought
as moments of an overarching process that both preserves, suppresses, and supersedes them so that there is an ongoing dialogue (exchange) between them. This
movement of dialogue and exchange, presence and the presence of the present, is
what Derrida (1972) refers to as *différance*. Emotions assist us to orient in a world
where we take up position and in a world that itself takes shape with our positions.
Emotions orient us both with respect to what we do at the instant and with respect
to the goals (intentions) that we formulate—they constitute the reason for thoughts
no longer thinking themselves, as Vygotsky (1986) suggests that they would in
theories without emotion. In this chapter, I articulate how various aspects of the production of speech—speech rate, intensity, pitch, and other aspects of the frequency
spectrum—co-express both a particular positioning in the world and the emotions
that go with them. Because they are expressed, that is, objectively available in the
sound produced, they also serve to bring interlocutors and listeners into alignment
or to express misalignment between interlocutors. As expressions of emotion, these
prosodic features constitute the principle means for producing emotional *con*texts
and therefore for culturing emotions, that is, for cultivating, propagating, growing,
developing, refining, and improving individual|collective emotional experiences.

Taking|communicating a position in/on the world

When we become conscious of ourselves, some time during our youth, we always
already find ourselves in a world shot through with significations. We find ourselves

always already at home in a world, a world that we inhabit with, and constitute through, our bodies; and this world is not the conjuncture of bodies and buildings, is not a series of representation but the concretization of intentionality (Merleau-Ponty 1945, original emphasis). Affect, as we saw in Chapter 4, is central to the way in which we take up a position in the world, regulating how we position ourselves consciously and unconsciously and in formulating more or less explicit goals. Affect (attunement, mood)—together with understanding, entanglement, and discourse—is constitutive of the way in which we go about everyday life (Heidegger 1977b). Here, then, "what is termed an affective state does not have the dull monotony of a state, but is a vibrant exaltation from which the self emerges ... the I is the very contraction of sentiment" (Levinas 1971: 91).

Communication generally, and talking specifically, effects itself in a panorama common to the interlocutors marking, re-marking, and remarking sense. This sense is not attached to the words, gestures, body orientations and positions, intonations, and so on but always emerges from the totality of communication in setting. In this, talk does not have a closed interior, reflecting the outpouring of a private thought but rather "it *is* the subject's taking up of a position in the world of its significations" (Merleau-Ponty 1945: 225, original emphasis). The term *world* here is to say that "the 'mental' or cultural life borrows from natural life and its structures and that the thinking subject has to be founded on the embodied subject" (Merleau-Ponty 1945: 225). Speech concretizes, both for the speaker and the listener, a certain structuration of the experience in the objectively experienced social and material world that the interlocutors take as common. That is, it is through the body that I understand others in the same way that I understand things; and it is in and through the body that I articulate my thoughts and myself. But the sense does not lie behind the sound-words understood: sense "fuses with the structure of the world that the gesture marks and that I take up on my own account, it is spread all over the gesture itself" (Merleau-Ponty 1945: 217).

In the verbal gesture, the sound-word is only one of many ways in which the person can mark, re-mark, and remark sense and signification. It is, in fact, the occurrence of temporally coincident markers—structures in the physical setting (world), intonation (speech rate, pitch, pitch contour, speech intensity), sound-words, pointing (deictic) gesture, iconic gesture, body orientation, body movement, body position, and so on—that we track relevant marks and markers, which mutually constitute each other as such (Roth and Pozzer-Ardenghi 2006). We can understand this mutual constitution of signifying marks by considering the following case.

For a five-year period, I conducted an ethnographic study of knowing and learning in a fish hatchery. As part of this work, I not only observed but also interviewed the fish culturists. Among others, I was interested in the database one fish culturist in particular uses to model the three coho populations that she is responsible for. At one instant of our conversation, she moves her arm/ hand/finger forward until the "index" finger reaches the computer monitor (Figure 7.1). I immediately understand this gesture as pointing, because, simultaneously, I can see something to be pointed to in the prolongation of the finger. That is, the pointing finger and the thing pointed to mutually constitute each

Figure 7.1 Pointing and the thing pointed to mutually make each other relevant.

other—if there were nothing to be pointed to, empty space, and absence of some mark, then there would be no sense in pointing. But without some form of pointing, the specific marks on the computer monitor are not relevant in and to the conversation. Similarly, we see in previous chapters, situations where the rising or falling of pitch constitutes a marker that interacts with the sound-word markers allowing us to hear questions, emphasis, and the like. Changing pitch levels make certain words stand out, and words make salient changing pitch levels.

The world we inhabit—and we inhabit and dwell in language in the same manner (e.g., Heidegger 1985)—provides many possible structures that may become markers that are tracked and become markers or traces of signification. These include, for example, the sound-words we produce, things in the setting, people, perceptual properties (aspects), pitch, speech intensity, rate of speech, body orientation, body position, body movements, deictic (pointing) and iconic (figurative) gestures, and so on. Now it is precisely the coincidence of two (as in the foregoing example) or more markers that makes something salient (Figure 7.2). But it turns out that some of these markers withdraw. Their function and effectiveness resides precisely in their withdrawal. Thus, I do not consciously attend to the fish culturist's finger but to the thing pointed out, thereby (literally) losing sight of the pointing finger. Similarly, various prosodic features are used in speech to draw attention to certain sound-words while withdrawing themselves so that the sound-word can stand out as emphasized. We hear an emphasized word, we do not attend to the change in pitch, speech intensity, or speech rate by means of which the emphasis is implemented and realized.

Some readers may think that words do signify on their own. But we have already seen in Fragment 1.1b that the sound stream itself, considered completely independent of the setting, nature of the speaker, and so on, provides very little for an understanding of what is happening in the situation from which the sound stream was culled. In producing these different markers—as seen in Chapter 2—we also produce the *con*text within which our sound-words and language come to make sense. These

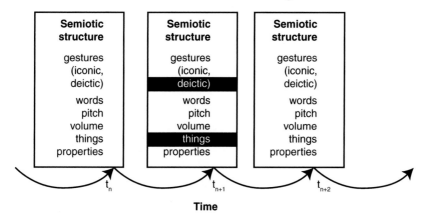

Figure 7.2 Two or more mutually relevant signs mark, re-mark, and allow to remark signification.

other markers are part of the pedagogical function of speech, which not only communicates content but also teaches how speech is to be understood. This is clearly evident, for example, in the those instances where we hear an utterance as an ironical comment versus hearing it as one made seriously, in jest, polemically, and so on.

The sound-words that constitute language, however, constitute a privileged system because it is highly conventionalized in form and content. This is so because in the course of human history, sound-words have accumulated all the voices of their speakers and, thereby, all the exchanges in which they have been part (Bakhtine [Volochinov] 1977). Sense therefore *appears* to be detachable from the word because we presuppose all the contexts in which it has appeared. This is not so for other possible markers of sense, because these communicative modes do not have a strict grammar and the semantic is not as clearly defined as that of words (captured in dictionaries). Experts in communication studies agree, therefore, that there is nothing like a "body language," though gestures, such as those in American Sign Language, clearly constitute a language. There are also emblems that have very specific sense, such as the middle finger sticking out from a fisted hand (with or without the verbal equivalent "f*** you") or the index finger pointed to the temple or forehead, which, in the German culture is equivalent to and often goes with the expression "*du hast einen Vogel*" (you are nuts/crazy). But as a whole, all bodily productions in and relative to the setting contribute to marking sense and pointing to significations. They mark the unique and once-occurrent *theme* to which the particular sound-word points.

We do not understand the communicative productions of others by means of intellectual acts of interpretation. The bodily productions allow us to *immediately* understand—*unmediated* by interpretation—anger, sadness, assertion, and the like, as aspects of the situation rather than making us think about anger, sadness, assertion, etc. We experience another person as angry; we do not have to think about the person as being angry. The bodily productions in and relative to the setting *are* anger, sadness, assertion, and so on. It is precisely this phenomenon that allows us to be empathic and solidary with the emotions of others and, in fact, to reproduce and transform these emotions collectively. That is, with our production of communicative markers generally, and with prosody particularly, we reproduce and transform the emotional *con*text within which we act and speak. That is, when we understand speech and other communicative productions *out of the situation as a whole*, then we can find sense in and make sense of sound-words and other signs. The other way around is impossible: sense, theme, and signification cannot be specified without some context. This fact immediately arises from the iterative (context-independent) properties of sound-words, which make them usable in many situations, therefore denoting none of them in particular.

Producing conflict and its resolution

There have been suggestions that convergence of pitch in particular is characteristic of conversations involving participants institutionally located such that they are said to have different degrees of power. Some of my research in classes co-taught by two or more teachers shows that working together over longer periods of time (about three months) leads to a convergence of speech patterns and prosodic displays (e.g., Roth et al. 2005). Prosody, as other non-verbal communicative means, is a resource that interlocutors deploy for pragmatically dealing with issues at hand. Divergence and convergence of prosody are associated with practical action in more complex ways than considering only differences in institutional positions.

The event analyzed in this chapter exhibits and exemplifies precisely this feature: increasing pitch levels when differences appear in the content of talk, then a "heating up" of the situation is paralleled by rising pitch levels, increased speech volume, and increased speech rates. When speakers increase their pitch levels, speech intensities, and speech rates substantially over those enacted by the previous speaker, then they "heat up" the situation (i.e., context) and "up the ante," literally trumping the commitment made before with higher prosody values. Shouting matches and shrill voices are familiar instantiations of this phenomenon. But speakers tend to calm the situation when their conversational contribution is produced with lower speech volume, pitch, and speech rates. This, too, is a familiar situation when, for example, parents or teachers calm youngsters involved in a fight by particular quiet and low-pitched ("soothing") voices. The changing nature of face-to-face communication involving periods of conflict and periods of agreement within the same conversation then can be considered a natural laboratory for studying the role of emotions expressed by prosodic and other non-verbal means on the reproduction and transformation of the specific situation at hand and, taking into account the comments made in Chapter 1 about schooling, of society more generally. The changes in prosody with respect to conflict and its resolution are articulated and exemplified in the following episode in which Pauline, a teacher in training, enters into and, in fact, fuels a conflict with students. The sense of solidarity that exists among students, documented in the ethnographic and interview data, is exhibited here in rhythmic alignments of the listeners' body movements and speaker's voice.

The episode as a whole can be glossed in this way: an African American student (Oprah)—always intending to be involved, checking on homework, wanting to pass the course, and avoiding detentions that would keep her off the basketball team—has an idea and attempts to explain it. Pauline challenges the explanation, thereby encouraging Oprah to enact an argument ritual that is similar to how she might have argued if challenged by someone outside of the classroom. We therefore have a mutual focus of attention—the explanation—but the transient attunement, emotion, and mood are not shared. Continued prosodic misalignment and the correlative expression of anger feed back and aggravate the situation, thereby producing conflict. Although Axel, the supervising teacher, is in the room, he does not participate in the series of episodes featured here. The exchanges involving students and Pauline are most salient in this episode, especially the exchanges involving Pauline, Oprah, and three other students. Oprah sits near the back so that most students cannot see her without turning around (Figure 7.3).

Just prior to the conflict beginning to articulate itself, Pauline has presented a "trick" to use a periodic table of elements to figure out the number of valence electrons that an atom of a specific element posses. Oprah then announces that she has figured out a systematic way to remember the valence. Pauline reiterates that the placement in the table determines the valence, but Oprah counters that this is not what she is talking about. There is another turn pair, in which Pauline points out that what she has said "*is* the trick." The transcript in Fragment 7.1 picks up at this point (the underlined speech elements are represented in terms of pitch and speech intensity over time in Figure 7.4, and each alphabetical label refers to the panel of the same letter).

Fragment 7.1

a	01	O:	<<p>theres another way you can figure it ↑out>
	02		(0.96)
b	03	P:	this IS the way to do ↑this
	04	A:	<<p>i hope so.>
	05		(0.34) ((Sasha and Tracy turn their heads toward Oprah))
	06	Ta:	[.hh h[h
			[((turns, smiles at Oprah))
c	07	O:	[arright ((smiles))

Figure 7.3 Seating arrangement of some of the key players in the episode.

In a quieter voice than she has used before, Oprah restates that there is another way to figure "it" (valence) out (turn 01). After a considerable pause—nearing the one-second mark (turn 02)—Pauline firmly asserts, "this is the way to do this" (turn 03). As Figure 7.4b shows, the pitch rises by almost 100 Hz during the utterance of "is" and is also accompanied by considerably higher than normal speech intensity. There is another stressed word: rather than falling to the end of the turn, the pitch rises again dramatically to 270 Hz on "this," which we hear as an emphasis. Pauline thereby emphasizes that her way, the one she just explained, is the only way to remember chemical valence. Far in the background, Axel comments calmly and with an almost inaudible volume, "I hope so" (turn 04). In this he sustains Pauline's claim but also provides a potential resource for avoiding a heating up of the conflict that appears to announce itself. First Tracy and Sasha, then Talia turn their bodies and heads while Oprah is in the process of orienting and situating herself for the account of her method to be produced. She announces the intention to articulate her method uttering "awright" (turn 07), and then explains how subtracting the number "2" from the atomic number of the first row of elements generates the chemical valences of the associated atoms. With the utterance of "awright," Oprah moves her body right to left and her hand into a forward position, and then erects her body again. Much like the physics professor in Chapter 3, she takes not only a physical but also a conceptual position. In Oprah's case, this is a position from which, after the fact, she will have launched the articulation of her method of recalling and remembering chemical valences.

Watching the videotape, we can feel that something is in the making. In turning their bodies and heads to look squarely at Oprah, the three peers exhibit this expectation that something is forthcoming. In this, they explicitly co-articulate encouragement for this something to begin. That is, what has happened so far and how it has happened has allowed such an expectation to emerge. It is now upon Oprah to speak and thereby to evolve the situation. The resources for such an expectation clearly have been made publicly available in the immediately preceding exchange. Up until this point, however, Oprah has stayed calm despite the determination and irritation that we can hear in Pauline's voice. Contrasting Figures 7.4a and 7.4c reveals that following the low pitch and low volume intervention on the part of Axel, Oprah's pitch has decreased to below 200 Hz. But within the culture of these students in this school, which values above all *respect*, the teacher perhaps has articulated a challenge, which Oprah has to take up.

Oprah has been subtracting two from the atomic numbers in the first full row of the period table of elements (lithium, beryllium, boron, carbon, nitrogen, and oxygen). Tracy is the first to ask Oprah in a low-pitched and low-intensity voice, where the "two" was coming from. Fragment 7.2 begins as Pauline repeats the question but, as shown in Figure 7.4d, her pitch rises to near 300 Hz and speech intensity increases above normal levels, especially as she utters "two" (turn 01).

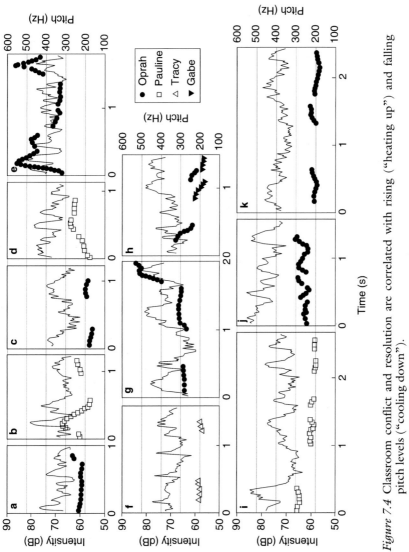

Figure 7.4 Classroom conflict and resolution are correlated with rising ("heating up") and falling pitch levels ("cooling down").

Fragment 7.2

d   01 P: where is the ↑twO coming from.
    02   (0.52)
    03 Ta: <<p>from.>
    04   (0.19)
e   05 O: <<f>I=M JUST SAYing just do the number ↑TWO: (0.14) ↓i:
             ↑you=don=t=wan=me=da copy text from noWHERe, or yOU can
             take t=the two come from the (0.16) the ↑rOW,> i mean
    06   (0.42)
f   07 Tr: <<p>that wont wORK fr (0.57) for=ALL=of them.>
    08   (0.42)
    09 P: it=doesnt=work for=ALL of them.
g   10 O: ↑well what. you <<f>want> then the ↑TWO-
    11   (0.30)

There is a brief pause, interrupted by Talia's "from" uttered at low speech intensity. At this point, Oprah launches her body forward and raises her voice, and her
pitch repeatedly moves to 500 Hz and beyond as she utters, "I'm just saying, just
do the number two" (Figure 7.4e). Correlatively, and confirming this hearing
and feeling of irritation/frustration, the first vocal resonance, which is associated
with the differential pronunciation of sounds, increases by nearly 30 percent.[1]
Oprah co-articulates the frustration that we hear in her voice (prosody); and the
production requires energy. In the present situation, the power in the air (i.e.,
energy in the air per unit of time) at the onset of turn 05 increases by more than
tenfold over the power normally used in her speech. That is, the expression of her
frustration, an integral moment of her taking up a position in this world, drains
energy, here used in the production of her utterances.

   Oprah continues in an accusatory way saying that her teacher did not want her
to copy text, with the possible implication that what she (Oprah) searches for is
understanding and having a surefire way to remember valence. The frustration also
is apparent from the way she uses her body to direct others' attention, for example, to a particular place in the periodic table (Figure 7.5). That is, the difference
between the taking of a conceptual position and the taking of a physical position
(including a variety of expressive modes) is undecidable. By now, Oprah's speech
rate has increased from an average of five syllables per second to over eight syllables
per second, consistent with the generally observed large increases of this parameter
with (hot) anger. As Émile Durkheim (1893) notes, when a belief is at stake, others cannot question it without bringing about an emotional reaction (more or less
violent) against the offender. It is precisely because of the stakes that thought and
emotion come to be two faces of the same coin. And this emotional reaction, as
shown here, is co-expressed and communicated not semantically or syntactically but
prosodically. Her voice expresses appreciation and social evaluation which, in fact,
"defines all aspects of the utterance, totally permeates it, but finds its most pure and
typical expression in expressive intonation" (Bakhtin [Medvedev] 1978: 122).

Figure 7.5 Oprah's emotional engagement can be read, among others, from the way she uses her body, arms, and hands to direct the attention of others.

Following the outburst, Tracy, who has turned around to face Oprah, suggests in a very low speech intensity that this way does not work for "all of them"; her pitch is more than 200 Hz lower than the final syllable Oprah has uttered (Figure 7.4f). Pauline restates that Oprah's method does not work for all instances. The pitch returns to 230 Hz and then descends to 185 Hz at the end of turn 09. That is, after the fact, Tracy's turn can be understood as a resource that has had a calming and defusing effect. Here voice not only is an expression of a particular positioning in this world but also constitutes a modulation of the context that allows the conflict to subside. Oprah, too, returns to a lower pitch level. Her speech rate has decreased to 3.5 syllables per second. The question "well, what?" already appears to be more conciliatory (consistent with an *F1 mean* of 1561 Hz), and this possibility for a resolution can be heard in the prosody. It is not only that the individual calms down but the situation as a whole cools down—the difference, here between a person taking up position and the world that is co-constituted simultaneously, becomes undecidable. Yet irritation can be observed again toward the end of the utterance (turn 10), where the pitch moves beyond 500 Hz when Oprah comes to the point of the number "two," associated with an increase in speech intensity to above 80 dB (Figure 7.4g) and an increase in *F1 mean*.

The voice intensity and sharply rising pitch at the end of Fragment 7.2 are resources for understanding that the conflict has not yet been resolved. We can still sense some of the agitation that has been present. But further contributions, uttered at lower pitch levels and speech intensities appear to add to the calming effect. Thus, Oprah still begins turn 04 of Fragment 7.3 above 300 Hz but progressively descends, following the pitch of Gabe (moving considerably above his normal pitch range), which overlaps hers and then drops progressively to a value below 200 Hz (Figure 7.4h).

Fragment 7.3

```
       01      (0.30)
       02  S:  <<p>(then? then? youre gonne be)
       03  P:  <<f>but once> <<dim> we start getting in here it doesnt work
                anymore>
h      04  O:  i aint talking about ((points to the left part of the periodic table))
                [this i=m talking about that] ((points to the right part of the
                periodic table))
       05  G:  [<<p>no she talking about ] row, and according to rows it says,
                the (simple?) rows it checks (??)
       06  O:  <<f>why, why do three then?>
       07      (1.55)
       08  O:  if thats the ca[se  ]
       09  P:               [no,] no
       10  O:  i dont know (0.46) <<f>well [i>      ]
i      11  P:                              [<<f>say] fast-> (0.40) ↓you=you
                asked for the (0.16) the best way to learn how to put valence elec-
                trons. each box counts as one as you go across the per- as you go
                across the period. (0.64) one valence electron, (0.55) two (1.06)
                then you jump over, (1.36) three, four, five, six, seven, eight.
                (0.61) thats what i=m talking about.
       12      (0.46)
j      13  O:  arright, so n=ä would be ^nine.
       14          (1.51)
       15      right? so then you have nine for a long [time.  ]
       16  P:                                          [alright.] this is one
                valence, one=
```

Following two brief, partially overlapping turns, Pauline begins to explain again that she has provided an explanation to assist Oprah in the *best* way to learn about valence electrons. She is thereby rearticulating *her* position, staking it out as a terrain not to be intruded upon. Pauline does this by speaking with a higher than normal pitch and high speech intensity, but descends for the second part of the utterance and lower speech intensity (Figure 7.4i). She has taken a position and thereby changes the world available to others present. However, as if she had realized during the brief 0.40 second pause the potential of her prosody to rekindle the conflict, Pauline's prosody parameters change to take on lower values that can be heard as less aggressive and therefore are more conducive to conflict resolution. It is not only that she is taking a different position but the world (situation), too, changes as a consequence. Oprah has not yet given up on her alternative explanation, as seen from the fact that she proposes a way of using it for the second row in the periodic table of elements, the row that begins with sodium (Na) (turn 13). The pitch level remains higher than normal and the speech intensity is very high (Figure 7.4j).

Other students "come to help," as is apparent from the final part of the episode. In their contribution they change the world that they inhabit together with all other participants. Thus, sitting in front of Oprah, first Stacy (turn 01) and later Ivory (turn 03) and Gabe (turn 05) together with Pauline (turn 04) suggest that Oprah has to "skip the middle," meaning the section of the periodic table where the transition elements of metallic nature are listed. Pauline answers Oprah's question about why this is the case by explaining that the elements in the middle of the table constitute a special category of elements (i.e., they are transition elements), which are not the current topic of their chemistry course (turn 08), and that they would return to these elements in more detail later (turn 10). Oprah, though still not giving up on her method in the content of her talk (turn 13), has lowered her pitch and speech intensity (Figure 7.4k). In this turn, her speech rate has returned to her normal level at around five syllables per second. At this point, the discussion continues for another minute, taking as its content the fact that Oprah's method works for a particular section of the table and why only for this and not other sections. The tension, which has been apparent previously, written all over the situation, now has been resolved as seen in the return to normal levels of pitch level, speech intensity, and speech rates on the part of all participants.

Fragment 7.4

```
       01  S:  ((oriented toward Oprah, who cannot see her))
                   you sk[ip the middle.    ]
       02  P:          [and thats as far    ] as (0.25) you
                       [skip    the middle]
       03  I:  ((oriented toward Stacy))
                   <<p>[i wasn=t ?     ] for skip[ping
       04  P:                      [you skip the middle]
       05  G:                      [you skip the ?ch    ]
       06  O:  why?
       07      (0.48)
       08  P:  because=this is a special class and we dont care about them when
                   we=re talking about this right now.
       09      (0.48)
       10  S:  right.
       11      (0.43)
       12  P:  we=ll go into it in more detail later o[n. ]
k      13  O:                                     [but] what i was sayin
                   about l=i b=e, b=e: whateversthere. what i=ve said works.
       14      (0.38)
       15  K:  .hhh it wor[ks] for the fi[rst  ]           [yea]
       16  P:             [it ]          [few] it works for the first [few] places
```

As shown in Chapter 2 during the analysis of the physics professor, position and status *cannot* determine social and societal phenomena, thereby allowing for successes or failures to emerge contingently from the sequentially ordered turn-taking. The evidence provided here is further indication that prosody generally, and pitch in particular, are resources in the process of managing interaction rituals. Among these social orientations is resistance to comply with the standard question–response sequence or exhibiting a stance that indicates the particular effort made of accommodating the other not only by responding but also by aligning the pitch or repeating pitch contour. Theories concerned with interactions as rituals suggest that the preferred state in communication is the alignment of rhythmic and prosodic features, because such alignment produces and intensifies emotional contagion, positive emotional energy, and, consequently, solidarity. Considerable changes in prosodic parameters (e.g., pitch, beat) on the part of one participant with respect to others means breaking out of the rhythmic repetitions and, therefore, breaking out of attunement and, as Heidegger would say, out of mood. It also indicates that the person is not responding to the cues of others, who are frustrated in the process. Thus, "the failure of solidarity, down to the minute aspects of coordinating mutual participation in a conversation, is felt as a deep uneasiness or affront … as a feeling of shame" (Collins 2004: 110).

These analyses, featuring the emergence and resolution of conflict in and through talk, provide further support to the contention that prosody generally, and pitch in particular, are conversational resources available in face-to-face meetings and for pragmatic purposes. We can think of these resources as constituting the context of the verbal utterances (text), but it may be better to think of them as parallel resources to sound-words that mark and re-mark sense in this situation. Conflict is associated with increasing pitch levels over the previous speaker, whereas conflict avoidance and conflict resolution are associated with lowering pitch levels. But we should not think of this situation as one in which conflict is the cause of changes in prosody—conflict and prosodic changes are but two moments of the same taking up position in a world partially constituted in the process. Thus, when an experienced teacher like Axel disagrees with a student statement, his pitch remains in his normal pitch range or, if outside, descends into a lower register. On the other hand, in conflict situations, pitch levels characteristically move into higher registers. This is apparent here, as Pauline initially and Oprah subsequently both fuel the articulation of difference as their pitch levels move higher and higher as if they were pushing each other on a swing that moves higher and higher. Conversely, the present episode shows that repeated contributions at lower pitch levels and speech intensity are correlated with a cooling effect that led to the ultimate defusing of conflict.

Exchanges between Pauline and Oprah produce affect with negative valence or negative emotions that result from emotion contest and conflict situations typical of face-work or dominance contests. It is apparent from the inflections of her voice—in addition to pitch and speech intensity—that Pauline is increasingly annoyed with what appears to be Oprah's resistance to accepting the articulated trick as the best way to learn chemical valences. It is in her intonation that she makes public an evaluation, inherently social because it is available to everyone present and to all those with access to the videotape. The annoyance (irritation, anger) is available to others in and through her expression that there is one correct solution; and it is the one that Pauline has articulated. The unfolding conversation shows that Oprah takes the teacher's stand as an outright rejection of her method, even before she had the time to fully articulate it. This may be heard as a lack of attention to her ideas, which would constitute "a breach in the mutual commitment of the participants" (Goffman 1963: 90). When her method is questioned, Oprah takes|articulates a position: she bursts out, her pitch tripling in value, the speech intensity quadrupling, her body movements vigorously oriented toward the teacher, the arm and hand aggressively moving forward and pointing toward the front. In all of these productions—resources for subsequent actions—Oprah takes|articulates for others an emotional stance, which incorporates anger and readiness to defend herself against the experienced danger, whatever it might be. These productions require energy, which, as my measurements show, increase tenfold in Oprah's prosodic articulation of frustration and irritation (anger). All of the verbal productions require higher than normal levels of energy, so that one legitimately articulates the situation as charged and characterized by high levels of energy. Anger, in fact, is the capacity to mobilize the energy to overcome barriers to an ongoing effort; and in its most intense form, Oprah's anger is an explosive reaction against the frustrations experienced in gaining acceptance for her method for remembering and recalling chemical valences.

In this situation, Oprah can be seen and heard as producing high levels of emotional energy with negative valence; and negative emotional energy is expressed largely by vocal means and gesture. She articulates a position and, in so doing, changes the context within which others find themselves and which they, through their own contributions, can in turn take position and shape. It is within these contextual features that the content of the sound-words take place. Here, where significant amounts of emotional energy are drained from Oprah, the quiet, low-intensity and low-pitched contributions from several classmates produce a lowering of the values of the same parameters in Oprah's speech. These productions, therefore, can be considered resources that oriented the class as a whole toward the current state of the conflict and toward the continued effort of defusing it. The students both take a position and calm the situation and, in this, provide a situation that allows Oprah to calm down. Allowing the participants to come out of the loggerheads by providing resources may be a form of commitment to the group and the group processes, that is, a form of solidarity that allows both parties in the conflict to cool down and resolve issues.

Prosody, entrainment, and alignment

In Chapter 3, we encounter the production of beat gestures. At that place, one of the questions I raise concerns the function of these gestures. I suggest that they may contribute to the coordination of multiple individuals in a group. These gestures, therefore, may have an important role in the question about how humans are able to create and bring about the human forms of transaction that reproduce and transform everyday ordinary society. Emotional valence of jointly lived situations and the emotional valence tied to the setting of goals and the likelihood of achieving them appears to be part of the answer. Accordingly, theorists in the sociology of emotion and face-to-face conversations suggest that emotions—articulated and therefore communicated by prosodic and other observable verbal and non-verbal means—constitute the essential feature that binds individuals into a collective (Turner 2002). Social binding, cohesion, and alignment derive from resemblances and "social similitude." "Gluing" and cohesion and the alignment that results from it are said to be possible because multiple pitches and other rhythmic phenomena have the tendency to align themselves when the different instances are not too far apart. Physicists—who observed, in the seventeenth century, that two pendulum clocks close to each other on the same wall will become aligned in their swings—use the concept of *entrainment* to explain such alignments. Social scientists concerned with time and temporality of human interaction have borrowed this notion to describe the observable fact of synchronization in human behavior. The preceding section shows how speakers exhibit and produce alignment and misalignment in their positions in and on the world. Other rhythmic phenomena—for example, in the movement of various body parts—align themselves with rhythmic patterns articulated and exhibited by the speaker(s). This is the case even when a recipient does not or cannot see the speaker and, therefore, gestures and facial expressions that often constitute the primary resources for accessing the emotions of others. To exemplify the presence of collectively enacted rhythmic patterns that align with those of the current speaker, I return to the events in the chemistry classroom.

After Oprah and Pauline have had their initial exchange about the method for remembering the valence associated with the atoms of a particular element, Oprah begins to articulate her method. (In terms of the overall event, Fragment 7.5 immediately follows Fragment 7.1.) Oprah orients toward the periodic chart of elements in the front of the classroom and moves her eyes from Pauline to the periodic table as she counts out the atomic numbers from three to six, from each of which she proposes to subtract the number two (Figure 7.6). The speech intensity for the entire episode is depicted in Figure 7.7, which also includes the words and numbers on which the spikes in speech intensity occur.

Figure 7.6 Oprah produces a beat gesture ending in the forward position precisely with the utterance of the result of each calculation.

Fragment 7.5

> 01 O: u:m (0.45) You see thrEe right; you take two away from three:;
> (0.32) jst gonna be one (0.16) thats how many valence electrons
> you got. (0.29) take two away through four (0.32) and it=d be two.
> (0.50) take two away of fl:ve and it be three. (0.37) take two away
> of=the=six; (0.36) <<dim>and it be (0.39) <<all>t=gotta=be> and
> so and so on> (0.55) i lost my numbers.

In this episode, Oprah presents her method of arriving at valence, orienting and
staking out her own ground. She does so in a rhythmic way, bounded by the
rises, an initially increasing involvement (production of intensity), and, decreasing
involvement as she gets into the zone on the periodic table where her method no
longer works. Here she reduces the power of the speech in the air to less than one-
twentieth of what it was during the outburst, the sound fades away, and the pitch
drops. When the stressed and unstressed syllables are represented using a meter
notion from poetry, the rhythmicity of the speech production clearly is evident:

/   ^ / ^ / ^ / / / ^
Take two away from three and you got one

/   ^ / ^ / ^ / / / ^
Take two away from four and it be two

/   ^ / ^ / ^ / / / ^
Take two away from five and it be three

/   ^ / ^ / ^ / / / ^ / / ^ / / /
Take two away from six and it g'na be and so on and so on

In this situation, the ingredients for a focused encounter and the production of
alignment are all present: bodily co-presence, barrier to the outside, mutual focus
of attention (periodic table of elements), and shared mood. In and through her
talking position, Oprah shapes the context that allows others to become attuned
to her world. Rhythmic movements, as seen in Chapter 3, are part of the way in
which speakers mark salience. In the present episode, too, there is a basic rhythm
that underlies the reproduction, coordination, and transformation of social alignment (i.e., social similitude) within the classroom. Mutual focus and shared mood
are linked through a feedback of intensification through rhythmic entrainment, a
rhythm set as shown by vocal means. But Oprah produces rhythmic patterns by
other non-verbal means, too. These features therefore become available for those
who are in a position to see her—in addition to expressing the basic rhythm characterizing her emotional investment. Thus, the hand moves forward and reaches
the foremost position exactly at the stressed utterance or vowel in the numbers,
falling together with the intensity and pitch peaks (Figure 7.7). That is, the cycli-
cal hand movement visible in Figure 7.6 is patterned such that the foremost
position and the stressed syllables fall together.

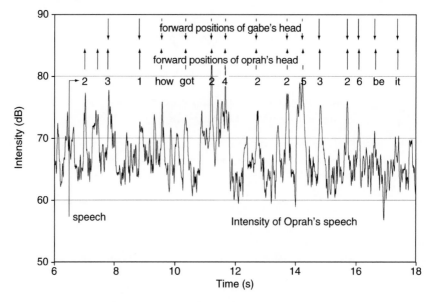

Figure 7.7 Oprah vocally produces a rhythm that she also produces gesturally; Gabe, who cannot see her, precisely reproduces the same rhythm.

When we think about the classroom not as a box for Oprah to act in, but as a world that she partially constitutes in and through her actions, we can easily understand that others sense and share the changes in this world. If we think of a classroom not as a sum total of independent individuals but as a relational totality, then the changes in one individual are co-constitutive to a change of the totality and therefore of others as well. We can see this at work in the present classroom, where there are signs that show how others are in synchrony with Oprah, even when students are seated and oriented such that they cannot see her. This "beat" of her verbal production is available to others in audible form. With each number in the series three (lithium) to six (carbon), Oprah briefly glances at the periodic table, as if verifying what the next number is. The heads and gazes of other students also move, expressing their regard to focus on the periodic table of elements. They move their gaze simultaneously with Oprah although they do not see her and although there is no indication in the speech content itself that suggests others ought to look at the table of elements. That is, Oprah not only talks but also shapes the context, thereby changing others who are attuned and exhibit synchrony. And it is in this world, that is, in part, the result of her actions, that Oprah now dwells.

There are other signs of synchrony. For example, Gabe rocks his head slightly back and forth. As Figure 7.7 shows, even though Gabe cannot see Oprah, his rhythm perfectly (within the measurement error imposed by the one-thirtieth of a second video frame rate) reproduces the forward position of Oprah's hand, which itself is aligned with the rhythm with which the account of her method is produced. Gabe also produces the identical rhythmic pattern with his right leg, which swings in a left-to-right motion matching in its extreme left position the foremost position of his head. Thus, when we mark the point in time when his chin reaches the foremost position, these temporal positions coincide with the forward position of Oprah's hand, and the peaks in her speech intensity and pitch. When Oprah arrives at "and so on and so on," Gabe stops rocking his head, the last coincident movement having been a slightest movement with a coincident closing of eyes following an upward movement of his head to direct his gaze to the periodic table. As there are no visual means that could have provided him with the resources for the coordination, prosody is the likely candidate that allows synchrony to emerge. Here, the class as a whole is aligned with Oprah in the production of her alternative and they can empathize with Oprah who experiences Pauline's actions as an affront.

In the following fragment (which partially reproduces Fragment 7.4), the production of patterns of synchrony is evident when the students are entrained into Pauline's re-articulation of her "short cut trick." The episode follows a first presentation by Pauline about how to find out the valence electrons from the columns of the periodic table. Oprah has proposed to continue counting after the end of the first row, attributing to sodium (Na) the number 9. Here, Pauline then reiterates that the maximum number for calculating the valence of an element is eight. In the course of Fragment 7.6, two students and Pauline suggest to Oprah that for the rows where there are metal elements in the center of the periodic table (for example, scandium to zinc), she has to "skip the middle," meaning that in this part of the periodic table, counting is suspended. The students, who assist Pauline in articulating an explanation for dealing with Oprah's problem are, in fact, aligned with her semantically; and this alignment is articulated also at the non-verbal level where rhythms are enacted in unison with others.

Fragment 7.6 (extending Fragment 7.4)

```
01  P:  the maximum amount is eight, thats why this is a shortcut trick.
        (0.24) one (0.21) this column is one; (0.48) this is two;
02      (1.28)
03  T:  three
04  P:  [three, four, five, six, seven, eight
05  X:  [three, four, five, six, seven, eight ((several students throughout
        the class in unison))
06  S:  ((oriented toward Oprah, who cannot see her))
        you sk[ip the middle. ]
07  P:        [and thats as far] as (0.25) you
              [skip            ] the middle
08  X:  ((oriented toward Stacy))
        [i wasnt] ? for skip[ping]
09  P:                      [you ] skip the middle]
10  G:                      [you ] skip the ?ch   ]
11  O:  why?
```

As the teacher utters, "this column is one," Talia, who already has nodded repeatedly affirming Pauline's statements immediately prior to the beginning of Fragment 7.6, moves slightly backwards then forwards, her lips silently forming "one" as her head reaches the foremost position (Figure 7.8). Similarly, her head movement and silent lip formation parallel the utterance of "two." Her hand then moves away from the body, fingers stretch out and point forward toward the periodic table. In synchrony with the teacher's hitting the chalkboard with the chalk, Talia utters "three." In this one instance, the teacher's utterance of "three" actually is uncoordinated with her beat of the chalk against the chalkboard, but the student is coordinated with it precisely. As the teacher counts out "four," "five," "six," "seven," and "eight," Talia moves her lips forming the words and simultaneously enacts a beat gesture, the hand reaching the down position precisely (within the one-thirtieth of a second of accuracy that the video allows) with the words. Behind Talia, Ivory, and another student begin to count at "three" and Ivory abruptly nods her head in unison with each uttered word, the chin reaching the forward position precisely at the emphasized syllable.

Other students in the class also fall into unison counting beginning with the number three. It is as if the two initial utterances had provided the resources for students to capture the rhythm so that they could produce their articulations of the number in unison with Pauline. Here, too, there is a mutual focus object, the periodic table of elements. The beat may articulate attention to the common object and, by co-articulating this attention to the same object, teacher and students also become mutually aware of their common focus. Apart from social alignment, the situation produces shared cognitive experience, that is, understanding of a chemical concept as a symbol of social relationship, something that has also been called a sacred object. It leads to the kinds of episode that the students in this and similar classes selected as successful teaching and learning events.

Figure 7.8 Talia produces a beat gesture in synchrony with the teacher's counting and action of hitting chalkboard with chalk.

In these episodes (and many other similar ones in this database), alignment and synchrony are observed beyond the pitch levels and contours presented in the earlier sections. Rhythmic patterns of beat gestures with the hand, rocking movements of legs, rocking head movements, beat of chalk against the chalkboard, and stressed syllables are produced and reproduced by members across the classroom who are in synchrony in the same way as jamming jazz musicians. Not only members who have the speaker in view reproduce and transform the synchrony—e.g., students counting aloud in synchrony with the teacher—but also members who do not have the current speaker in view. We now see that beat gestures and other rhythmic features of a performance, such as seen in the physics lecture of Chapter 3, have important functions in the alignment of those who are co-present in a situation. It is important to note that any synchrony, therefore, is not mere cognitive alignment—something that is processed consciously, interpreted, and applied—but, in fact, is an embodied and unconscious phenomenon. The body that reproduces the beat has to act in a way that *anticipates* the occurrence of the driving source frequency. It is not just one beat becoming the driver of another; both beats have to be produced so that synchrony can occur. The situation as a whole, collaboratively produced by members, becomes the driver of members' beat production. This, therefore, is the everyday life equivalent of a jazz jam session, where the rhythm produced becomes the driver for coordinating the rhythm; that is, the rhythmic features are both resource and result of the collective action.

In the present analyses, synchrony is a resource for all co-present individuals to experience and recognize alignment and agreement. Thus, the synchrony between Talia's counting and movement and Pauline's rhythmic patterns is consistent with Talia's repeated head nods following Pauline's statements about how to remember and recall atomic valences. Social alignment here is articulated publicly, available for all to use as a resource in subsequent actions. Social alignment, then, not only is constituted and thereby communicated by means of agreements in the cognitive content of statements but also, and perhaps more importantly, by a variety of rhythmic bodily means. From an analytic perspective, therefore, individual participants not only orient themselves and each other to existing public exhibits of (collective) alignment but also concretely realize individual exhibits of alignment. It is out of this alignment that other students are positioned to produce resources that allow Oprah, for example, to calm down prior to producing an altercation of the kind so prevalent in inner-city schools, altercations that frequently result in the suspension of students and their exclusion from schooling. Talking, therefore, not only produces text but also, and simultaneously so, produces context. This context not only has cognitive value, as captured in the linguistic term signification, but above all it has emotional value.

Emotions, prosody, and power/status

Emotions are central to the ways in which human beings orient to situations; and they are modified by the articulation of emotions of other participants in face-to-face meetings. Besides facial expression, prosody is a major pragmatic resource for displaying and experiencing emotions. There have been suggestions that participants with less power and status converge in their prosodic parameters to align with those of more power and status; and differences and conflict between conversationalists having roughly equivalent power and status (e.g., children participating in hopscotch games) are characterized by very high values and differences in the pitch levels of participants. As I show in Chapter 2, differences in participants' institutional positions do not determine the way in which conversations unfold or the contents that they cover. In the present chapter, prosody is an expression co-extensive with taking up a position in the world that is shaped in and through the taking of a position. Prosody is but one of the moments of communication, all subordinated to the same task at hand and, therefore, being different expressions of the same societal-psychological or ideological unit. That is, sound-words, prosody, body position, hand gestures, and other communicative resources articulated at some point in time are different expressions of the same underlying orientation, emotional valence, and significations. The sense marked out by vocal gestures, therefore, does not lie behind but is "intermingled with the structure of the world outlined by the gesture" so that "the smile, the relaxed face, gaiety of gesture really embody the rhythm of action, the mode of being in the world which are joy itself" (Merleau-Ponty 1945: 217). Sound-words are only one part of a texture that they contribute to constituting.

This chapter shows that we need to theorize the reproduction and transformation of prosody not only as part of a larger communicative unit but as part of taking up | expressing a position in and on the world. Rather than viewing power and status as factors that *determine* pitch levels and convergence, the production of pitch levels, pitch continuation, pitch level repetitions, and so on are co-expressions of difference/resistance and accommodation. The concept of social alignment denotes high levels of unity or agreement. Convergence in prosodic parameters among two or more participants is an expression of—and serves as a resource for—the further production of alignment, itself an expression of the emotional synchrony of participants. In cases of conflict, some participants may, through the production of lower pitch levels and speech intensities, change the context and with it cool the situation and calm down an angered, excited, or animated member.

We find social alignment—as a phenomenon that participants continuously reproduce | transform—within the student body. This alignment occurs in a variety of ways, including prosody. These alignments may well be sources for solidarity that the students experience within their peer group. Thus, the synchronous rhythmic features simultaneously found at various places in the classroom suggest that the students are "in tune" or "in sync" with one another. They also express anticipation of particular events, such as when numerous students turn around to face Oprah as if they had predicted a likely pattern of response, that is, as if they "saw something coming." Anticipation inherently means *being attuned to* and *participatively understanding* the situation in a phenomenological sense, that is, an intuitive lived sense of what is happening and what dangers might loom ahead rather than a reflective understanding. I note above the sense of anticipation that three students express when Oprah starts her explanation; and this sense is available directly to the viewer/listener of the videotape in Oprah's performance as well. At the same time, these various expressions, observable from Oprah's position in and take on the world, may have been resources encouraging her to take up the challenge and propose her alternative description of remembering and recalling valences.

Prosody is an important phenomenon for producing entrainment, a driving force within the set of interaction ritual ingredients that have solidarity and positive emotional energy as part of their ritual outcomes. But in the agency | passivity || resources | schema figure, we can understand such outcomes also as context, where feedback intensification through rhythmic entrainment plays a crucial role in the reproduction and transformation of mutual focus and transient emotions. Entrainment is not describable in terms of a causal link, as the production of synchrony, other than in a mechanical system, it requires anticipation. Thus, in one instance, Oprah produces a particular rhythm, which Gabe also displays. It is not that Oprah's rhythm *causes* Gabe to rock in the same rhythm, because Gabe, looking toward the front of the classroom, has no other resource than Oprah's voice. If he had to consciously attend to making his rocking coincide with her activity peaks (intensity, pitch), he would be out of synchrony by something on the order of a second or two. Even if there were non-conscious ways of causing synchrony, he would still be behind her, for he could only know when Oprah's pitch peaks after having heard it in its entirety. This means that Gabe has to anticipate peaks, which is a production of his own, requiring that he already be in tune. Being in tune is a phenomenon distended in time rather than a punctual momentary one. The synchrony of his movement with Oprah's prosody is a consequence of being in tune. Such an anticipation clearly is observable at the instance when Talia utters "three," just as Pauline hits the board with the chalk but prior to the latter's utterance of the same number word, and inconsistent with all other instances where number word and the hitting of the board fall together. That is, Talia anticipates the correct placement of the count with respect to the noise from the chalk, but Pauline, who produces the chalk noise, is out of alignment with her speech, which only follows the rhythm of the beats produced by the piece of chalk hitting the chalkboard surface.

8   When is grammar?

Das *Wesen* ist in der Grammatik ausgesprochen
[*Essence/Being/Life* is expressed in/by grammar].
(Wittgenstein 1958, 116 [§371], original emphasis)

One does not follow rules in order to achieve meaning.
(Rawls 1989: 160)

In the first introductory quote, Ludwig Wittgenstein makes an important point about grammar. However, the official Anscombe translation ("*Essence* is expressed by grammar") does not capture the semantic field covered by the German original. Two paragraphs later, Wittgenstein notes that grammar tells us what kind of object something *is*, which, etymologically deriving from the Latin *esse*, would, in fact, confirm the translation. The German equivalent of *essence* would be "*Wesenskern*," but Wittgenstein used the term *Wesen*, which covers a field including being, creature, nature, personality, and air. But there is also a verb, *wesen*, and Heidegger (1985) uses *Wesen* as noun form of *wesen*, to live, to be at work. In this form the verb, having arisen from the Proto-Indo-European *ues* or **sues-* (to stay, live, spend the night), is etymologically related to inflections of the verb "to be" (Engl., *was*, Gr., *waren*). In this root of the verb to be, "the noun *Wesen* does not originally signify quiddity, essence, but the constitutive staying of presence (*Gegenwart*), pre-sence (*An-wesen*) and ab-sence (*Ab-wesen*)" (Derrida 1972: 244).[1] To discuss the essence of language, language as such, therefore, "means getting ourselves to the location of its being present (*Wesen*): gathering in the event" (Heidegger 1985: 10).

Language is both the essence and the being of humans. "*Essence/being/life* is," to return to Wittgenstein, "expressed in/by grammar"; linguistic form and forms of life are mutually constitutive and irreducible. We cannot, therefore, study linguistic form, i.e. grammar, independent of life as a whole (Vološinov 1976). This is also why translation—both between languages as within a language—is full of contradictions, because of the different grammars of language and life across cultures. The semantic field of the German verb "*aussprechen*" does not only cover the English "to express," but also is used in the senses of the verbs to pronounce, to voice, to speak, to submit, and so on. Heidegger associates it with *hinaussprechen* putting something in speech and, therefore, into the open—in this way producing a link with the Greek *apophansis*, letting be seen, allowing this display (speech). Grammar, then, allows us to see the essence of being and life. This leads Wittgenstein to suggest that the differentiation between a surface grammar (the use and place of a word in a sentence) and a deep grammar (what one *means* by using a word) becomes undecidable. This, too, is the position taken by the Swiss linguist Ferdinand de Saussure (1996) who suggests that there are two irreducibly connected grammars—because of the dual nature of language—one pertaining to the material signs used as part of everyday life and the other to the ideas. A similar idea is expressed in McLuhan's (1995) dictum that the medium *is* the message, that is, the grammar of the medium and the grammar of the message are ineluctably and irreducibly intertwined. Grammar, then, is irreducibly subject to present conditions, "grammar does not say how language has to be constructed to fulfill its purpose to have such-and-such an effect on human beings. It only describes but in no way explains the use of signs" (Wittgenstein 1958: 138 [§496]). But ideas, as consciousness, are related to everyday life so that we may expect grammar in mundane talk to be irreducible from real, ongoing, societal activity itself. The organizations of life, body, and language, i.e., the grammars, are irremediably intertwined (Deleuze 1990) and the differences between them become undecidable.[2] Ideas, talk, and consciousness contingently arise from the dialectic of real-time production-in-setting.

Punctuation is an important aspect of grammar in written language. But in speaking, there is no punctuation. A well-known example of literature that embodied the absence of punctuation exists in Chapter 18 of *Ulysses*, which presents the internal monologue of Molly Bloom, the female protagonist of the novel:

> ... sure the women were as bad in their nice white mantillas ripping all the whole insides out of those poor horses I never heard of such a thing in all my life yes he used to break his heart at me taking off the dog barking in bell lane poor brute and it sick what became of them ever I suppose theyre dead long ago the 2 of them its like all through a mist makes you feel so old ...
>
> (Joyce 1986: 622, lines 632–7)

Readers familiar with the English language will parse the text into familiar units, pulling together fragments that appear to belong together because of the content. In this situation, the text presents us with the thoughts of a person, and we know from experience that we do not think in terms of periods, commas, quotation marks, parentheses, capitalization, and so on. Moreover, we do not think of grammatical features in everyday conversations with others. It is therefore not without accident that I reproduce conversations throughout this book without punctuation marks but include the information about prosody that speakers actually make available to each other. Whether something is a statement, question, order, and so on partially is available in intonation and in form (grammar), themselves a function of the situation as a whole, including the physical body producing these forms. Ultimately, therefore, it is the totality of significance relations that is responsible for the theme marked by the speech event. But even if not marked, grammar is pervasive. We do hear a speaker quote someone else, even if there are no quotation marks. There is structure in turn taking that mediates the form and content of sentences. This aspect of grammar is precisely what this chapter is about.

Language, or rather, that which is properly language in language (de Saussure's *langue*), often is thought of as a system comprised of semantics, the sense of words, and syntactics, the grammatical structure underlying the mobilization of language. Much of structural linguistics in the second half of the twentieth century has been influenced by the work of Noam Chomsky on *generative grammar*—an idea that dates back to the rationalism of the seventeenth century and was part of a theory that the German philosopher and mathematician Gottfried Leibniz developed. Many readers have taken the term in the sense of an internal system that is able to generate morphologically well-formed sentences. Recent work in the cognitive sciences shows that grammar does not have to be innate for speakers to come to use grammar with language (e.g., Elman 1993). This work shows that a properly designed artificial neural network exposed to structured sequences of words learns to distinguish nouns and verbs, the subject of a sentence from the object, and so on. Thus, mere participation in social interactions where iterable and iterated noises are produced with certain regularities—the experience of children before they are conscious of words *as* words—may lead to regular usage of these noises. As is well known, children generalize grammatical features even without being taught, and frequently despite being taught differently. Thus, a child at a certain stage might say that her mom "buyed some candy" rather than "bought some candy" for her. But this approach, too, assumes grammar to be an inherent feature, here arrived at by induction and generalization, which, depending on the situation (i.e., over-generalization), is produced faultily.

But does grammar in fact have to *underlie* the use of language? Or may we not assume that a grammatical feature specifically, and grammar generally, is itself a *product* of social interaction and therefore life? The reflection that opens this chapter certainly suggests so. Moreover, throughout this book, there are conversation fragments that allow us to ask the question about the pragmatic production of regularities in speech. In this chapter, therefore, I take a closer look at grammatical features that arise from social interaction. Speaking, I suggest, does not merely *follow* (unarticulated, tacit, invisible) rules but produces these (unarticulated, tacit, invisible) regularities that, after the fact, can be said to be consistent or inconsistent with certain rules as interlocutors orient to and accomplish the activity that they know to be participants in. However, and most importantly, interlocutors understand one another even when an utterance does not implement formal grammar. In everyday use of language, (grammatical) rules, if there are any, follow rather than precede use.

From "from the other" to "for the other"

One of the important aspects in the reproduction and transformation of language is brought about by the transition of language (fragments) from direct reported speech (quotation) via indirect reported speech to unattributed (owned) speech. Direct reported speech plays various roles and has different functions, including the direct attribution of a statement to a person, for whatever pragmatic reasons this might be. We do hear when others quote even though there are no quotation marks. Pragmatically, the modalization of others' speech in more or less direct form serves different purposes in different contexts. Thus, for example, in the sciences, reported speech serves to soften the factual nature of statement, which thereby come to be modalized (Latour and Woolgar 1979). Thus, in the sciences there is a clear hierarchy of facticity of increasing nature in the sequence "X said, 'objects fall'," "a considerable number of studies suggest that objects fall," and "objects fall." At the same time, in directly quoting, unquestioned and unquestionable authority may be conferred to a statement, attributed to the voice/signature of another high or higher up in the social hierarchy of the field of inquiry: "The stronger the feeling of hierarchical eminence in another's utterance, the more sharply defined will its boundaries be, and the less accessible will it be to penetration by reporting and commenting tendencies from the outside" (Bakhtin [Medvedev] 1978: 122). In this modalization, a second aspect of reported speech comes into view: it not only tells us what someone else has said but also constitutes a form of social evaluation, of its reception in the speech of another person.

Reported speech clearly is a grammatical phenomenon, as it structures the utterance of the speaker. Here, therefore, structure, content, and context come to mediate each other. The upshot is that it does not make sense to analyze any one of these features independently of all other features of language, itself to be understood as a one-sided expression of the communicative unit as a whole. In fact, the lecture in Chapter 3 shows how the genre interacts with the place the body takes in the lecture hall and with the orientation that the body takes with respect to the audience; these interactions, in turn, are reflected in the grammar actualized. In the following, I focus on the main forms of reported speech: direct, indirect, and quasi-direct reported speech. I exemplify and discuss these grammatical phenomena with examples from different chapters.

Direct reported speech

Direct reported speech may have very different functions depending on the context. In this book, I use it to mark off sentences written by others from sentences for which I take authorship. But quotation marks, which always signal some form of citation (Derrida 2003b), also are used in this book to set words in our discipline apart—e.g., "to construct" and "to position oneself" in the opening pages of Chapter 4—thereby *mentioning* rather than using them. Learners who directly repeat what someone else has said use direct reported speech. A statement may be attributed to someone else for particular, pragmatic reasons and functions. The direct reported speech structures the utterance within which it plays a particular role. It structures the utterance in the sense that the reported speech fragment appears as a whole and the remainder of the utterance needs to fit around and mark the reported speech as such. In the following fragment from Chapter 6, Preston provides an account of some discussions he has had with peers. The transcript already marks, using quotation marks, what we hear as an instant of direct reported speech. In fact, the quotation marks exhibit the cultural competencies of the transcriber. These competencies reproduce those of the interlocutors, who understand that a quotation has occurred, for otherwise the transcriber could not really do his or her job, that is, transcribing a *con*versation.

Fragment 8.1 (excerpt from Fragment 6.4)

01 P: and I said, "what about religion, have you ever thought about what you actually want to believe? Have you ever thought about what your destiny is? Science can't provide you that."

Here, no further context is provided so that we could only hypothesize as to the function of the use of direct reported speech, in addition to indirect and quasi-direct speech described below. One function of direct reported speech is dramatization; another function is authenticity deriving from the reproduction of the utterances that initially has occurred in some other place at another time. The direct quotation may also be heard as having a dramatic function in his account of the debates that he has had with peers. Two issues need to be kept in mind. First, Preston does not spill out prefigured text but speaks in real time and without time-out. Second, because there is no time-out, he does not have time to reflect on the actual production of his account. That is, if he articulates the account in terms of these various means, it may be because he is thereby transported back to the original discussion and, simultaneously, because speaking in this way makes the events present again and allows him to transport all interlocutors into the event he recounts. The grammar here may directly reflect his taking of a position on the world, essence/being/life expressed in and through grammar. That is, taking|expressing a position happens not only during talk, as seen in Chapter 7, but it also shapes the way in which a speaker accounts for a historically preceding conversation.

The quoted source does not always have to appear. But in the way in which utterances are structured, certain parts of it can be heard as direct reported speech. In the following fragment from Chapter 5, the interviewer prefaces a stretch of talk by saying "so the question is very simple." In this utterance, the source of the question remains unknown, it may be that of the interviewer but it may also be that of the Internet site where some of the answer alternatives are displayed. The interviewer thereby achieves several things. First, he formulates that a question is forthcoming. Second, he prefigures that which is forthcoming—a question that the interviewer has on his interview protocol, "could you explain to me why we have day and why we have night."

Fragment 8.2 (excerpt from Fragment 2.1)

01 I: so the question is very simple. (0.24) .hhh could you explain me:?
'why:: (0.55) 'why: we have day and why we have night;

In this instance, the formulation announces something definite to come "*the* question" rather than "a question" or any question or anything at all. The announcement ends as a statement before we can hear a question unfolding. We can hear the question even though the structure of the utterance does not conform to formal English. Moreover, the utterance as a whole is structured in that it consists of an announcement and the content of what is announced. This hearing is justified when we take a look at the next fragment which is structured very similarly, an announcement to think about something and then the articulation of the content to be thought about. This content is the item from the questionnaire, which Preston has already responded to both in checking one of three forced choices (agree, disagree, no opinion) and explaining his choice. As in Fragment 8.2, there is a descending pitch toward the end of the formulation (though less so), a definite article ("the") preceding the ordinal stating the number of an item ("number four,") followed by what has been announced as coming, the content of the item number four.

Fragment 8.3 (excerpt from Fragment 6.3)

09 T: So when when you think about the, ah- the number four; "Scientific laws and theories exist independent of human existence, and scientists merely discover them"; would you say that is true, or ...

In this instance, there is an additional marker that points to the preceding part of the utterance as something standing apart and, therefore, as being quoted. The interviewer asks, "would you say that is true, or." By using the demonstrative pronoun *that*, the teacher points back to what has immediately preceded, recycling it back into the present utterance without actually pronouncing it, and then asking whether the statement thereby referred to is true.

In the preceding examples, specific features of the utterance point to another feature, marking the coming or passing of a clause consisting of direct reported speech. How else may interlocutors hear reported speech? How do they recognize that something said is actually the saying of another presented again—re-presented and represented—at a different place and time? We already see in the structure of the speech in Fragment 8.1 grammatical markers of change from the speaker's voice to the reported voice (in this instance, the same speaker at different instants in time): the speaker is denoted followed by a verb in the simple past tense ("I said") followed by a statement in the tense of the original speech (present perfect simple ["have you thought"], present ["science can't provide you that]"). But there are other means as well, which we may not be aware of while participating in a conversation, but which characteristically feature alone or in combination to mark a

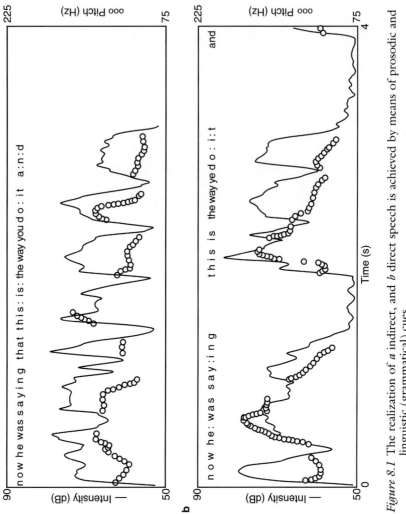

Figure 8.1 The realization of *a* indirect, and *b* direct speech is achieved by means of prosodic and linguistic (grammatical) cues.

stretch of talk as direct reported speech. In Fragment 8.4, we hear/see the marker for the speaker ("he") and the verb in imperfect (continuous) past ("was saying") followed by the reported speech (in present tense), itself succeeded by the main narrative in past tense ("he went on talking"). (An example of the same utterance as indirect reported speech is provided later.)

Fragment 8.4

01   now ↑he was saying. (0.49) <<f>↑THIS is the way ye do it.> (0.62) and
     then he went o::n: a=talking about other things.

In this fragment, we easily note two instances of a temporal marker that sets the reported speech apart: more or less brief pauses of 0.49 and 0.62 seconds. The reported speech is also set apart in louder than normal voice (<<f> ... >). The announcement of the event ends with a downward pitch (period in transcript), the pitch jumps upward at the beginning of the quoted material that ends, as statements do, in a downward trend of the intonation (period in transcript). All of these features clearly stand out in the analysis of the voice track when we use a linguistic software package, here PRAAT (which, incidentally, means "talk" in Dutch, the language of the developers). The software allows us to detect clearly other features that mark off the part of the utterance made of direct reported speech (Figure 8.1b).

First, the formulation of the index pointing to the person quoted ("he") is emphasized by the rapidly increasing pitch coinciding with "he," setting it apart from this or any other person involved. A detailed analysis of the conversation may show that the emphasis allows a particular male person to be isolated among several. There is a past tense "was saying" followed by a clear pause. The pitch then increases again to drop toward the end of the quoted piece, separated from the subsequent speech by another pause. The pitch of the next word is higher again than that of the sound-words at end of the direct reported speech. Also, we see the increased speech intensity for the quoted part, which is about 2 dB higher on average (73 dB compared to 71 dB means almost doubling in loudness) than that of the speech preceding and following it.

In this instance, we have a number of features all assisting in marking off the reported voice from the person's own. These features do not have to be present all of the time but, the more there are, the clearer the separation of the quote from the remainder of the speech. As these features disappear, the difference with other forms of reported speech becomes undecidable. It is important to know that temporal constraints do not permit the speaker to stop and reflect on/think about what will be said in the fractions of a second that follow. Therefore, these grammar-producing features are produced unconsciously. But the position taken again organizes this production, and the production itself articulates the position.

It is not just that we report the speech of others directly, but in so doing we also provide evaluations of the utterance itself and, because of the attribution of speech acts to individual intent (illocution) and production (locution) as source, to the individual him/herself. In Fragment 8.5, we return to Chapter 1, where the teacher quotes the speech of the immediately preceding speaker Connor. After some talk, which we may hear/gloss as "prodding," Connor finally and with a very low voice utters "squares." The teacher begins her next turn with the same word. She thereby reports back to the assembled group what he has said/ she has heard him saying. But she does more, and this is articulated in the pitch contour (intonation), which first descends as if a statement was unfolding but then rises again, as if a question were to be realized. The following sound-word exhibits the same contour in addition to a stretching out of the heard "and."

Fragment 8.5 (excerpt from Fragment 1.1c)

```
53  C:   <<pp>s:::::><<p>quares>-
54  T:   ˇsquare [ˋan꞉꞉d
             [(((Cheyenne has moved forward, jutting her index finger
         repeatedly to the card next to the cubes inscribed "square, cube"))
```

With rising intonation, we may hear the reported speech as a question, as glossed in this example: "so you said 'square'; and what else did we say?" When the intonation is falling (ˋsquare) or falling and finishing the utterance (square.), then we may hear the reported speech as an acknowledgment of what has been said and a positive evaluation thereof as in the gloss "you said 'square.' This is correct [what I wanted to hear]." Here, the social evaluation may actually pertain to the speaker as person. As part of the IRE sequential order of talk, this third part of the sequence constitutes the evaluation, which is not only one of the utterance as such, but also one of the student, who, in providing the incorrect or incomplete response, can be said to be less than fully knowledgeable about the subject.

But there is more. Although correct, there is something else to come, as flagged both by the rising intonation that flags questions and the conjunction "and" that is not followed by the term it flags to come. That is, Connor has answered correctly, but only partially so, which we understand in the articulated unarticulated word and which we hear as missing and to be supplied by the other. In Chapter 1, we see that the answer is supplied twice, by other students, once in and by means of a pointing gesture to the sheet containing the name of the group ("square, cube") and the other by means of the sound-word, the sought-for one, as recognizable from the turns that follow.

Here we also see that the same word or phrase has a different function than its first occurrence, which means, in Bakhtinian terms, that it has a different theme, marking something different. Thus, Connor's "square" was part of an answer, whereas the teacher's "square" was an acknowledgment of the answer, an evaluation of the answer as appropriate with respect to the sought-for answer, the existence of a definite, sought-for answer rather than any answer, an evaluation that the answer provided is only a partial one, and a request for supplying the other part of the sought-for answer.

A quoted stretch of speech may itself undergo transformation depending on the particular function of the quoting voice. Thus, for example, when one speaker questions what another person has said, then the quotation is subject to the constraints of appearing in an utterance designed as a question. One such situation arises in Chapter 2 when the girl AJ responds to a question about the summer being hotter than the winter.

Fragment 8.6 (excerpt from Fragment 2.1)

```
→   05  I:    ↑why is it hotter (0.19) in the summer.
    06        (0.67)
    07  AJ:   because we orbit the ↑`sun
    08        (2.63)
→   09  I:    what about the winter we dont orbit the sun? (0.35) during the
              winte:r?
```

AJ responds that it is "because we orbit the Sun" (turn 07). The interviewer quotes AJ but negating her statement "we don't orbit the Sun" in the context of a different season, "during the winter?" (turn 09). We do hear the interviewer quote AJ directly even though the phrase is not identical. The quote and question could be realized differently as well, for example, in the utterance "in the winter, we orbit the Sun?" with a falling pitch in the first part, perhaps with a little pause following winter, followed by the direct reported speech. In fact, we can imagine further variations, where the interviewer could co-articulate irony, criticism, doubt, and other evaluative moods by modulating the sound-words by means of the inflection, thereby realizing very different themes even though sound-words and grammar would be identical.

Direct reported speech has additional functions. Elsewhere I provide an extended analysis of a classroom conversation where students use direct reported speech for a variety of purposes, for example, to ascertain the authority of the speech or textbook content presented (Roth 2009a). They preface what is to come by stating, for example, "he [the teacher] said," "Einstein said," or "in the book it says." In the attempts to convince others, these forms of direct reported speech weigh more than the indirect speech described in the next subsection.

Flagging something as direct speech does not mean that what is being reported is precisely what has been stated elsewhere. In fact, if another interlocutor knows the source of direct reported speech, the precise nature of what has been said can become an issue in its own right. For example, in the cited study, one student embroiled in a charge of racism says about his interlocutor, "he puts words in my mouth and then believes it." In this case, the interlocutor is challenged for not having directly reported speech but that he has "put words" into the mouths of his peer. What the function of direct reported speech is and whether it is, in fact, accepted as direct speech is a pragmatic issue that interlocutors settle as needed, and which, from a methodical perspective, we, therefore, need to take as an empirical matter rather than a matter of truth or lie.

Indirect reported speech

In indirect reported speech, the speaker reports what someone else has said without actually quoting the person directly. In so doing, the words and structure of what has originally been said comes to be changed, and in this change there is both an intrusion of the voice of the current speaker into the original utterance and an evaluation, which results from the fact that what is reported appears in and as a product of the voice of the reporting speaker. The original voice begins to disappear in the social evaluation that comes with the appearance of what has been said in the present speaker's utterance. Thus, "[t]he analytical tendency of indirect speech manifests itself above all by the fact that all the *emotive* and *affective* elements of speech do not transpose themselves intact into indirect speech, in so far as they are expressed not in the content but in the *form* of the utterance" (Bakhtine [Volochinov] 1977: 177, original emphisis). In the following fragment from Chapter 6, Preston reports on conversations he has had with others (in his dorm) but he does not quote them directly, he does not use markers that set off a stretch of talk as direct reported speech. On the other hand, he uses a verbal marker typical for indirect speech, "that."

Fragment 8.7 (excerpt from Fragment 6.4)

01 P: there was a couple of people who where completely atheists who thought about that they were really good science; they wanna be scientists; and I said, "what about religion. have you ever thought about what you actually want to believe? Have you ever thought about what your destiny is? Science can't provide you that."

In Fragment 8.7, Preston articulates for the interviewer (and anyone else reading the transcript) that he has had a conversation with "a couple of people," whom he characterizes as "complete atheists." He then makes known to us what they had said, not directly, but in essence, "who thought about that they were really good at science." Rather than directly reporting what other people told him and how they let him know that they are "really good [at] science," Preston—flagging the indirect way of referring to their speech by a preceding "that"—then glosses some distilled form thereof. This indirect way of referring to the speech at that other instant comes to the fore in the contrast that his subsequent direct reported speech sets up. In one breath, he states that these former interlocutors were atheists, that they were good at science, and that they wanted to be scientists.

In Fragment 8.8, Preston uses indirect reported speech to relay to us what his parents ("they") have told him, that he cannot become a doctor because … he does not have the marks for it. We can almost hear his parents, who may have said something like "you have to be realistic. You cannot become a doctor. You do not have the grades for entering in a medical program."

Fragment 8.8 (excerpt from Fragment 6.3)

08 P: And so I wanted to be a doctor, so I decided to pursue it, and then I tried to take that advantage and now they are taking that dream away from me that I can't become a doctor because, now they are coming back to reality, that I don't have the marks for it ...

As in the previous fragment, the indirect discourse can be used to gloss the outcome of a longer conversation and to distill it into a shorter statement, which itself appears in an evaluative statement, "now they are taking that dream away from me." That is, we hear what the parents are glossed as having said within an evaluative comment, whereby they have taken a dream from him rather than him having done poorly for one or another reason. We can clearly hear that his parents did not say something like, "we are going to take your dream," but rather, Preston communicates an assessment of the effect of his parents' comments reported indirectly here: taking away his dreams. One possible function of indirect speech is that it is not open to criticism in the way that direct speech is. In the latter case, stating what someone has said allows the interlocutor to question whether the statement, in fact, constitutes an action that takes or can take a dream away, whereas the speaker can fashion—not consciously but by orienting to the situation holistically—the indirect quote to be consonant with his own voice.

Indirect speech can also be used to articulate what might be said in the future without anticipating the precise ways in which this will be done. Thus, in the following fragment from Chapter 6, Preston tells us what he can and cannot say at some future point if the interviewer were to pursue the line of questioning. At issue is not just the statement "Newton is artificial," but the provision of an account for such a statement that this indirect reported speech anticipates, *the essence of which* would be that Newton's science is artificial.

Fragment 8.9 (excerpt from Fragment 6.2)

04 P: I would think that religion is completely by the book of God, is not artificial, because I have grown up that way, and therefore I can't say that- Newton, I can say that Newton is artificial ...

There is more to Fragment 8.9. We can actually hear Preston refer to something that he cannot say, which is that religion is artificial. He uses indirect speech to bring the text of the statement from the questionnaire item into his own talk, animating it in and with his own voice.

As before, in the case of the direct reported speech, we may ask whether there are markers other than the verbal ones that distinguish indirect from direct reported speech. To exhibit the similarities and differences between the two forms, I reproduce Fragment 8.4 but this time in indirect speech yielding Fragment 8.10. We already see in the transcript that the two pauses marking the direct reported speech are absent in this case. Absent, too, is the change in average speech intensity, though other prosodic markers remain, such as the emphasis on "he," produced by a rapidly increasing pitch and the similar emphasis on "this" produced in the same manner. These two emphases— already seen in direct reported speech—are highlighted in both instances and may suggest that these are semantically important features in the narrative. The software analysis exhibits these similarities and differences (see Figure 8.1a).

Fragment 8.10

01   now ↑he was saying that ↑this: is: the way ye ↑do: it a:n:d then he went o:n: talking about other things.

When we measure the number of syllables per time unit, we find that there is a constant rate in the indirect reported speech across the entire unit (Figure 8.1a) but that there is a slower rate in the voice of the speaker, a faster rate identical with the indirect sample for the reported speech, and a faster rate (not visible in the figure) for the subsequent speech (Figure 8.1b). That is, speech rate, too, can be used to mark the difference between direct reported speech and the speaker's own speech that does the reporting. Further analysis of this speaker may show that the slowing before direct reported speech is an additional feature situationally made available to mark the speech of others.

Quasi-direct reported speech

Somewhere between indirect and direct reported speech lies quasi-direct reported speech. It is not merely a mixture of the two forms but has a double-faced nature, or, in more modern ways of theorizing, it is an undecidable phenomenon where both constitutive moments resonate at the same time. In the examples Bakhtine [Volochinov] (1977) provide, this form of reported speech is characterized by the simultaneous presence of two voices, that of the current speaker and that of another person. An interesting example in the philosophical literature— interesting because the two voices belong to the French author and that of the English-speaking editor of the book (David Wood) to which the author has been invited to contribute—can be found in *Passion* (Derrida 1993: 84): "'its remit, *dit-il du livre*, is neither to praise nor to bury Derrida, but...' (but what, *au juste?*)." Here the direct quotation, the English part, is broken into two pieces separated by the author's own voice (here in French). In this book, I use quasi-direct speech on the opening page of Chapter 1 in writing "Heidegger answers his question by saying that *language speaks*" (emphasis added), which, using "that" marks indirect speech but the "language speaks" that follows is a repetition of the quote. (See also second voice-over in Chapter 10.) That is, in the same phrase, we find both direct and indirect speech. The Anglo-Saxon scholarly writing in the social sciences makes little if any use of this strategy,[3] though the following quote from *Ulysses* does, in fact, implement it:

He laid both books aside and glanced at the third *Tales of the Ghetto* by
Leopold von Sacher Masoch.
—That I had, he said, pushing it by
The shopman let two volumes fall on the counter.
—Them are two good ones, he said.

(Joyce 1986: 193)

In most instances, the separation between the two voices is not undecidable. Do
we hear the voice of the quoted or that of the quoting speaker? Do we hear the
voice of the author, the protagonist, or another person quoted? There are two
voices, each reflecting upon the other, a feature that is dominant in the dialogic
monologues characteristic of Fyodor Dostoevsky's novels (Bakhtin 1984a).

One of the features of formal scholarly English is that it uses quotation marks,
which immediately denotes the difference between voices (French differs in this
as the above example shows). In spoken English, however, quotation marks do
not exist so that it comes perhaps not as a surprise that quasi-direct reported
speech can be detected in actual conversations. In the following fragment from
Chapter 6, we can hear the change in Preston's voice as he begins twice with
a grammatical feature that would introduce a direct reported speech fragment
("they can say," "they can't say"), but then continues with an indirect reported
speech ("*what* you are made of," "*what* you are going to be," and "*where* you are
going to be") that also could serve as a direct reported speech fragment.

Fragment 8.11 (excerpt from Fragment 6.4)

01 P: All they can say is what you are made of, they can't say what you are
        going to be, where you are gonna go.

The transition between authentic voice and quotation also is undecidable in the
following fragment from Chapter 7, as Oprah is quoting herself. In turn 05, she
formulates what is to come as something she is "just saying" and then she repeats
the statement—which, in fact, constitutes the solution to the problem of how to
arrive at the chemical valence of an element—"just do the number two."

Fragment 8.12 (excerpt from Fragment 7.2)

d 01 P: where is the ↑twO coming from.
   02   (0.52)
   03 Ta: <<p>from.>
   04   (0.19)
e 05 O: <<f>I=M JUST SAYing just do the number ↑TWO: (0.14) ↓i:
           ↑you=don=t=wan=me=da copy text from noWHERe, or yOU can
           take t=the two come from the (0.16) the ↑rOW,> I mean

She has already said it, but, in this case, the two situations—quoted and quoting voice—become undecidable because of the present tense in the formulation. So what comes is both an instance of direct reported speech and a form of authentic speech, and both are from the same voice. This phenomenon can also be found in the literature. Analyzing *La folie du jour* by Maurice Blanchot, where the narrator uses in one of the last paragraphs precisely the same sentence that begins the text, Derrida (1986: 270) notes: "[T]hese are the same words, in the same order, without quotation marks, this starts and restarts a quasi-narrative [*quasi-récit*],[4] which, again, engenders the entire sequence including this new start, and so on." Moreover, returning to our case, this self-citation itself is only a special case of repetition that always already occurs in the use of language, whether the citation is acknowledged—by using quotation marks and an author's name, which itself is not unique but a special case of the iterability of the word (Derrida 1988b)—or not—by speaking "plain everyday language," which continually reproduces and transforms itself in speaking.

Function of direct, indirect, and quasi-direct reported speech

There is a central role in direct, indirect, and quasi-direct speech to the reproduction and transformation of language (Bakhtine [Volochinov] 1977). This is not just a philosophical statement; it is a description of actual and concrete practice that we encounter, for example, in Chapter 1. The teacher says, "what did we say this group was about?" and thereby offers up, and requests Connor to state, what has already been stated. He may do so using either direct or indirect speech, such as in "we said that this group is about squares and cubes" or "Cheyenne said, 'This group is called squares and cubes'." Because the teacher already formulated the coming of direct or indirect speech, the answer could actually be provided in an elliptical form, "squares and cubes," being the replacement for the "what" in the question. This can be seen in the sequential order of turns that follow the questioning, which unfolds until the two sought-for, previously stated items—more accurately, what will have been the two sought-for items—have been articulated. I note above how reporting what someone else says until a statement becomes fact mediates the speech/writing of another person. Therefore, what is important as an object of study is the role and function of the dynamic relation between these two aspects of speech, the speech reported and the reporting speech: "The reported speech and the reporting context are but the terms of a dynamic interrelationship. This dynamism reflects the dynamism of social interorientation in verbal ideological communication between people" (Bakhtin [Medvedev] 1978: 119).

In an extended study of conversations in physics classrooms, where the students completed a concept-mapping task, the purpose of which was to summarize the entire content of a chapter, students saw themselves forced to settle disagreements about concepts (Roth 2009a). That study clearly shows how direct and indirect forms of speech are used to convince peers. The change from direct to indirect speech coincides with students' control over the physics language, which, after some experience, they fully articulate in their own voice without relying on what others have said (written). A full analysis of the function of these forms of speech in the development of new forms competencies has yet to be completed within the educational literature.

The function of the different forms of reported speech will also change depending on the context. For example, I show in this section the various ways in which Preston brings the speech of others (peers, parents, and, not shown here, teachers) into the conversation about science and religion. Because any utterance is configured for the audience, we cannot engage in a decontextualized analysis of features but must always look for the pragmatic uses and effects that such features have, and the latter can be determined only in and from the responses of the interlocutors. This pragmatic use is a function of the situation so that the grammar of language is subordinated to and interacts with the grammar of social life. This aspect of grammar is featured in subsequent sections concerned with the beginning/ending of turns, utterances, and topics.

There is, of course, a reflexive dimension of this topic in the presentation of this book. Throughout this book, I use direct and indirect reported speech/ writing (paraphrase) to bring the works of other scholars into my own. Readers may ask themselves in each case what the particular function of this use of reported speech/writing is. In fact, there may be multiple functions in any one case, such as exhibiting the work on which one is building, to place a more contentious statement in the mouth/hand of an eminent scholar, or as a narrative strategy to include different voices.

When does the turn (utterance) end?

Conversation analysis and ethnomethodology are not deterministically and teleologically oriented sciences (e.g., Garfinkel and Sacks 1986). They recognize the inherently achieved manner of social interaction. Yet much of the educational literature focusing on talk appears deterministic, even if it claims to be grounded in one or both of these sciences—which may not be surprising as the reactive approach to the interactional constitution of sense has dominated the social sciences (Rawls 1989). Typical for the determinism unwanted in the two allied disciplines is the sequential order of turn-taking, which, in the educational literature, has been taken up saliently in the IRE concept. Close study of actual conversations *in real time* show, however, that turns at talk are not rigidly fixed and who speaks when and about what is always open. Whether something a teacher does or says is taken up as an initiation (i.e., reified as an initiation) is itself open and has to be understood as a pragmatic achievement. In the following subsections, I show that speaking turns are not mechanically organized into deterministically linked slots. Rather, turns at talk are contingent achievements that interlocutors pragmatically accomplish in real time and without time-out for reflection. The end of one utterance (turn at talk) and beginning of another is not something that is inherently given, so that speakers have to pragmatically solve the question about when and where to take/give up a turn at talk. It is achieved in the sequential ordering, by means of the sequential order itself.

Turns as contingent achievement

Important parts of the micro-constitution of social situations in institutional talk are beginnings and endings of turns and turn sequences. The literature tends to take these as parts of events (objectively, transcendentally) as given when, in fact, they are concretely achieved through the cooperation of the participants of talk-in-interaction. This is no more evident than in those research articles that make assertions about the presence of teacher initiation–student response–teacher evaluation sequences. There are no natural boundaries that mark the end of one and the beginning of another utterance. Who is going to speak next is itself an achievement, and this is clearly evident in turn 50 of Fragment 8.13, where the teacher stops to speak and the denoted student (Connor) does not speak. Eventually, the teacher speaks again. But rather than abandoning the question, she provides what we can hear as another translation of the question. She could have instead provided the correct answer, for example, "in the interest of managing the time given that there are another 10 students who did not yet have a turn." That is, these turns, as the pauses that separate the sound streams, are collective achievements that are pragmatically and contingently rather than mechanically realized involving the interlocutors present.

Fragment 8.13 (continuation of Fragment 1.1c)

```
      49  T:                    ^[₄WHAt ] ↑was the (0.15) ^WHAt ↑did we
                     put for the name of that group.
 →    50       (1.51)
      51       whats written on the] [₅card.]
               ((still points))      ₁] [₅((Pulls hand back, no longer points))
      52       (0.26)
      53  C:   <<pp>s:::::><<p>quares>-
 →    54  T:   ˅square [˅an::d
                        [(((Cheyenne has moved forward, jutting her index finger
                        repeatedly to the card next to the cubes inscribed "square, cube"))
      55  J:   cubes.
```

We can hear turn 51 as a way of "coaxing" the other into taking a turn, which he has not taken when space is available in turn 50. In this case, the turn that the student may take comes with a risk, for the subsequent turn, if it is an IRE sequence that is beginning to realize itself (even this we cannot know, even though it might be likely), an evaluation will follow. An older student in a "difficult" school may, in fact, take a turn but say "f*** you," in which case no IRE sequence would be realized.

Pauses constitute multiple possibilities. On the one hand, they provide opportunities for a change between speakers, as one speaker appears to have stopped. A
brief inspection of Fragments 2.2 and 2.3, however, reveals that the pauses considerably vary in length. They do so both between and within speakers. For example,
in Fragment 2.2 alone there are three within-utterance pauses near the one second
mark and one pause is longer than 1.7 seconds. In fact, it would be better and more
accurate to say that at these pauses *will have been within-utterance*, as we can never
know when precisely the next person comes to take a turn at talk.

On the other hand, there are between-speaker pauses that range from between
0.88 seconds on the long side of utterances to overlapping speech at the other
end. In fact, marking longer pauses as occurring within the turn (utterance) is
based on an arbitrary, in any case a posteriori, decision. Thus, the 0.93 second
pause within turn 33 of Fragment 2.2 could have been placed on its own line,
because Annemarie has come to the end of one complete clause and then begins
a very different—we might be tempted to say metalevel—clause, "I am right,
then?" At the same time, there is a 0.98 second pause within Daniel's turn 40,
but it occurs within an unfinished clause.

Fragment 8.14 (Fragment 2.2)

```
      31  A:  death rate increasing (0.69) and the birthrate increasing and the
                birthrate is increasing (0.57) faster (0.95) than the death rate.
      32        (1.71)
  →   33        so they=re both increasing but the birthrate invar is faster increasing
                than the death rate so presumably that means that the population is
                increasing. (0.93) is that right then?
      34        (0.88)
      35  D:  hhum
      36        (0.43)
      37  A:  round [this    ] region?
      38  D:         [khmm]
      39        (0.73)
      40  D:  u:m; yea=if you=take (.) well (.) shall=i=think=i=use the half
                if=you=take the birth minus the death (.) rate (0.63) `well the birth
                plus the death (.) rate which is negative, you=re gonna get (0.13)
                some positive (0.98) growth rate; right?=
      41  A:  =^yea ^[i=]m looking at the slopes of the curve[ss ].
  →   42  D:    <<p>[so]>                                    [uh]=<<p>okay.>
```

Saying arbitrarily, however, that grammatical completion is the crucial contextual
feature that allows speakers to make the decision whose turn it is does not lead
us to a general rule. For example, in turn 54 of Fragment 8.13, Jane takes the
next turn even though the teacher has not produced a grammatically complete
phrase. In this instance, there is no pause between speakers. But we can easily
imagine that the teacher would have refrained from speaking to allow students

to produce one or more words to fill the slot she designs for them to place a response in the way she provides Connor with more than 1.5 seconds to come up with a response (turn 50). Similarly, the interviewer in the first part of this chapter (Fragment 8.6) allows time for AJ to respond (e.g., turn 06) and does not immediately speak when there is a pause following an utterance by the little girl, even though it extends to what in other social situations would be an awkward 2.6 seconds (turn 08). In this last instance, it is easy to see how the pause provides possibilities that go both ways. By not speaking, the interviewer allows AJ to add to what she has already said and he thereby indicates that he is making space for her to continue. In not continuing, AJ indicates that she has said all that she has to say and that she makes space for the interviewer to ask the next question or to elaborate on the one he has previously asked. As the pause unfolds, the pause provides opportunities for both interlocutors. In this instance, the interviewer breaks the silence in and by asking about the Sun in the winter, which is the opposite case to the summer that he has previously asked about and to which AJ has provided a response.

In some instances, two speakers speak at the same time, and this too provides opportunities and constraints on both speakers. By overlapping another, a speaker indicates that she wants to speak, in fact, has begun to speak; in continuing to speak after another person has started, a speaker indicates that he wants and intends to finish some thought in the process of articulating and realizing itself. (See Chapter 3 the emergence of thinking in and through talking.) In turn 09 of Fragment 8.15, Daniel stops when Annemarie begins to speak, although he has not produced a grammatically complete unit. But in stopping, he allows Annemarie to try herself and, perhaps, to get back on track with her tutoring session.

Fragment 8.15 (excerpt from Fragment 2.3)

```
      07  A:   oh; okay
      08        (0.28)
  →   09  D:   s:o, the (0.45) the sl[ope ]
  →   10  A:                         [this ] is the rate of change of birth?
                 (0.23) °i see.°
```

In beginning to speak (turn 10), Annemarie expresses her realization of something not yet expressed, which provides Daniel with further opportunities of gaining insights into Annemarie's thinking, which he might welcome both as a researcher and as a tutor. Similarly, although he appears to start an explanation in turn 42 while Annemarie still is talking, Daniel stops again, thereby providing his interlocutor with an opportunity to articulate what she is looking at. At the same time, by continuing to speak rather than abandoning the turn to Daniel, Annemarie asserts herself (not necessarily consciously) in articulating that what she has been talking about is different from what Daniel has been talking about, which therefore provides them to align each other with respect to what the topic really is, or ought to be.

We observe an interesting case of the disentanglement of turns in Chapter 4; a phenomenon totally incomprehensible if we were only studying the verbal transcript in the way the early conversation analytic studies did, which focused on telephone conversations. In those studies, because of the context, talk, and pauses—prosody generally was not studied—were the only features co-participants made (could make) available to one another. When interlocutors are co-present to each other, additional means of managing interaction and, therefore, managing turn-taking and the grammatical structure of talk become available. On the video track, we see that between turns 04 and 06 of Fragment 8.16, the two speakers come to be entangled with each other, they talk to one another. Lisa utters a phrase that we can hear as a question because of the grammatical structure (rather than the intonation). In producing a phrase that we can hear as a response to Lisa, Nina reifies the preceding utterance as a question. Between the two utterances, Lisa has turned around and Nina has placed her arm around the girl's shoulder (Figures 8.2b, c).

Fragment 8.16 (Fragment 4.1)

```
→   04  L:   do [we ((b)) do it ¯again
                 [((Figure 8.2b))
    05         (0.65)
→   06  N:   you find [if you ↑want or you can go find `out what
                      [((Figure 8.2))
             <<dim>`the bridges should do.>
    07         (0.92)
→   08       ^learn from them.
    09         (1.21)
→   10  L:   <<all>we can do it [again [if we want, we are
                                [((Figure 8.2))
             allowed to]>
    11  N:                      <<len>[this=is a::
             sample>   ]
```

There is a longer pause in turn 07 followed by another statement in turn 08 that augments and comments upon the earlier turn 06 ("learn from them"). At what will have been the end of the utterance, Lisa turns to her right and begins to walk away, 1.12 seconds later calling out to another girl "we can do it again if we want, we are allowed to" (turn 10). As Figure 8.2d shows, Nina has turned toward and talks to a boy (thereby overlapping with Lisa), whereas Lisa is already several meters away. That is, the end of the turn 08 also constitutes the end of their conversation, at which point each person turns to the respective other. The disentanglement is enacted in and through the mutual bodily turns toward the recipients of their next utterances, the boy in Nina's instance, the peer in Lisa's. The changeover from turn 08 to turn 10 is apparent in the totality of the situation, the presence of the other individuals and the bodily turns that disentangled the two interlocutors, freeing them up to become entangled (entangle themselves again) with new interlocutors.

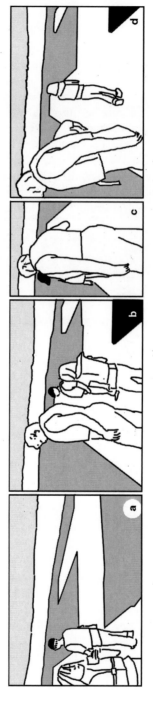

Figure 8.2 Nina and Lisa are interacting at the dock.

Completion of a statement

In traditional cognitive psychological (scientific) approaches and in folk psychology, thinking occurs in the head. This makes it difficult to understand the alignment that we often observe in conversations, for example, when one person completes the utterance of another. In the following fragment from Chapter 6, Preston utters in turn 04 what we hear to be the completion of a question of which the teacher, in turn 03, produced the first part. An affirmation that Preston has produced the completion of the teacher's formal grammatically incomplete statement is provided in turn 05 ("yea") and then is translated into a similar but non-identical form ("what you can do in science"). The completion, therefore, is possible, but perhaps not quite the one that the teacher is oriented to producing without having had the pattern to say it in the way the utterance is actually unfolding.

Fragment 8.17 (excerpt from Fragment 6.3)

```
      02  P:  That's something that I have wrestled with for a long time.
  →   03  T:  But doesn't that affect your overall, the way-
  →   04  P:  I think about science?
      05  T:  You can, yea, what you can do in science.
```

How is it possible that people complete each other's utterances (questions, statements, etc.) without having had the time to reflect and without having had something complete? Traditional cognitive approaches do not have explanations, as the "interpretive machinery" required would be much too slow. Even something as simple as the orientation of a figure in a Tetris game would take more than one second to interpret, and, as recognizable throughout this book, human utterances are much more complex than a figure made of between two and four squares. A computer, for example, cannot evaluate a statement unless there is a clear end; it then takes time to do the evaluation. In contrast, human beings appear to understand in real time. If we take the pragmatic approach of Martin Heidegger, the later Ludwig Wittgenstein, or Mikhail Bakhtin, then we understand that signification is written all over the situations in which we take part and which we continue to reproduce and transform in our communicative and practical actions. How do we know what to do with the words at our disposal? Participants are *attuned* to these significations, and it is out of their mutual attunement to the situation that they take as shared that mutual statement completion arises.

Competence in a cultural practice arises precisely when the gap between the generality of rule and the solicitude of the moment is minimized. How is this possible? I am thinking here of the difference between digital and analog computing devices. The former are based on analysis, requiring the availability of all information that is then evaluated. The latter are connected and directly express the state or states of the system as a whole—an example is the volume indicator on a hot water kettle. Mikhail Bakhtin (1993) offers the concept of *participative thinking*, which goes precisely in the same direction, thinking directly, expressing the situation as a whole. Participative thinking is possible because "we are already together with the Other beforehand, concerning the being [*Seiende*, that which is] that the talking is about" (Heidegger 1977b: 164). Mutual attunement means attunement to each other and the situation as a whole, which, for Preston and his teacher is the current topic, the nature of science, religious beliefs, and achievement in science courses. The term *participative* thinking expresses engaged, committed, involved, concerned, and interested thinking—something that Bakhtin (1993) contrasts with the detached cognitional act as theorized in psychology. He characterizes the psychological approach with the adjectives of "crude" and "inadmissible" because, thereby following Karl Marx, he understands life as determining consciousness, cognition, and speech (language) rather than the other way around.

In some instances, completion is actually sought for and, when it does not occur, the concerned participant will engage in the work that facilitates completion to come about. In Chapter 1, we encounter a situation where the teacher explicitly sets up a situation where a specific, already prefigured answer is sought for a question designed to elicit it (Fragment 8.18, turn 49) and then, after only part of the sought-for answer is provided, a slot is created to be completed by Connor or, as he does not answer, by two students one by pointing (turn 54) the other by uttering the sought-for word (turn 55).

Fragment 8.18 (excerpt from Fragment 1.1c)

    49 T: ^[₄WHAt] ↑was the (0.15) ^WHAt ↑did we
                    put for the name of that group.
    50   (1.51)
    51   whats written on the₁] [₅card.]
        ((still points))   ₁] [₅((Pulls hand back, no longer points))
    52   (0.26)
    53 C: <<pp>s::::::><<p>quares>-
  → 54 T: ˇsquare [ˇan::d
                    [(((Cheyenne has moved forward, jutting her index finger
                    repeatedly to the card next to the cubes inscribed "square, cube"))
  → 55 J: cubes.

The participants can complete the statement because of their attunement, which, when it does not already exist, can be fostered to emerge. This case, where alignment does not already exist, exhibits the normally invisible work that participants complete and the conditions that have to exist in situations, such as between the teacher and Preston, where the latter completes a question of the former, which did not have a prefigured response. Here, work is required to achieve attunement to the sought-for answer, and this work is exhibited in the teacher's communicative actions, the words and prosody she makes available to the children so that Connor or, here, someone else, may produce the completion. Underlying this phenomenon, often observed in classroom, is the production of participative thinking; students are so much aligned with the teacher about the current topic that they provide the words and phrases that will complete what the teacher has begun.

When is the end of the topic? (Topic shift)

Conversational topics do not just end. There are no absolute and fixed beginnings and endings of topics, but these beginnings and endings are interactional achievements, contingently produced as a matter of course. One conversationalist may initiate an end but requires the collusion of the other in bringing the end about. In Fragment 8.19, an excerpt from Chapter 6, the transition occurs when the teacher leads from the conversation concerning the second item on the forced-choice/explain task to the third item by explicitly invoking it and, in using the same word "commitment" from his previous turn, links these two parts—talk about item 2, to talk about item 3 of the questionnaire—of the conversation.

Fragment 8.19 (excerpt from Fragment 6.2)

```
      06  P:   And that's the only argument I have is because that's the way I've
                grown up, that is why.
      07  T:   But you have to make that– you have to make that basic commitment.
      08  P:   That's right.
  →   09  T:   See, question three actually asked you, "Do scientists have to make
                similar commitments? Do they have to believe that what they come
                up with?"
```

In moving to the next item, the interviewing teacher not only offers bringing the topic to a close, but also indicates that this topic has come to a moreorless satisfactory end. This may be either because the conversation does not appear to produce more of the sought-for information or because the item in the (interview) protocol has been satisfactory—perhaps as far as the interviewer can tell. Preston does not have to accept this offer to end the conversation. For example, in saying something like, "there is something else I wanted to add about the second question," he could extend the topic. In the interview involving the girl, AJ, in Fragment 2.1, we can see a transition from one item to the next that is much more abrupt than the previous case. AJ first responds to a question about the reasons of having day and night. In what will have been her last words in turn 03, AJ repeats an immediately preceding statement, "we can bump into something." This repetition follows a 1.5 second pause, interrupted by an ".hh=yea," which we can hear as an affirmation of what she has just said is indeed what she wanted to say. It can be heard as a completion, "yea, you can bump into something, this is what I have to say, and nothing more."

Fragment 8.20 (excerpt from Fragment 2.1)

    01 I: so the question is very simple. (0.24) .hhh could you explain me:?
                ↑why:: (0.55) ↑why: we have day and why we have night;
    02   (1.28)
    03 AJ: kay (2.06) ((licks lips with smack)) be (0.16) cause .hhhh (0.84) we
                need ↑day to pla:y: anweneed night to sleep. (0.69) .hhh and then
                if we dont have ↑day we dont have the flash light or we can bump
                to <<dim>something or something>; (0.47) .hh=yea; (1.04) we can
                bump to something;
    04   (0.75)
→   05 I: ↑why is it hotter (0.19) in the summer.

The pause that follows is much shorter than the one marked as having occurred within-turn. That is, whereas the interviewer treats the 1.04 second pause as within turn, the 0.75 second pause in turn 04 becomes a between-turn pause. The interviewer, without further formulating what he is doing, asks the next item on his list. In moving to the next item, he also communicates that the previous topic has been completed, at least for the time being and perhaps, unknown to the participants at this time, for good.

In the fragment from Chapter 4 that I already feature in the previous subsection, Lisa starts the topic with an utterance that Nina realizes in her turn as a question–answer pair. She tells the girl that she/they can repeat what they have done or "find out what the bridges should," and then follows up, "learn from them" (turn 06). The topic is completed as Nina turns to the boy, and Lisa walks away, talking to another member of her group (turn 10).

Fragment 8.21 (excerpt from Fragment 4.1)

    04 L: do [we ((b)) do it ⁻again
              [((Figure 4.1b))
    05   (0.65)
    06 N: you find [if you ↑want or you can go find `out what
                  [((Figure 4.1c))
           <<dim>`the bridges should do.>
    07   (0.92)
→   08   ^learn from them.
    09   (1.21)
→   10 L: <<all>we can do it [again [if we want, we are
                       [((Figure 4.1d))
           allowed to]>
    11 N: <<len>[this=is a::
           sample>]

In this and the preceding subsection, we see how pauses play a role in the transition between utterances and topics. However, pauses are not sure fire markers of transitions, as those that turn out to be within turns are often longer than those that turn out to be pauses between turns. The pauses in speech are a function of the contingencies of the unfolding situation as a whole. Moreover, as we see in the next subsection, pauses may constitute resources that interlocutors take as communicating something not available otherwise.

Pauses as resources for attributions (knowledge, understanding)

In the previous subsections, we see that pauses play an important role in the organization within and between turn utterances. In fact, we may fruitfully think of these pauses in speech as glimpses of the (generally untheorized) silent ground against which speech comes to appear as figure.[5] Speaking itself cannot lead us to an understanding of language. Speaking comes together with the possibilities of hearing/listening and being/keeping silent. While one person speaks, another generally is/keeps silent allowing her to listen/hear the speaker. It is out of this triple relation that the constitutive function of language in interaction for the existential nature of existence. Moreover, communication encompasses more than the verbal means, and much of what is to be communicated is available in the totality that a situation offers to those who both make it (like a habit [garment]) and inhabit it with their habits (Roth 2004). Pauses, then, can be used to make attributions to the other. For example, in the referenced study, there are often long pauses in a scientific laboratory while images are passing by on a computer monitor perceptually accessible to all three members to the setting. The study shows that absent talk actually indicates alignment of the participants and talk occurs precisely when there are, what comes to be known subsequently, as different assessments of an image that has just disappeared. The perceptual gestalts on the computer monitor are an integral part of the participative thinking that occurs even though the members of the laboratory do not speak.

In the present book, too, we find instances where participants take a developing pause as an indication that another person may not know or may not have understood. This is the case in Fragment 8.22, an excerpt from Chapter 5, where something we can hear as a question based on the structure of the utterance and its intonation (turn 01) is followed by a long, 2.29-second pause (turn 02) before the interviewer speaks again. He formulates the pause as a possible indication that AJ may not know an answer ("if you don't know it's fine"), and, to ascertain that not knowing is indeed the case, invites the girl to say "I don't know." (This actually is another case where quasi-direct speech is at work, here in a prospective mode, as indicated by the present tenses in the assessment "if you don't know" and the formulation ["you just say"] of what is to be done ["I don't know"].) Here, *being dumb*, in the dictionary sense of not speaking, reticent to speak, is treated as an indication of being dumb, in the dictionary sense of ignorant or stupid.

Fragment 8.22 (excerpt from Fragment 5.4)

```
        01  I:   so which one you think (0.93) uh p mo show (0.61) the shape of
                 the orbit?
→       02       (2.29)
        03       if you dont know its fine. you just say i dont know- (0.72) o:r- uh;
```

In turn 02, there is a possibility for AJ to take a turn or to make a bid for a next turn. But a pause develops, which means, *both* members to the setting keep silent. Silence not only belongs to talk as existential possibility, it assists us to better understand the constitutional function of talk in being. It is the absence of AJ's talk that the interviewer takes as a possible indicator of lack of knowledge. "The one who in interlocution keeps silent can more authentically 'let understand,' that is, develop understanding, than the one who never runs out of words" (Heidegger 1977b: 164). In keeping silent, AJ "lets" the interviewer "understand" that she does not have something to say and is not in the position to articulate an answer.

We encounter a similar case in Chapter 2, when Annemarie asks Daniel whether she is right after having provided some reading of the graph. This question already follows a 0.93 second pause, as if she offered an opportunity for the other to take a turn. There is another pause following her question, ended by an interjection ("hhum") followed by more silence. Annemarie then utters with a rising intonation characteristic of a question, "round this region?" In this, we can hear her specify the content of her question, which presupposes that this specification is not just gratuitous, but required were David not to have understood what the question is about. The latter does eventually answer, so that the respecification does, in fact, achieve the outlined effect of clarifying the question. Here, then, the pauses, if understood as Daniel's silences, would signal the possibility that he has not understood.

Fragment 8.23 (excerpt from Fragment 2.2)

```
        33       so they=re both increasing but the birthrate invar is faster increasing
                 than the death rate so presumably that means that the population is
                 increasing. (0.93) is that right then?
        34       (0.88)
        35  D:   hhum
        36       (0.43)
→       37  A:   round [this] region?
```

Silence at the instant where the possibility is created for another to speak, for example, in the opening offer to a question–response pair, may also be taken as an indication that the interlocutor does not know, or rather, as in Fragment 8.24 from Chapter 1, as an indication that the nature of the question itself, what it is asking for, has not been understood. In turn 49, the teacher asks, "what did we put for the name of that group?" A pause begins to develop, which is 1.51 seconds when it ends, an ending brought about when the teacher takes another turn, "what's written on the card" (turn 51).

Fragment 8.24 (excerpt from Fragment 1.1c)

```
     49  T:                      ^[₄WHAt ] ↑was the (0.15) ^WHAt ↑did we
              put for the name of that group.
→    50      (1.51)
     51      whats written on the₁] [₅card.]
              ((still points))      ₁] [₅((Pulls hand back, no longer points))
     52      (0.26)
     53  C:  <<pp>s:::::><<p>quares>-
```

In this statement, we can hear a translation of the earlier question into a new one that has the same content, the name given to the group of objects in which Connor's object has found its place. (The conversation that follows lets us know that this is the content of the question.) Such translations occur precisely when misunderstanding or non-understanding is detected as a way to remedy the situation and to bring about the desired mutual understanding (participative thinking). We know that this is likely the case, as Fragment 8.25 immediately arises from a preceding teacher–question that Connor succeeds by posing a question in turn, "what do you mean like?"

Fragment 8.25 (excerpt from Fragment 1.1c)

```
     46  T:  em an ↑what did [₁we say that [₂group was about.]
                            [₁((points toward objects on the floor,
              Figure 1.1, maintained until turn 51))
                                        [₂((makes tiny circular movement
              with index finger))
→    47      (1.00)
→    48  C:  <<p>what do you [₃mean li[₄ke?>]]
                            [₃((touches "his" cube, Figure 1.2))
                               [₄((looks up to T))
```

In asking what the teacher means, Connor makes explicit that the content of her question is not clear to him. Connor's request already has been preceded by a one second pause, another indication for a possible lack of understanding. Thus, turn 51 actually constitutes a possible repetition of turn 47 in the sense that it communicates the same state of affairs; Connor does not know what it is that the teacher is asking him about. The silence also allows us to understand the relationship between speaking and knowing (e.g., the link between logos and logic in the Greek language and the ensuing logocentrism) or between being dumb and being dumb. But talking may also produce stupidities, so that talking itself does not mean that the speaker knows. Therefore, keeping silent more than talking exhibits the existential possibilities of humans that come with language, which the early Greeks captured in the saying that constitutes humans as the speaking animal (*zōon logon ekhon*).

Grammar as contingent achievement in context

In this chapter, I provide analyses—using conversation fragments from preceding chapters—of the occasioned achievement of grammatical structure within and across utterances and turns at talk. Thus, one utterance may turn out to be grammatically incomplete but is completed, as a grammatical statement, by another person. The incompleteness may be by design, a designedly incomplete statement, and therefore an achievement of grammatical incompletion within the turn, completed across turns, and, therefore, in a collaborative manner. In this chapter, I also mobilize examples of difference in grammatical structure that emerges from the reporting of speech, including the mobilization of tenses and tense changes, and the associated openness to questioning (e.g., the achievement of direct reported speech versus indirect reported speech). Pragmatically, therefore, grammar, situation, content, and veracity of this content are irreducibly intertwined. That is, text and *con*text are inseparable, when both forms of text are of the linguistic sort, but especially when *con*text is of nonlinguistic sort available in the situation, and even more so when it is of the sort completely inaccessible to, and situationally not accessed by, consciousness. This is precisely what matters to the evolution of language, the individualization of possibilities, rather than the stable forms of grammar (Bakhtine [Volochinov] 1977). Subsequently, the realizations are solidified in formal grammar, while halting on this point the evolution of language.

Turns, topics, and phrases (statements, questions) are indeterminate. There are no pre-set boundaries. Whether they are achieved, how they are achieved, and the structure they achieve has to be theorized as something contingent and, therefore, matters of empirical analysis rather than presupposition. The achievement never is that of a single person but rather it is one that all members to the setting/conversation accomplish by acting in a given situation in its totality. This exemplifies a state of affairs in previously articulated philosophy of language where the utterance itself is understood as an evolutionary process embedded in, and structured by, other processes at a very different scale. Writing about the method for studying the real evolution of language at different time scales, one text notes that

> The social relations evolve (as a function of the infrastructures), then communication and verbal interaction evolve within the frame of social relations, the form of speech acts [*actes de parole*] evolve from the fact of verbal interaction, and the process of evolution is reflected, finally, in the change of forms of language [*langue*].
>
> (Bakhtine [Volochinov] 1977: 137–8)

Thus, the real substance of language [*langue*] does not exist as an abstract system of linguistic forms or as isolated monologic utterance or as psycho-physiological act of utterance production—the standard approaches to language—but as a social phenomenon of verbal interaction realized in and through utterances and turn-taking. Verbal interaction, therefore, not syntax, semantics, psychophysiology, and the likes "constitute in this way the fundamental reality of language [*langue*]" (Bakhtine [Volochinov] 1977: 136). In this way, "the structure of the utterance is a purely social structure" (Bakhtine [Volochinov] 1977: 141). But it is not a social structure that determines interactions; rather, it is a structure always achieved in and through contingently ordered interactions. Consistent in this conversation analysis (Rawls 1989), grammar is not a precondition for sense and signification, but is itself a contingent form of ordering interaction order.

The upshot of this book in general, but of the present chapter in particular, is a world always in the making, always open, unfinalized and non-finalizable, contingently achieved in and through acting-in-setting that draws on all available (semiotic) resources for marking, re-marking, and remarking sense, which may, but does not have to be, in the form of talking. It is this world, continually in the making, that we learn to navigate in walking the walk while we talk the talk—an issue that I now turn to in Chapter 9.

9   Con/textures

Der Mensch spricht [Man speaks]
Die Sprache spricht [Language speaks]

(Heidegger 1985: 9, 10)

Throughout this book, we see people in specific societal circumstances engaged in the business of talking, and, in so doing, not only engaged in realizing the talk of business but also in bringing the very business into existence. Or, rather, we see people in various forms of conversations. In and through their conversations, sequentially ordered turn-taking, through diachronic and synchronic communication features, they produce the very structures of (immortal) society that social scientists note and describe. To do so, these scientists require the same conversational skills that the people they study display. The essence/being/life of language, therefore, is the relation of speaking to language. Talk realizes and singularizes the possibilities of language in a concrete way. It is only one moment in the totality of life, which constitutes a network of significations in which that which is properly language in language and everything else constitute a text. This text *is not*—is not in the sense of a finalized entity—but continually becomes, undergoing continual transformation, having both a limited thematized moment and an unlimited (bottomless pit) of unnamed and unnamable dimensions. The resulting con/textures reflect the tissue of language and life it theorizes. In this penultimate chapter, I weave together—thus con/texture—a phenomenological and, therefore, pragmatic perspective on language from the works of such philosophers as Martin Heidegger, Jacques Derrida, and Mikhail Bakhtin. Much of this perspective goes against the mainstream current of present-day thinking on language, learning, and context. In this chapter, I weave together different texts—my own analyses and those of language philosophers—creating con/textures by means of which I create con/jectures (literally, a throwing together, Lat. *conjicĕre)* concerning language, learning, and contexts.

The dominating mainstream current of thought places primacy on intentionality: it is the starting point, driver, and ending point of theories of language use, discourse, and talking. It is "phallogocentric" (Derrida 1996: 131), for it emphasizes language (*logos*) and reasoning (*logos*) as we have come to know it through the history of Western thought in the Greek tradition, culminating in the ratiocinations of Immanuel Kant (the Logodaedalus). But the examples provided throughout this book exhibit the fact that intentionality cannot be the paradigm on which to build a solid theory of language, its concrete realization in speech, and the various other forms of thinking about language, learning, and context that appear in the frameworks of constructivism in all of its different brands (social, radical, etc.). In a relevant pun on Heidegger's formula, Paul de Man (1979: 277) writes "*Sprache verspricht (sich)*," which can be heard both as "language promises" and "language makes a slip of tongue." Language is about ... something and makes and simultaneously promises the truth of the said. Derrida (1988b), picking up on this pun in his *Mémoires for Paul de Man*, notes—against speech act theory—that difference between the constative (saying about) and the performative (promise) of language becomes undecidable. There is never just one meaning but always already an excess in language, thereby undermining the traditional view of language as a code or tool.

In Chapter 2, we see how in talking *about* something, the interlocutors *make* the very situation that constitutes the framing condition—the *con*text, the text surrounding text, literally the tissue, from Latin *texēre*, to weave—of their content talk. This context, therefore, constitutes another form of the excess of language. Words (text) contribute to making the very context that allows us to understand them and their sense. In talking the talk, we walk the walk; and this walk is not causally (pre-) determined but an exploration that lays the garden path in walking. The situation between Annemarie and David (Chapter 2) in particular shows how we can never know whether the situation in which we enter is actually sustained in and through our talking, so that we might *find* ourselves in very different situations *of our own making*. This same kind of auto-affection is at work in the Chapter 3, concerned as it is with the evolution of the speaking | thinking unit, an auto-affection that allows the very possibility of changing the genre or producing a major error in a lecture. Here I show (a) how talk is but one of the forms in which a position in and onto the world is articulated and expressed; (b) that the very structure of the utterance needs to be understood from a more holistic phenomenon of communication, which also includes (deictic, iconic) gestures, prosody, body position, body orientation, and structures in the setting including those produced in and for the situation at hand (like the diagrams, notes on a chalkboard); and (c) that speaking and thinking have to be thought together as a speaking | thinking unit. Not only is language subject to the situation as a whole, speakers are subject to the possibilities of language—there is, as I show in Chapter 4, an essential passivity involved in using language. First, the language is not that of the singular (solipsistic) subject but always already has come from the Other and is both for the Other and, in and through our speaking, returns to the Other. This dimension of language shapes the utterance, because it cannot ever be what *I* want to express but is inherently recipient designed. Second, I show in Chapter 4 that the locution and intent do not capture the entire phenomenon of the utterance but that the effect (the perlocution) and the social evaluation also need to be taken into account. Speakers, however, are passive with respect to this effect, much as listeners are passive with respect to it. Interlocution therefore constitutes an ethical relation through and through.

In Chapters 5 and 6, we see how knowledge and identity are not entities, traits, or characteristics that someone "has," but that there are, in talking, essentially social aspects in what comes to be elicited and how it is elicited. Knowledge and identity are expressed even if a speaker has never thought about pertinent issues before, which means, that he or she does not have to have a previously "constructed" mental framework (conception, misconception) to participate in a conversation. Moreover, what interview participants say about identity is itself shaped by the auto/biographical genre available for telling a life, so that the interview text is shaped more by the requirements of genre and interaction rituals than by the singularity of a person's experiences. We see in these two chapters that "nothing verbal in human behavior ... can under any circumstances be reckoned to the account of the individual subject in isolation; the verbal is not his property but the property of his *social group* (his social milieu)" (Vološinov 1976: 86, original emphasis). Talk about phenomena or identity can figure as topic or as resource, and therefore have very different function in and on the conversation as well as on the unfolding topic. In Chapter 7, we see how prosody becomes an important resource not only in the expression of a person's position in and take on the world but also in the coordination of social situations. Prosody and rhythm are resources for social coordination, which we can observe across a variety of bodily phenomena; and the observed coordination at the bodily level is consistent with the degree of solidarity that members to the situation express when, reflexively, talking about events that have happened.

In Chapter 8, I use examples from the preceding chapter to show how different grammatical phenomena are interactive achievements even when we focus on the utterance of one speaker who uses direct, indirect, or quasi-direct reported speech—because this speaking is always designed for another, it is shaped by requirements of the listening. The completion of a topic, the beginning and ending of utterances, and the pauses within and across turns are all achievements rather than predetermined and determining slots that speakers enter. But as collective achievements, none of these phenomena is entirely under the control of a single person, so that any person is as much an agential subject producing it (*signatory*, author) as a patient subject (counter-signatory) to the *event-context* that emerges at a superordinate organizational level.

Every chapter of this book, therefore, provides material supporting the suggestion that we need a different way of thinking about language—it is more than the tool in the hands of the agential, intentional, and individualist go-getter typical for North America. Language is more than a mere topic; it constitutes the very ground that makes words as tool and topic possible. But language itself is only part of a more encompassing phenomenon: life in its totality. Therefore, language constitutes a ground that itself is grounded in a bottomless pit of unthematic and unthematized human experiences in a world that is partially of human making.

On the nature of language

In the scholarly literature on learning (e.g., in science, technology, engineering, or mathematics), language is a curious phenomenon because it hardly ever is theorized. It is used as if it were a code (e.g., in the concept of "code-switching") or as if it were a transparent medium that allows researchers to get at the mental structures of individuals. Language, then, comes to be a mere instrument to make something else—"misconceptions," "meaning," or "identity"—lending itself to intentions that themselves are not theorized. But we are always already in language, which makes it difficult to bring language to speak about language. "How is language as language?," asks Heidegger (1985: 10) rhetorically, and then responds, "*Language speaks.*" (In fact, the issue is a little more complicated than it appears in English, for the German word for language, *Sprache*, is the noun accompanying the verb *sprechen*, to speak.) As the introductory quote to this chapter shows, this response appears on the page following another proposition with the same verb but a different subject: man speaks. We may hear these two statements as articulating a contradiction in that the second statement makes language speak independently of the question "*who* speaks?" If language speaks, it does so independently of the speaker, who but realizes language and linguistic possibilities in a concrete way. The speaker, therefore, does not control and intend language, what it says, which always exceeds what the speaker might have intended to say. If we say language speaks, then we allow there to be an excess over intentionality.

"Man speaks." Although we (scholars) speak it, "our relationship to language is undetermined, dark, *nearly speechless*" (Heidegger 1985: 150). This may sound strange, and one may be tempted to relegate such an undetermined relationship to simple speakers rather than to a scholar. To better understand language as language, we have to stop hearing (reading) what we already understand. This is the advice Heidegger gives, especially to the scholar who "attempts to speak of language, completely then, when this happens with the intent to show possibilities that permit to become thoughtful of language and our relation to it" (Heidegger 1985: 150). When in the course of our development we become aware of being, we always already speak, we always already are caught up in a world shot through with signification. Language and the world as we know it are inseparable. Moreover, we learn language before developing the capacities to understand its structure (grammar). Language, therefore, belongs to the closest neighborhood of the essence of being human. The upshot of this is that there is—as philosophers of language including Donald Davidson, Richard Rorty, and Valentin Vološinov say—no longer a difference between knowing a language and knowing one's way around the world, a point that the Swiss linguist Ferdinand de Saussure (1996) already made toward the end of the nineteenth century. Arguing in chemical language, and arguing about chemical representations, as Oprah does in Chapter 7, is indistinguishable from knowing one's way around a world of chemistry. In this, language does precisely what it is to do when it disappears (from consciousness)—much like a hammer that is ready to hand, allowing me to focus on hammering a nail into the wall for hanging a picture without itself demanding a place in consciousness, thereby vying for precious and limited space in my conscious experience. I am taking a position in the world and speak without thinking up words that I then pronounce to make available to another, much in the same way that I do not think about the hammer when I drive the nail into a wall. I do not see red lights ahead of me to be interpreted as the brake lights of a car about to slow down but I note a braking car and I brake in turn. When I speak competently, I participate in and I am absorbed by a particular situation in the world, rather than making this world present again by means of a reflexive turn of language.

The aforesaid makes it clear that we cannot come to an understanding of language and its structure by departing from the totality of life, of which language is an irreducible moment. Rather, we have to understand language out of its role as an integral part of the totality of life. "Language is the house of being," Heidegger (1985: 156) writes. Language and consciousness need to be understood out of dwelling *in* a world that makes any objective nature *of* the world possible—as Karl Marx and Friedrich Engels used to say, concrete life precedes and determines consciousness, it is not consciousness that determines life. "The idealizing subject that constitutes a priori its object and even the place where it finds itself does not, properly speaking, constitute them a priori but precisely, after the fact" (Levinas 1971: 126). The event always exceeds the knowing, the thought, and the idea in which the subject wants to enclose the event a posteriori. Spoken language is always an integral part of the world we inhabit, and we inhabit language as we inhabit the world.

So far I emphasize language. But language is but one among many ways of marking, re-marking, and remarking sense—though it certainly is a privileged one. Young children such as Connor (Chapter 1) or AJ (Chapters 2 and 5) do not develop an agential Self prior to language, they do not have articulated intentions prior to a language that allows them to articulate such. Therefore, to understand language and its structure, we need to think and theorize it from communication and life more generally. It is not an autonomous phenomenon with autonomous structure and semantics, but always already a heteronomous phenomenon, dependent on something always already outside it. But this outside only comes into existence with language so that language, as Derrida (1981) suggests, is without father. Language and its purpose arise simultaneously so that any author of a new language

> is typically unable to make clear exactly what it is that he wants to do before developing the language in which he succeeds doing it. His new vocabulary makes possible, for the first time, a formulation of its own purpose. It is a tool for doing something which could not have been envisaged prior to the development of a particular set of descriptions, those which it itself helps to provide.
>
> (Rorty 1989: 13)

At the point where poets, the creators of new languages, have arrived at this new language, they have already had tremendous amounts of experience in which the new idioms are grounded. The development of the new language itself constitutes an experience that contextualizes and grounds the language, but a grounding that can be understood and captured only after the fact. If exceptional people cannot understand the intention and purposes of a language prior to mastering it, how can it be otherwise for ordinary people? We can, therefore, use this way of thinking about language as an analogy for children and students learning new words, the sense and purpose of which they only come to understand once they use the words appropriately.

The essence of language—if there is such—is not that it produces the relationship between a word and a thing, word and some meaning behind. "The word itself is the relation, which in each case includes the thing so that it 'is' thing" (Heidegger 1985: 159). The question of how we can speak of language as language points us to the fact that language and world are tied together into a tissue/texture (Gr. *Geflecht*). Preston (Chapter 6) always already finds himself in such a tissue/texture and has had experiences to be articulated and drawn upon for talking about the topic that the teacher has broached; and part of this tissue/texture is such that it is both prior to being thematized in language and exceeds the questioning it enables. This tissue/texture denotes the interlacing of *Sprache* (language, tongue, speech), the world, and the path (*Weg*) that leads us to *Sprache*. "*Geflecht* is not one figure among others. We are implicated in it, interlaced in advance when we wish to speak of *Sprache* and *Weg*, which are 'already in advance of us'" (Derrida 2007a: 60). This, in essence, is what leads in Chapter 5 to the fact that speaking everyday language always already comes with resources to talk about scientific phenomena, and this talk frequently is inconsistent with the scientific canon. In Chapter 6, existing ways of talking lead to identity narratives that always already take familiar shape and content. But precisely because these ways of speaking are always already in advance of us, there is no sense in attempting to "eradicate" the ways of talking that students come to school with, that is, their "misconceptions" or in thinking about the identities of students as expressions of their singularity.

To sum up, language and life form an irreducible whole. Because this whole is irreducible, the path to language, therefore, is laid in talking. With respect to language, the idiomatic expression *walking the walk*, doing what one says one does, may well be replaced by *talking the talk*—which is precisely the subtitle of this book.

Intentionality, consciousness, understanding

> Intentionality, consciousness of … is attention to speech or welcome of the face, hospitality and not thematization … The subject is a host.
>
> (Levinas 1971: 276)

In much of the current scholarly literature, concerned as it is with agency, everyday life is thought of and theorized in terms of intentionality and intentional actions. This literature contrasts a long history of phenomenological analyses that exhibit the by-and-large tacit nature of much of what makes everyday cognition and the invisibility of the methods by means of which the structural coherence of everyday life is achieved. For example, we may read statements such as: "The concept of woman as positionality shows *how women use* their positional perspective as a place from which values *are interpreted* and *constructed* rather than as a locus of an already determined set of values" (Alcoff 2006: 148, emphasis added), or "Because engaging in agency *involves reflection* and the development of *awareness*, it necessitates that individuals *continually examine* their identities—who they are and how they change" (Basu et al. 2009: 360, emphasis added). In the first quote, women are said to *use* their positional perspective to *interpret* and *construct* values, thereby expressing an essentially intentional orientation to being in the world. Whereas critical women and feminists do indeed have intentions with respect to *aspects of reality*, much of what they do still is grounded in their familiarity with the world. Without this grounding in an always already familiar world, no intentionality would be possible because of the complexity of social life. (Who or what intends intentions?) This complexity comes to the fore in situations of breakdown, when the normal ethnomethods on which the regularities of society and social life are based—and which, in fact, produce this regularity—come to the fore because the normal ways of going about life no longer function. This is precisely the reasoning behind the method of the *breaching experiment* (Garfinkel 1967), which, in one way or another disrupts what people normally do—so that they find themselves exhibiting precisely the normally hidden and invisible ways by means of which societal structure is produced—to study the production of orderly society as a structured phenomenon.

In the second quote, which, again, is used as an example to stand for a whole approach to everyday cognition, the authors use intentional language whereby individuals are said to *reflect*, to *continually examine*, and to *be aware*. From a phenomenological perspective to everyday cognition, much of our everyday doing is a form of coping where the world and the things that populate it are pre-thematic, unthematized, and invisible; that which we can see and describe in words always already exists within a field, the visible *presupposing* the invisible (Merleau-Ponty 1964). The individuals featured in the chapters of this book—AJ and the interviewer, the professor, Mary and Penny, Preston, Oprah, or I—engage in conversations without thinking about the shoes (sandals) they are wearing, the clothing they don, the hairdo of the day, and so on. This is so even in the case of the glasses they wear, of which people generally become aware only if something is wrong—when these are fogged up, dusty, broken, or missing. Members to a setting talk without doing any of these things that sometimes are taken as indicators and indexes to their identities. They do not even reflect on the particular words they say and which they do not particularly choose— because the spontaneous emerges precisely "on the condition that it does not itself *present itself*" (Derrida 1972: 353). Rather, as we see in the conversations with Preston (Chapter 6), whatever is relevant is mobilized against everything else as ground; and the figure thereby created is in part independent of Preston, imposing itself upon him in total heteronomy. This does not mean that some teenager, for example, Oprah in Chapter 7, may not consciously think about how she does her hair or what jewelry she is choosing for the day. Rather, whether these aspects matter in the situation at hand has to be an empirical issue, and in this case, hairdo or jewelry or intentionality for speaking this way may turn out to be completely irrelevant to the topic, structure, and process of the conversations that the participants to a setting produce.

The intentionalist discourse has had a long history and, though it has been subjected to critique throughout the twentieth century, it continues to dominate much of the social science literature generally and the educational literature on language, learning, and context specifically. The essential element in the intentionalist approach—which can be found in the tradition of John Austin and John Searle—is

> consciousness, the conscious presence of the intention of the speaking subject in the totality of his speech act. From there, performative communication becomes once more the communication of an intentional sense, even if that sense has no

referent in the form of a thing or of an anterior or exterior state of things. The conscious presence of speakers or receivers participating in the accomplishment of a performative, their conscious and intentional presence in the totality of the operation, teleologically implies that nothing *is left* [qu'aucun *reste*] to escape the present totalization. Nothing is left, either in the definition of the requisite conventions or in the internal and linguistic context, or in the grammatical form, or in the semantic determination of the words used; no irreducible polysemy, that is to say, no "dissemination" escaping the horizon of the unity of sense.

(Derrida 1972: 383–4)

There is a limit to intentionality on other philosophical grounds as well. Thus, "any general framework, whether conceived as a grammar for English, or a rule for accepting grammars, or a basic grammar plus rules for modifying or extending it ... by virtue of the features that make it general, will by itself be insufficient for interpreting particular utterances" (Davidson 1986: 444). The problem is that what interpreters and speakers share in successful communication is not learned, which means it cannot be a language governed by rules known to the interlocutors in advance. On the other hand, what the interlocutors know in advance is not inherently shared so that it cannot be a rule- or convention-governed language. The only thing required for a conversation to be successful is the ability to converge, in situation and for the purposes on hand, on a sense—like the sense of a game in contrast to the physics of the game—of common understanding, a sense that can always be revised as needed when it becomes evident that the interlocutors have been at odds or at cross purposes in their mutual participative thinking. When Connor and his teacher find themselves talking at cross purposes, the former asks the latter, "what do you mean like?," which leads to an exchange that brings about a context within which the student comes to understand what the teacher wants him to do. In and with respect to what they bring to and find in a situation, the interlocutors are passive, as they cannot ever make thematic everything required in and to the reproduction and transformation of the situation at hand. The teacher does not design to be unintelligible to Connor; nor does she know what is required to become intelligible and so she provides several translations of the original request. With respect to the effect of her utterance, she is totally passive. Moreover, both are passive with respect to the language they use, its expressive capabilities—unless they make these capabilities thematic, something that generally takes tremendous efforts and work. Such work is possible in slow, exacting theoretical writing but is prohibitive in the unfolding of everyday affairs, where we act in real time without any time-out for reflection. Connor does not have to (and cannot) think about something to say, for which he searches and selects sound-words ("what," "do," "you," "mean," and "like") to say it, "thought and expression self-constitute simultaneously" (Merleau-Ponty 1945: 213–4). Speech expression, therefore, is a gesture that "indicates certain sensible points of the world, [that] invites me to join it there" (Merleau-Ponty 1945: 216). Here, the subjects learn from what they have said—an effect of the situation that derives precisely from the fact that nothing and nobody can be present to it-, him/herself.

In the theoretical approach taken here, intention does not disappear. Rather, it has "its place, but, from that place, it will no longer be able to govern the entire scene and system of utterance [*l'énonciation*]" (Derrida 1972: 389). The intention that animates an utterance never is entirely present to itself, that is, conscious of itself together with everything that makes the context. This is so because the "nerve center of any utterance, any expression, is not interior but exterior: it is situated in the social milieu that surrounds the individual" (Bakhtine [Volochinov] 1977: 134). That we cannot reduce intentionality to the subjective derives from the fact that language is reproduced, iterates itself, and therefore *comes with* a structure to which the speaker and audience are subjected and subject. It is iterability that leads to a certain degree of absence of intentionality so that, "above all, this essential absence of intention from the actuality of utterance, this structural unconsciousness, if you like, prohibits any saturation of the context" (Derrida 1972: 389). The exhaustive determinability of context would require, at the very least, a speech intention that is totally present and completely (immediately) transparent to itself and to its audience, as it is the germ of what becomes the context. It is not that there is no effect of consciousness, but rather that the things normally excluded in discussing intentionality presuppose what they are set against—non-intentionality, passivity, subjection in addition to being agential subject.

In speaking, therefore, language comes to be achieved, semantically (see especially Chapters 5 and 6) and syntactically (see especially Chapter 8). It is a fathomless ground, fathomless because it is itself part of the texture of material life, where much of what we practically know and understand, our sense of the game, never is nor can be thematic. Language is also the means, the tool, and a resource, for getting a job done, which may include the constitution of the relevant segment of the lifeworld at hand. And language may be a topic of talk (object) in its own right. Linguistic ability itself is the ability to converge on practical understanding (practical consciousness) in and of the situation at hand. This abandons the ordinary notion of a language and erases the boundary between knowing a language and knowing our way around in the world generally. There are no rules for how to arrive at shared practical understanding, so that "there is no more chance of regularizing, or teaching, this process than there is of regularizing, or teaching, the process of creating new theories to cope with new data in any field—for this is what this process involves" (Davidson 1986: 446). Davidson concludes that in thinking about a natural language—in contrast to the artificial languages that one might find in computing or logic—we have to give up the idea of a clearly defined shared structure that we learn and then apply to particular cases. Natural language applies to cases because it has grown out of them rather than because it has been developed as a general system to be applied to special cases.

The relation of speaking a language and understanding dates back to the ancient Greek, whose word for philosophical reflection and reason—i.e., *logos*—derived from the verb to speak (Gr. *legein*) and the associated noun for language (*logos*). Grammar, as science, was founded in and modeled on the logic of *logos* (Heidegger 1977b). But because of the existential role of speech to Being, grammar needs to be liberated from *logos* and become subject to the pragmatics of social interaction and the possibilities that arise to it from the pragmatics of speaking, from which, as I show in Chapter 8, grammar emerges as a contingent achievement—i.e., follows the incalculable (chaotic) logic of contingent emergence—rather than being a pre-existing structure that conditions observed and observable forms of speech.

The verbs *to speak* and *to talk* may already and prior to all thinking, shift our thinking and theorizing too much to the agential side. It is in fact hearing that is foundational to being and language as such. Thus, "hearing constitutes the primary and essential openness of Being-there for its own utmost possibilities of being, as hearing of the voice of the friend" (Heidegger 1977b: 163). Prior to anything else, children *hear* sound-words before they develop the capacities and competencies to speak and thereby deploy language. They hear and speak a language prior to being able to learn grammar, the latter process *presupposing* the very linguistic competencies that grammar describes. Being hears, because it understands: we normally do not hear random noises that we have to interpret so that they can become words—we generally hear words. The connection between hearing and understanding becomes evident in those situations where analysts cannot decipher what someone says even during multiple attempts of listening—only to hear precisely what is said should someone else offer a word. Moreover, from a developmental perspective, children hear (recurrent sound-words) precisely because they already have a practical understanding of the situation that they find themselves in as something that warrants recurrence.

The importance of hearing to speaking and understanding is immediately evident when we consider how we hear and understand the difference between direct and indirect speech as I describe it in Chapter 8. We hear when the interviewer directly quotes the fourth item from the questionnaire rather saying something else, as in Fragment 9.1.

Fragment 9.1 (excerpt from Fragment 6.3)

09 T: So when, when you think about the, ah, the number four, "Scientific laws and theories exist independent of human existence, and scientists merely discover them," would you say that is true, or …

We do not have stop and reflect to hear/understand. Talking is precisely premised by and on this possibility of the ability to hear/understand; and is structured by the same understanding. To understand literally means to stand amongst the things, and, deriving from the Proto-Indo-European root st(h)ā̄-, st(h)ə- "to stand," is found in other languages equally related to comprehension, including the German equivalent *verstehen* and the Greek *epi-stamai*, "understand." We understand not the individual sound-word, utterance, or turn but the situation as a whole; and it is out of this whole that individual words take their sense. Thus we can understand sentences even though we do not know, hear, or know the sense of each word.

Existentially, talking arises from the possibility of and for hearing. Hearing, and therefore speaking, is tied to understanding, which is evident from English expressions such as "I hear you" in the sense of "I understand what you are saying," or "I heard nothing more about it" in the sense of "I had no more information about it." Even more poignantly, the close relation of hearing and speaking comes to the fore in expressions such as "to hear tell/talk" as in "you may have heard talk about possible bankruptcy of General Motors" or in "he knew by hearing tell of it." Hearing/listening constitute the existential openness of human beings to the Other, forcefully captured in the expression "to hear to" in the sense of listen to, obey, take orders from. "*Dasein* [being-there] hears," writes Heidegger (1977b: 163), "because it understands. As an understanding Being-in-the-world with the Other, it listens to *Mitdasein* [being-there-with] and to itself and thereby belongs to these." It is for these reasons that we do not just hear noises that we interpret: we tend to hear *the wind* rustling in the leaves, *a motorbike* approaching fast, *a woodpecker* pounding away on a nearby tree. In the same way, we do not just hear noises but we hear the talk of an Other as something said and expressed to us. We already know what the talk is about. Even in pathological cases, we *hear* incomprehensible and inaudible or foreign words—which transcribers denote by possible hearings (as in "(injured?)") or a sign of omission (as in "(??)")—rather than noise and sound complexes.

The relationship between speaking and understanding the world (as) we know (it) is further clarified when we consider two very different senses of the verb "to articulate" (the noun "articulation"). On the one hand, to articulate means to express, convey, utter, or pronounce. In this way, to articulate is directly tied to and synonymous with talking. On the other hand, to articulate also means, in transitive use, to create an articulation, a joint, to bring together different pieces; in intransitive use, to articulate means to be united by a joint, to meet or form a joint. In this way, the verb is related to the structure of our lifeworld, where its joints lie allows us to tell where its different composites join and what its elements or moments are. We *articulate* something, that is, we tell something apart, precisely at its joints, places in the world that can be articulated in both of the senses of the word developed here. At the same time, we often do not articulate, see the complexity and composite nature of something whole unless we have a way of articulating what its pieces are.

This mutually constitutive relationship is evident on both historical time scales and at the scales of individual development (ontology), for example, in phenomena related to heat and temperature. Historically, there was only one phenomenon and only over time, especially in the seventeenth and eighteenth century, scientists were beginning to tell two phenomena apart, one pertaining to heat as energy and the other to temperature ("hot" and "heat" have the same etymological roots). In the nineteenth century, it became clear that an additional concept was involved, entropy. That is, what was initially one phenomenon/concept unfolded into three phenomena denoted by the terms energy (heat), temperature, and entropy. Similarly, in the course of their individual development, students come to *articulate* the differences between heat (energy) and temperature, and those in more advanced science courses learn that the energy required to change the state of a substance is related to the change in entropy. Here, being able to articulate (utter) words generally precedes the articulation of phenomena, but they know the word, that is, use the word appropriately only when they properly articulate the situation/phenomenon.

Meaning, theme, signification

In the scholarly literature that treats (of) language, learning, and context, the assumption is often made that familiar contexts allow students to "construct meaning," and, when they are confronted with new words, to construct the "meaning of words." Authors making such statements generally do not tell us what this "meaning" is, and, according to linguists, there is a general confusion about the meaning of "meaning" and understanding, not in the least because they are used inconsistently and, sometimes, in mutually exclusive ways (Nöth 1990). What precisely is it that students construct when they are said to have "constructed" "the meaning" of a word? What do the authors mean when they write that the term "conceptual reconstruction" "*indicates* the meaning we have in mind when using the term conceptual change in our work" (Treagust and Duit 2008: 386)? What is it that the term *indicates*? Why do the authors not tell us the meaning? How can we find out if it is *in* their minds but not out in the open? And what is the relationship between meaning, sense, reference, word, concept, and the sound wave (that we hear as a word)? *Meaning* sometimes is used synonymous with *sense*, sometimes with *reference*; and this is so even though semioticians clearly make a distinction between sense (the relationship of signs) and reference (the relation of a sign to the thing it denotes).

Yet despite all this ambiguity, *meaning* is an expression recurrently used in the current Anglo-Saxon scholarly literature—concerning what comes to be a product of language use. Thus, students are said to "construct meaning" where the nature of what they construct remains unarticulated. One of the ways in which the term meaning is evident in translations of foreign language works, such as *Marxism and Philosophy of Language* (Vološinov 1973) and *Limited Inc* (Derrida 1988a). In both instances, a word that in French appears as *sens* (sense, in the sense of dictionary sense) is translated—not always consistently and staying the same—as meaning. This multiplicity of the word-sign, for both Bakhtin and Derrida, precisely is the upshot of language as the possibility of communication. Derrida poses a question about *communication* and then states that to articulate this question "*il a déjà fallu que j'anticipe sur le sens du mot* communication: *j'ai du prédéterminer la communication comme le véhicule, le transport ou le lieu de passage d'un sens et d'un sens un*" [it was necessary that I anticipate the sense of the word *communication*: I had to predetermine communication as a vehicle, the transport or location of the passage of a *sense* and a *unique* sense] (1972: 367, original emphasis). The official English translation of the same passage reads like this: "I have had to anticipate the meaning of the word *communication*: I have been constrained to predetermine communication as a vehicle, a means of transport or transitional medium of a *meaning*, and moreover of a *unified* meaning" (Derrida 1988a: 1). What confuses matters are translations of other words, such as *vouloir-dire* (wanting to say, as in "what do you mean?"), which in the English text appears both as "meaning" and "intention."

But is dictionary sense what students are to construct? Certainly not, for children may know the dictionary sense of a word and, employ it in a literal way, often use it inappropriately, in inappropriate contexts, and in inappropriate circumstances. Dictionary sense is what is iterable and, though not unique, is limited precisely to the extent specified by the dictionary. Is it intention that students are to construct?

Certainly not, as intention is presupposed in the construction. What else might be associated with a word-in-use? Bakhtine [Volochinov] (1977), who place the iterable dictionary sense as the lower limit of the linguistic capacity to signify the opposite to the *theme*, which constitutes the upper limit of signification. That is, in contrast to the repeatable, self-identical, and, therefore, iterable word, the theme is what the word marks in singular, once-occurrent manner, in context and in event (*Ereignis*). And this is precisely what cannot be *constructed*, as both Bakhtine's *theme* and Derrida's *différance* denote and come with the irreducible absence of intention or conscious attendance to (presence of) the "most contextual [*événementiel*, 'event-natured'] utterance there is" (Derrida 1972: 390). Speech is the existential-ontological foundation of language. It comes with being attuned and (practical) understanding, a situation Bakhtin (1993) denotes by the term *participative thinking*. In talking, we articulate intelligibility; talking and intelligibility presuppose, produce, and transform each other in and for the practical purposes at hand, in the short term, and, observable especially on longer time scales, lead to the transformation of language as semantic, syntactic, phonetic, and so on system [*langue*].

Heidegger and Wittgenstein, two scholars concerned with showing how we make sense of the world and the function of language in our everyday coping, actually take a similar approach, both of which are appealing in the context of the present discussion. Thus, words do not have something attached to them that would be called "meaning, something students would 'construct'." Rather, whatever the term denotes: "Let use *teach* you the signification" (Wittgenstein 1958: 212).[1] It is in use, in actual practice that we come to utter sounds; and it is the regularity with which situations and certain sounds occur in our experience that both become familiar and come to stand in a special, recurrent relation. This is consistent with another way of relating words and a familiar world: "To the significations, words accrue. But word-things do not receive signification" (Heidegger 1977b: 161).[2] Thus, words, as signifiers, merely are part of some situation that make other parts (signifieds) stand out. Their function is, as Wittgenstein says, apparent in their concrete use. A look back at Fragment 1.1c allows us to clarify these issues.

Signification, therefore, precedes the use of words such that speaking presupposes the where-of (that which the talk is about), what is said as such, communication, and testimony. This has radical consequences for learning in that there is a priority for significations over words rather than the other way around. If students are to "construct meaning [of words]," leaving aside the philosophically untenable concept of construction, then the position worked out here means that students always already have to have a practical understanding of the world before words can be used to mark, re-mark, and remark the sense in and of specific situations. It is not that there are initially words, which come to receive meaning, but that there have to be significations to which sound-words accrue in the sense that they are useful signs/markers of an always-and-already existing sense. At the moment toddlers articulate the sounds mə'ma: or pə'pa: for the first time, they have already a considerable history of interacting with people generally and with those that we call "mamma" and "papa" specifically. They hear these sounds in the context of mamma's and papa's faces prior to knowing any sense (or "meaning"); the sounds go with these faces as milk goes with the mamma ('mæmə, i.e., breast). This relation of familiar worlds and the regular sound-words we use is also relevant to older children, as shown in the following ever-too-brief analysis.

In saying "that group," the teacher of Chapter 2 produces the material sound phonetically transcribed as "ðæt gru:p" to orient Connor to something else in the setting, apparently, as the unfolding events suggest, to "the group" of three cubes at the boy's feet. She also uses a pointing (deictic) gesture that goes with it, which we understand as but another way of making "that group" stand out from the ground of the classroom lifeworld as such. Finally, she produces a circular movement with her index finger, iconically grouping and representing grouped objects. All three, the sound, hand-finger thrust forward (Figure 1.3a), and the circling gesture (Figure 1.3b) function as things that expressly bring something else into view that before has been but part of the unattended to and invisible ground against which their talk is unfolding. But all three are material things and processes, and, as such, are but aspects of the material situation as a whole. In the same way, the question "what's written on the card?" asks the student, in his response, to bring to the fore something that has previously been marked (by the other teacher in the room) on some card, which, a cursory gaze, may find next to "that group," which actually assists in finding "the card." The sounds, heard as part of language, actually are an integral part of the situation allowing other parts of the situation to make themselves be noted (see Chapter 3). This analysis brings two very important issues to the fore, issues that are at the heart of this entire book.

First, if language, as sound, is but part among other parts of being, then it loses a bit of its special and mythical status that it currently has in scholarly discourse. With Donald Davidson (1986) we might say looking at the featured episode that there is no more distinction between knowing the language of geometry and knowing one's way around the world of the geometry classroom. There is nothing that we have to add to or construct for language, such as "meaning"; there is only the process of becoming familiar with a world that we inhabit, which includes familiarity with, and fluent use of, language. The world as a whole, that is, the ensemble of the material world, social relation, and communication, constitute an infinitely textured whole, something like a piece of cloth where both the warp and the weft exist of the same material. Thus, "the *interlacing* (*Verwebung*) of language of that in language that is purely language and of the other threads of experience constitute a piece of cloth" (Derrida 1972: 191). "Words" are just translated physical sounds, hand and arm gestures are produced by material bodies, intonation arises from variations in the pitch of the vibrating vocal cords, all interwoven into a tissue, with complex texture, text (from Lat. *text-us*, past participle of *tex-ĕre*, to weave). Therefore, every word as every sign "can engender new contexts ad infinitum and in a manner that is not saturable" so that in the end "there are nothing but contexts without any center and absolute anchorage" (Derrida 1972: 381). Language as a part of the textured whole that makes life leads us to realize another interesting feature: the indexical properties of all language (Garfinkel and Sacks 1986). Earlier, I show how "that group," the pointing gesture, the iconic gesture making a circle, and other aspects of the setting are signs that point to each other. All sound-words in this sense point to other sound-words, things, gestures, prosodic variations, and so on.

Second, there exists a reflexive relation between the different forms of signifiers we use and other things (i.e., signifieds) in the world, which may be objects, groups of objects (categories), phenomena, or other signifiers. Recognizable and iterable word-sounds can be used to bring to the fore objects, may be used to get other people to attend or do something, but these other aspects of the setting motivate the production of the sound. This includes the title of a book, which, identically, functions very differently in the text—I use repeatedly "language, learning, and context," including as citation in this sentence. And, strangely enough, we cannot ever say which of these two, the part of the text or the title is the original and which one the citation (Derrida 1986). Similarly, in any setting where a conversation takes place, there are things that make salient some parts of the sound stream, such as when intensity and pitch increase, thereby emphasizing and drawing attention to some word-sounds over other word-sounds.

The texture Derrida writes about, the contexts, constitute the very systems of signification to which words accrue for Heidegger. Iterable sense is only the lower limit whereas what students have to learn is connecting it with concrete particulars to form the *theme*. The words are only signifiers and students do not yet know the signifieds and, therefore, they do not know the sign—the signifier–signified relation—and signification. Proper word-use, therefore, brings together the iterable and repeatable in and of human experiences and the never repeatable, the once occurrent—it constitutes the coming together of the rule (sense) and the solicitude of the instant. To exemplify once more, I return to Fragment 1.1c. As in other places of this chapter, I return to "that group." The teacher asks Connor, "what did we say that group was about." Dictionaries may have different entries for the word "that," which may function as a demonstrative pronoun, adjective, and adverb, relative pronoun, or conjunction, each followed by a number of entries. Thus, for example, *The Oxford English Dictionary* (2009) lists eight major entries under *that* as a demonstrative pronoun, each with from two to six subentries. "Group" is listed separately as a verb and as a noun, the latter of which has six entries with up to six subentries. What the teacher says, or rather, what would be constant across different situations and settings, could be found among these entries. But what she says in the here and now of this classroom at this instant, what she means to say is something utterly singular. Here it is addressing Connor, taking his turn at this point following and followed by a number of other turns, with the intent to make him utter the words that are written on "the card," that is, she wants him to utter the name/characteristics that come with the group of objects geometrically proficient individuals generally denote by the word "cube." This is precisely what Bakhtin denotes by the word *theme*, the once occurrent function of the utterance mobilizing certain words that here solicit a particular response from Connor. What the student can learn, and learns, is bringing together the dictionary sense of the signifier with the signified in this situation. As he does not immediately (participatively) understand the theme, Connor asks for a translation, of which the teacher supplies not only one but two ("what did we put for the name?" "what's written on the card?"), before the intended response is provided, requiring another interaction and completion involving Jane.

10 Différance

Already it had to be marked that *différance is not*, does not exist, is not a being-present (on), whatever it may be; and we will have to mark everything that it is not, that is, everything; and consequently that it has neither existence nor essence.

(Derrida 1972: 6)

What is written as *différance* then will be the movement of the game that produces these differences, the effects of difference, by means of something that is not simply an activity.

(Derrida 1972: 12)

Throughout this book, we encounter situations that apparently involve contradictions. For example, the unit of analysis considers two and even three turns at once so that the speech act comes to be distributed across two individuals (see Chapter 4). The speech situation is not given but produced at the same time that speakers contribute to the making of the topic: text and context are not different but, in part, are produced in the same act. The speech act itself is a diastatic process, an event that is shifted with respect to itself in position (speaking/hearing), intent/production (locution, illocution) and effect (perlocution), and in time (perlocutionary effect apparent only after locution). I also show that there are simultaneously agential and passive aspects in the articulation of knowing, for example, about astronomy (Chapter 5), and in the articulation and mobilization of identity along the lines of self|other (Chapter 6). Moreover, the concept of thinking|speaking no longer allows us to speak independently about what a person thinks and what the person says (e.g., Chapter 3); and this idea grounded in Vygotsky is associated with a similar shift in language at the cultural–historical level, whereby language is renewed each time a word is used (Bakhtine [Volochinov] 1977). In any event, because speakers articulate thoughts for the Other, the said never can be understood from the intention alone but is always also structured by the recipients. When others do not understand, they can always ask the speaker what she means, thereby ask for a translation at the heart of the language and back into the language itself, a process that points us again to the heterogeneous nature of language that cannot be self-identical.

All of these phenomena suggest that we require a way of working able to capture, or at least to obliquely denote or enact, the observed hybridity and heterogeneity. Language is a multiplicity and, if we want to think language from language, as I cite Martin Heidegger to have said in the preceding chapter, then we need to build a theory that begins rather than ends in multiplicity. Where does this multiplicity come from? Many language philosophers agree that it comes from language itself, which, precisely because it is different from itself continually tropicalizes and metaphorizes itself in use (writing), a process Derrida (1972) obliquely refers to as *différance*. But *différance* is not a concept: it is, where Derrida emphasizes that the "is" itself needs to be crossed out, a movement of play that produces difference. We therefore require ways of thinking that are able to handle the difference produced by *différance* positively: difference in itself rather than difference derived from, and therefore less than, sameness.

Over the years, my thinking with respect to the nature of language has evolved from taking it as a transparent means into the mind of students (during my dissertation) to a tool for producing and reproducing reality (e.g., in discursive psychology) and to an integral part of the fabric of life composed of linguistic, pre-, and non-linguistic moments. I arrived at my "movement" in and through the play consisting of (a) a close, slow listening to and reading of recorded audiotapes and videotape transcripts, and (b) a close, slow reading of continental philosophy and its close attention not only to the agential aspects of language-in-use (which is the route Anglo-Saxon scholars have gone) but also its passive moments (see Chapters 4 and 9). In fact, much of the literature in which my work is grounded is the result of bringing together phenomenological concerns with those of dialectical and dialogical thinking, such as it has been developed in the lineage from G.W.F. Hegel and K. Marx. This lineage of thinking has led to the emergence, on the one hand, of the Russian social psychology that Lev Vygotsky and his students founded and the group around Mikhail Bakhtin, and on the other hand, to the emergence of the philosophy of difference that Friedrich Nietzsche and Martin Heidegger announced and that mainly French philosophers subsequently developed.

In much of the mainstream, the dominant and dominating views of language and scientific literacy are based on an epistemology that begins the presupposition of the identity of a thing with itself:

> VOICE-OVER: Because the thinking of metaphysics remains involved in the *difference which as such is unthought*, metaphysics is both ontology and theology in a unified way …
>
> (Heidegger 1957: 139, emphasis added)

Both the phenomenon of representation (inscription) and the figure of the scientist as rational thinker and actor are premised on this identity. Yet no text can be thought in and of itself. Any text always already is read in the *con*text of a world of texts that it itself contributes to producing, that the text, in fact, presupposes for the possibility of being read in an understanding way. The voice-over in this paragraph makes this relationship between text and context salient and a topic of the paragraph. Thus, the referent of any text is "no longer the *Umwelt* of the ostensive references of dialogue, but the *Welt* projected by the nonostensive references of every text that we have read, understood, and loved" (Ricœur 1986: 211). This inherent feature of all written texts is articulated in and by the use of voice over or parallel texts, texts within texts, that mutually refract each other—as exemplified in a number of texts that Jacques Derrida produced including *Glas* (Derrida 1974) and "Tympan" (in Derrida 1972) and which I, together with a number of colleagues (e.g., Roth and McRobbie 1999), have used in a variety of scholarly articles on knowing and learning in science classrooms.

Recent philosophical scholarship generally, and the French philosophers of difference and dialectics particularly—among them Gilles Deleuze, Jacques Derrida, Didier Franck, Jean-Luc Nancy, Paul Ricœur—take a very different perspective on the question of language. This perspective emphasizes that the opposite, the non-self-identity of a thing or person with it or him/herself is more compatible with our experiential reality—as articulated throughout this book in the empirical analyses. In this, these philosophers articulate an approach already chosen earlier by Mikhail Bakhtin, who recognized that unless language changed at the instant someone produced an utterance, we would not be able to understand the *internal* dynamics that make language a living, cultural–historical phenomenon. A language is dead, unchangingly frozen in a permanent state, precisely when it is no longer spoken (as is the case for classical Latin). For Bakhtin (1984b) as for Nietzsche (1954b), language is something living. Spoken language, therefore, inherently and unavoidably changes—in particular the spoken language of the people rather than the written works of the middle and upper classes—and for Derrida (e.g., 1981), it is the concatenation of writing, "that movement which situates every signified as a differential trace," that produces continual change in language and thought. Yet change is precisely the least theorized linguistic phenomenon in the literature on learning—yet it is this that we are confronted with on a daily basis. But if continual change is the case, if living language changes at the very instant that someone realizes it, then language cannot be self-identical. Such a perspective is not wishy-washy hand waving and fuzzy talk with the label "postmodern." It is a serious position that better theorizes the learning of language in the indeterminate manner in which they concretely (observably) realize themselves, whether the observational sites are school science classrooms, community controversies over environmental resources, or the workplaces of scientists and technicians. In the present chapter, I further develop an approach to language and literacy articulated in my recent writing, adding to the sets of concepts (a) *bricolage, métissage,* and hybridization, (b) diaspora, (c) heterogeneity and hybridity, and (d) mêlée (Roth 2008a, 2009b).

The theory built from this set of concepts is suitable for providing explanatory descriptions of learning as instances where students come face to face with a foreign and strange idiom that has facts, theories, and concepts as its topics and resources. But because the radically foreign always lies inexorably and unreachably beyond our horizons, the relatively strange is appropriated only when the relatively familiar already contains an element of the relatively strange, that is, the individual not yet capable of speaking a specific idiom already has the possibility to speak this foreign idiom. Language, therefore, is a mêlée of the simultaneously familiar and strange, it is a continuous process (rather than a thing) non-identical with itself: it is a river. This river continually changes, each time someone speaks, with each word; and it is only because language changes with each utterance that it is undergoing historical change, from the inside so to speak. Change is built into language and does not require great poets and writers. The perspective I develop in this chapter has another advantage that other theories currently do not have, but which a forward looking, change-oriented theory of language and literacy requires for understanding the constant and increasingly exponentially changes these undergo: an internal dynamic. The perspective that I outline has serious consequences for the way in which we think about learning and assessment of knowledge and literacy.

Toward an approach of thinking difference in and for itself

Language is a continuously changing phenomenon, as we can witness and note (become conscious off) almost daily. There are ever new words and expressions, ever new forms of mobilizing language, and ever new contents: the relation between the two is mutually constitutive, as new expressions enable new contents and new contents enable new expressions. But linguists are generally concerned with language as a stable and constant phenomenon, and even those who mobilize the concepts of discourses and Discourse do not provide explanations how and why language and its forms change. As Bakhtine [Volochinov] (1977) realized, you cannot get from the synchronous approach to a diachronous approach. Here, I am not looking for causal factors that change language from the outside, such as in explanations about great poets, novelists, politicians, or scientists who introduce this or that new word, concept, or form of expression. In this case, the source of change is something other than the language, the inventiveness, expertise, or genius of some person. Such an explanation cannot ever explain the continual change that we see and experience language to undergo. Rather, it is only when we begin linguistic theorizing with speech communication, which constitutes a continuous flow that can we think of linguistic change as *inherent* to the phenomenon of language, language as the condition for linguistic change: "Language cannot properly be said to be handed down—it endures, but it endures as a continuous process of becoming" (Bakhtine [Volochinov] 1977: 81).

As a consequence of such a position, we no can longer think of individuals as receiving a language that they reproduce, in the image of the child who encounters language in a relation with ("more experienced") others that the child subsequently moves to an internal plane. Rather, individuals "enter upon the stream of verbal communication; indeed, only in this stream does their consciousness first begin to operate" (Bakhtine [Volochinov] 1977: 81). To understand the proper relation between individual and collective and the language that both produce and the result of this relation, it might be helpful to think of language as a collective phenomenon that uses individuals to concretely realize itself. Because no individual is like any other, these concrete realizations are inherently different, every single time:

> The organic connection of meaning and sign cannot become lexical, grammatically stable, and fixed in identical and reproducible forms, i.e., cannot in itself become a sign or a constant element of a sign, cannot become grammaticalized. This connection is created only to be destroyed, to be reformed again, but in new forms under the conditions of a new utterance.
>
> (Bakhtin [Medvedev] 1978: 121)

How can we think/theorize such a curious phenomenon that changes at the very instances that it realizes itself? That is, language is at the same time that it is not, because it is already changing while it concretely realizes itself. Georg W.F. Hegel (1979a) provides an early answer to this question in the context of mind and consciousness (how does mind develop?). Hegel realized that consciousness could be something that develops when it is different from itself, involving itself both as subject (that which thinks) and as object (that which is thought). There were two immediate consequences. First, in thinking the subject as something that externalizes and, therefore, objectifies itself (estranged itself from itself); but at the same time, the subject reappropriates, that is, subjectifies the external object in thinking about it. There is, therefore, a continuous dynamic across the inside/outside, internal/external, or intra-psychological/inter-psychological divide that most mainstream research employs. Second, we could not ever know how to intelligibly express something for another if we did not already take upon our own expressions the perspective of another—a mother talks to her son using age- and topic-appropriate language and thereby is taking his perspective on life—so that every expression inherently becomes a social rather than an individual act.

In the course of the nineteenth century, Karl Marx further develops this approach in using the concept and phenomenon of value by showing how the capitalist economy of his time could have evolved from the humble (barter) exchanges between members of early tribes. Accordingly, in every exchange of two goods (commodities), value expresses itself in two forms: use-value and exchange-value. The bag of grain serves the farmer as exchange-value to purchase the coat that keeps him warm, which constitutes for him use-value. On the other hand, to the seamstress, the coat serves as exchange-value for getting the bag of grain to make the flatbread that is use-value for her and her family. Metaphysical philosophers who tend to think in terms of dichotomies—to every *A* there exists a *not-A*, *tertium non datur* (a third thing is not given), and $A = A$ but $A \neq \neg A$—will invariably say that what something *is* (its nature, ontology) depends on the perspective of the person and on the context (time). Thus, such philosophers tend to argue that from the perspective of the farmer, the grain is exchange-value and the coat is use-value, whereas for the seamstress it is precisely the reverse. For the same person, different things constitute different forms of value, whereas the same things change what they are when they change possession. Marx, on the other hand, suggests that a thing could not be different unless it was already different within and for itself. Value is both use-value and exchange-value; and it is neither simultaneously. Use-value and exchange-value simply are a *one-sided* expression of the same thing, value, which may express itself differently depending on context just as the physicist's light expresses itself as particle or wave depending on the experimental condition. Because it can be different things simultaneously, for the same or different persons, for same or different situations, it is not identical with itself, that is, in other words, it is non-self-identical. Mathematically expressed, this leads to the dialectical statement $A \neq A$ in contradi(stin)ction to classical logic.[1] An entity never *is*—Derrida (1972: 6) erases the "~~is~~"—but always *becomes*, therefore different from itself at the instant that it concretely realizes itself. We therefore require concepts that capture this diastasis of difference that appears at the very instant of realization; and to be able to capture this real-world phenomenon, these concepts themselves need have the same structure (Ilyenkov 1982): here, they need to be diastatic.

This way of thinking about a variety of cultural phenomena comes with advantages in that we no longer can, or have to, essentialize key aspects of knowing: language, learning, and context. It allows us to think difference for itself: phenomena and concepts such as culture, identity, and language all are thought as non-self-identical mixtures in which there is a continuous exchange and movement between the different forms in which the unit expresses itself (Nancy 1993).[2] At the biological level, each human being is already a mixture of the genetic material of its parents, whose genetic possibilities realize themselves in new and different forms with each additional child they have and across generations. This means that there is no pure (first or second) culture, as any culture always already is an inherently heterogeneous mixture, the result of continuous *métissage*. And language, as I show above, always already is different from itself, continuously borrowing, transforming, erasing, mutilating, creolizing, hybridizing, existing forms in the very instant of being expressed. Thus, "a language is always a mêlée of languages, something halfway between the goal of total confusion of Babel and the immediate transparency of a glossolalia" (Nancy 1993: 15). Translation, such as that accomplished by the teacher in Chapter 2, therefore, comes to "translate itself in an internal … translation by playing with the non-identity with itself of all language" (Derrida 1998: 65).

The individual, who expresses herself using language, which in form and content is a societal phenomenon, thereby expresses identities that are collective possibilities rather than singularities—"because," as I quote the words of Rimbaud (1951: 254) in Chapter 6, "JE est *un autre* [I is *an other*]." Both culture and language are phenomena that realize themselves in and through each human act, so that the identity of the human being itself takes on its common feature: non-self-identity. It is because of this non-self-identity with ourselves that we can be different within and across space and time, changing as we realize the unfolding possibilities in our bodies and experiences—precisely in the same way as Marx's value.

The differences within a non-self-identity do not simply co-exist but continually mediate, modify, and influence each other. It should comes as little surprise, therefore, that Nancy (1993) proposes the metaphor of cultures that cultivate each other, clearing one another's ground, irrigating, fertilizing, and draining each other. They also plow each other, culture being the cultivator, the tool for breaking the ground; and cultures graft themselves onto each other. Each non-self-identical phenomenon is a mêlée, a process that even configures itself so that in a correct sense it never *is*. I like to use the analogy of the river for thinking and talking about the mêlée: there is continuous flow, sometimes appearing as laminar, sometimes as back current, and sometimes as eddy. The flow of the river is all of these things and none of them simultaneously. It is in a state of continuous *becoming*, something that never is (*be-*), but something that always remains to *come* (Fr. *à venir*), always lies in the future (Fr. *avenir*).

Philosophers have recognized the fruitful nature of thinking in this way, because it allows us to understand the nature of human existence, including such difficult issues as "free will." Thus, for example, thinking about forgiveness allows us to ponder the difference between being determinate beings, cultural, sociological, or psychological dopes who act in the way this or that statistical model predicts. If the victim of an act can forgive the perpetrator for his deed then there is nothing to forgiveness: "Forgiving the forgivable, the venial, the excusable, that which one can always forgive, this is not forgiving" (Derrida 2005: 32). It is only forgiveness of the unforgivable that constitutes true forgiveness. But forgiveness that forgives the unforgivable inherently is self-contradictory, non-self-identical: forgiving the unforgivable is an inherently contradictory and therefore non-self-identical situation that is fruitful precisely because there is no final answer to it, no end that would allows us to walk away peacefully. There can be no recipe telling us what to do, no mechanically derived, prefigured answer. The relation between forgiving and the unforgivable is dialogical, one returning to the other, without end. The decision to forgive the unforgivable cannot be anticipated, is incalculable, indeterminable from prior conditions. It is a historical act that the wise person resolves in taking account the singular nature of the case while violating the rule to the least extent.

Thinking different knowledge differently

The genre of the standard, peer-reviewed research article requires the statement of future questions or other forms of research that a piece of work gives rise to. Here, too, I articulate the direction in which the work in and on this book is taking me with respect to language, learning (knowing), and context; that is, I articulate some possibilities that a different way of thinking—difference in and of itself—can take our field. I do so in tracing out how we might go about thinking aboriginal forms of knowing (e.g., traditional ecological knowledge) differently than attempting to subordinate it to *science*.

Over the past five years, I have had the opportunity to engage in close readings of many of the classical and recent philosophical texts that are based on a dialectical way of thinking. This understanding arose together with my close reading of conversations in a variety of settings—classrooms, laboratories, workplaces—consisting not only words but also of a variety of communicative means. In the process of my developing understanding, I also came to better appreciate the writings of "postmodern" philosophers such as Jacques Derrida, which are not "fluffy" and "unspecific" at all, as some colleagues like to say. Rather, in themselves these writings testify (a) to a deep understanding of the philosophical "giants" that preceded them (those of Plato, Aristotle, Hegel, Marx, and Heidegger to name but a few), and (b) to a rigorous (not rigid) way of reading/writing that is consistent with its content, difference in and for itself. Together, these developments in my understanding have allowed me to evolve new ways in thinking language, learning, and context. I am interested in understanding these issues within a democratic society and in understanding the very idea of democracy—which, to be consistent with itself, cannot *be*, but always lies in the future (Fr. *avenir*), always has *to come* (Fr. *à venir*). In this section, I exemplify my ways of thinking/writing language, learning, and context as well as culture and democracy in an analysis of the concept of "indigenous science," a form of knowing that is radically different from scientists' science yet uses the same noun to denote itself (as a form and move of legitimation). My fundamental position is that in a democracy (at least in the one ever to come), indigenous knowing can stand on its own and therefore does not have to legitimize itself by denoting itself as "science." Words constitute ideologies (Bakhtine [Volochinov] 1977) and therefore it is important to interrogate which words we use and how we use them.

On rejecting "tofunaise"

Indigenous *science*. For some time now, I have been wondering why some educators have insisted on using the term *science* to denote the knowledge of certain people— that of American Indians, Canadian First Nations, Maori, Hawaiian—by the same term that also denotes the field that those use who produce substances and plants that are destructive for people and the environment (e.g., Monsanto scientists). Why would anyone want to claim to be part of a category of people, knowledge, or way of dealing with the world that also includes people and groups who produce what environmentally conscious people call "Frankenfood," food derived from genetically modified organisms? Why would anyone want to have his or her knowledge in the same category as that which has given to humanity the destructive and now banned dichloro-diphenyl-trichloroethane (DDT), agent orange (mixture of 2,4-dichloriphenoxyacetic acid and 2,4,5-trichlorophenoxyacetic acid), thalidomide (2-(2,6-dioxopiperidin-3-yl)-1H-isoindole-1,3(2H)-dione), and other equally and more dangerous substances? Furthermore, why would we use the term *science* to denote a form of knowing that is as different from the discourses that reign in laboratories and scientific journals as the mundane discourses of just plain folks concerning phenomena and areas over which "scientists" have traditionally claimed authority? Why *ought* everyday talk about the environment and the "indigenous" forms of knowing developed by fishermen—who may have fished an area for 40 years—be something other than science whereas the knowledge of a First Nations person fishing salmon in the same area constitute a form of *science*?

University-based "scientists" do not always know best even when it comes to their own domains, as I learned while being part of a major research effort that brought together biologists, Earth and ocean scientists, philosophers, sociologists, historians, educators, anthropologists, and members of other disciplines to study the phenomenon of single-industry communities on both Canadian coasts. It turns out that locals (fishermen, fish culturists) have better and deeper understanding about certain fish, fish culture, fish life cycles, and fish habitat than the university and government scientists who have made it their life purpose to study these and similar fish species. Moreover, I have had repeated occasion to note that the fish culturists I studied have a better understanding of which research designs would work and make sense than the laboratory scientists who come to the hatcheries to conduct experiments (which have turned out to be flawed for the reasons that the fish culturists have stated before). Local knowledge is not inherently inferior to scientific knowledge.

> AUTHOR's VOICE-OVER: Difference as such, Heidegger writes, is unthought. Because it always is thought as difference from the same, difference is unthought as difference, that is, in and for itself.

Tofunaise. Tofurkey. Tofu chicken burger—some ads say, "looks like chicken burger without the chicken." I have wondered why products from soy protein attempt to imitate or take the place of dairy and meat products and dishes rather than taking a place in their own right? Tofurkey, also "faux turkey" (technically, tofurkey is a spoonerism because "faux" is pronounced "fo" [i.e., tofurkey and fo-turkey]), is offered in supermarkets with everything required to make it look like turkey. It then may take the place of turkey in the traditional American Thanksgiving meal, with stuffing from grain or sauce-flavored bread to give the eater the impression of eating turkey when one is not really eating turkey. But, as its alternative name suggests, it is not the real thing, it is "faux," false, imitation. Why *indigenous science*, where "science" is a term not only denoting forms of knowing but also forms of taking position in the world, methods, epistemologies. Those using the term "science" modified by the adjective "indigenous" definitely do not take the same position as the scientists do in university and commercial laboratories, for example, at Monsanto. Why, then, call it an indigenous form of knowing science? Would those who use the term "indigenous science" also accept the term "mundane science," "everyday science," to denote what others in the field of science education term "misconceptions," "folk beliefs," "alternative conceptions," the forms of knowing featured in Chapter 5?

Thinking about knowledge and curriculum

Educators often suggest that we need to rethink who and what drives the agenda for thinking and designing curricula in schools. They propose, for example, to rethink education from a more encompassing societal perspective that takes into account social justice. Thought from such a perspective, as but one of many forms of knowing and human endeavors, gives formal school knowledge its due place within a greater effort in reproducing and transforming society. Thinking in such a way then would allow us to recognize what happens and is produced in (university, industrial) research laboratories as, but the enactment of, one form of knowledge-producing method and knowledge product among many other forms of knowing that we appreciate in our culture today, including philosophy, the fine arts, literature, ethics, politics, social sciences, and so forth. It would also allow us to acknowledge the many forms of everyday knowing that are exhibited in the ways we communicate about and act toward the natural world.

In my responses to such efforts, I suggest that we needed to go much further than calls for social justice by beginning with a different epistemology that acknowledges a non-hierarchical relationship between different ways of knowing, as these articulate themselves in talking, which all have different merits and which are taken into account as needed in specific, always local issues. Rather than focusing on specific disciplines and ways of knowing to organize school curriculum, we could take a problem-based approach and appreciate the different contributions and different ways of knowing make to the specific issue. This knowledge, then, might come from the local ecological knowledge that white European residents have evolved over decades of living in a particular area, which, as I observed in one particular contentious community issue concerning water supply, by far exceeded the spotty knowledge scientists and engineers have brought to and built while working on the case. In the same way, local fishermen turn out to have developed a tremendous local ecological discourse concerning particular fish and other marine species that by far outstrips what university and federal fisheries scientists have developed during their relatively brief engagement with the relevant ecosystem.

I know of at least one effort that attempts to combine very different forms of knowledge. At the University of British Columbia, fisheries scientists attempt to reconstruct the Strait of Georgia ecosystem (the ocean between the North American continent and Vancouver Island) by entering (qualitative) traces of indigenous discourse side-by-side with (quantitative) traces of scientific discourse into a database to reconstruct what the Strait may have looked like 100 and 500 years ago. The purpose of the reconstruction is to develop policy choices for the future of fisheries in the Strait, an approach that takes its name from the method: *Back to the Future.* This back-to-the-future method takes into account all stakeholders and their different forms of language—scientific, qualitative, historical, or anecdotal—when it evaluates local benefits that may be extracted from alternative ecosystems, designs practical management instruments, and monitors the recovery of ecosystems and compliance. Because of this comprehensive method, the approach garners powerful support and consent among an unprecedented broad range of stakeholders.

Central to the approach of the *Back to the Future* project is the recognition that traditional ecological knowledge and ecological science are not structured in the same way. It is on the basis of difference that it considers similarities between the two, here denoted by the name of the scientific modeling program *Ecopath* and the acronym for traditional ecological knowledge (TEK):

> Both Ecopath and TEK are concerned with the relationships, ratios and connection within the ecosystem than with achieving an absolute understanding of individual elements. *In their own way* both TEK and Ecopath are comprehensive, just as local fishers consider an entire constellation of factors along with the target species, prey, associates species, weather, current, tide, phase of the moon, to name but a few.
>
> (Haggan et al. 1998: 10, original emphasis)

As a result of its approach, "The *Back to the Future* methodology supplies a practical direct use for the knowledge of maritime historians, archaeologists, ecological economists, fisheries ecologists, and the TEK of indigenous peoples" (Haggan et al. 1998: 2). In fact, traditional ecological knowledge rather than being denied a voice is "strengthened in the BTF [back-to-the-future] process by a cross-validation with ecological science, and may thus be endowed with a real and valuable role in shaping future fisheries policy" (Haggan et al. 1998: 2).

Does Tofunaise become more acceptable and "better" because its suffix "aise" relates it (and makes it similar) to mayonnaise? Some people do not like Tofunaise because of its taste of tofu, and with the "naise" does is make it a "niaiserie" (chiefly literary word, derived from French, denoting foolishness). Or does tofu not become a mal*aise*, a discomfort, an uneasiness of and for mind and spirit by the addition of the suffix "-aise" (linked by the insertion of -ni-)?

For all the praise I attribute to the back-to-the-future method, in my way of thinking it does not yet go far enough, because cross-validation of two domains is possible only when they are considered on some ground that allows validation of one by another. But that ground would have to be independent of the two others, providing it a space to be compared. What might such an epistemically disinterested ground be? Inherently it is impossible. There is no metalanguage possible, for it would imply that exact and unequivocal translation is possible and, in fact, unnecessary—we all would only need to speak this language to instantiate perfect communication. Instead, I propose to consider different ways of knowing as inherently, that is radically different. It is so different that the two forms of knowledge are not only different from every other way of knowing but also different from themselves; each form of knowing is non-self-identical because it allows translations within itself. The only way that two forms of knowing are the same is that they are different from every other form. That is, I am arguing to think epistemology from an ontology of difference—which never *is* but always becomes.

Thinking from an ontology of difference

> We can only say "the same" if we think difference ... The same banishes all zeal always to level what is different into the equal or identical. The same gathers what is distinct into an original being-at-one. The equal, on the contrary, disperses them into the dull unity of mere uniformity.
>
> (Deleuze 1994: 66)

In the first voice-over of this chapter, Martin Heidegger notes that difference had not been thought in and for itself. Grounded in prior work of German idealist philosophy, he appears to have been the first scholar to call for a thinking of difference in and for itself. His statement has become programmatic for a substantive amount of philosophical work conducted particularly in France. It includes the writings of the philosophers Jean-François Lyotard, Jacques Derrida, Giles Deleuze, and Jean-Luc Nancy and of belletristic writers such as Hélène

Cixous, a postructuralist feminist theorist known for her *écriture feminine*, who is intellectually very close to Derrida. (Cixous plays with the phonemic properties of language, thereby drawing additional layers of signification that escape strict lexical analysis; she might have enjoyed combination of pairs of words employed here, such as tofurkey and faux turkey.) Underlying this work is a wariness with forms of thought that reduce the diversity inherent and constitutive of the world and its languages to the sameness underlying representation and its effects in the unifying concepts and theories at our hands.

Attempting to adjoin indigenous ways of knowing of science—by means of adjectives "aboriginal science," "indigenous science," and so on under the guise of equality—disperses, as Deleuze notes in the quote opening this section, what is inherently distinct "into the dull unity of mere uniformity." The use of adjectives may, in fact, reduce and annihilate difference to the same (concept) rather than celebrate difference by using different concepts. Changing aboriginal ways of knowing so that they can be cross validated with ecological (industrial, university) science, though a tremendous step forward to overcome the hegemony of *modern* science discourse (*logos*) and its logic (*logos*), really means bringing it into a dull unity of mere conformity and uniformity.

The road toward thinking difference in and for itself is not easy, as the origin of this difficulty, at least within Western cultures of the Greco-Roman-Christian lineage, lies in language:

> Our occidental languages, each in its own way, are languages of metaphysical thinking. It has to remain open whether the nature of Western languages is in itself marked only metaphysically and therefore permanently by onto-theo-logic, or whether these languages offer other possibilities of telling and that simultaneously means of a telling silence.
>
> (Heidegger 1957: 66)

Despite subsequent critiques of his work on difference, Heidegger led the way for proposing a way of thinking difference as such—*singulare tantum* (Heidegger 1957: 36), a singular term that denotes a plurality or multiplicity, that is, a *singular plural*. These examples concretize this idea difficult to understand within the ontology that underlies current Western (scientific) thought.

Thinking difference in and for itself leads us to a way of looking at "conceptions" as singular plurals, constituted by and constituting single and singular experiences, each of which can function as a synecdoche to refer to all experiences, much like the word cube or the view of one side of a cube refers us to the "concept of a cube," always only available in the way it (one-sidedly) expresses itself. The result is a network where one experience can take us to any other experience or trace thereof. The network does not merely sum up experiences, but because of the interdependence of the connections, each additional experience mediates the effects of all other experiences on each other. That is, the "value" of the whole network depends on the value of each individual node (experience), but the value of each node depends on the value of the net as a whole. Ideas, therefore, "are multiplicities: every idea is a multiplicity or a variety" (Deleuze 1994: 182). Importantly, "multiplicity must not designate a combination of the many and the one, but rather an organisation belonging to the many as such, which has no need whatsoever of unity in order to form a system" (Deleuze 1994: 182). We cannot, therefore, understand the whole independently of its parts, nor can we understand an individual apart from the whole. The "individual" experiences that Connor and his peers in second-grade geometry have had with rolling objects, therefore, are not "elements" from which the conception is (can be) built up. Vygotsky (1986) proposes "unit analysis" to replace the psychological analysis in terms of elements, where, in the present case, the unit would be the conception as a whole. Such a conception—in contrast to how it would appear in traditional (constructivist) theories—is not just mental; rather, it subsumes all forms of experiences, including emotions. Each "conception"—realized, as we see in Chapter 5, in many different ways of and in speaking—is a multiplicity that cannot be reduced to any of the ways in which it expresses itself. There is no "one" conception that a singular person "has," but a continuously changing, non-self-identical multiplicity that is different from the continuously changing non-self-identical multiplicity of any other singular person. This multiplicity is repeated in the collective of speakers within a language and between languages.

These two examples now allow us to think of language, learning, context, culture, and identity as multiplicities that cannot be reduced to individual elements and components. They are, therefore, inherently different, not merely from other cultures, languages, forms of knowing, and identities, but also different from themselves; they are non-self-identical. What any "one" culture, language, forms of knowing, or identity has in common with any other culture, language, form of knowing, or identity is this: it differs. This, then, has as a consequence that we need to recognize all "indigenous" forms of knowing, including that of just plain folks of White Western (Judeo-Greek) cultural heritage. Their everyday ways of knowing have suffered from the same kind of hegemonic onslaught and colonialism of laboratory "science" as the ways of knowing of other sections of society including women, people of color, aboriginals, and immigrants.

In the process of coming into contact with other cultures, languages, forms of knowing, and identities, blood already and inherently mixed becomes even further mixed, creolized, mingled, commingled, blended, merged, coalesced, amalgamated, and fused. These processes are continuous; they traverse our lives. The resulting mixture is more than simply rich with diversity: it ceaselessly eschews and escapes the diversity it mixes. As a result, cultures do not add up: "They encounter one another, mix with one another, alter one another, reconfigure one another. They each cultivate all others, they clear one another's ground, irrigate or drain one another, plough or graft themselves onto one another" (Nancy 1993: 282). In extension, I add: language does not add up; learning does not add up; and context does not add up.

Epilogue

What nobody knows is precisely the peculiarity of language—that it cares only about itself.

(Novalis 2001: 426)

I begin this book with Heidegger's question about how language is and lives. Here at the end of this book, after numerous investigations into the appearance and use of language in everyday situations—classrooms, lectures, interviews—we can respond to this question perhaps best by saying that the life of language is the language of life. Neither life nor language *is*—both always become. This is so because, as we see throughout the chapters of this book, there is no difference in knowing a language and in knowing one's way around the world. Material life and language are interwoven as *con*text and text. But material life never stops; it continuously flows and unfolds. The opposition between signifier and signified—which in fact parallels other oppositions, such as that between speaking and thinking, body and the mind, mind and the world, intra-psychological and inter-psychological (sociological), a word and its "meaning"—is undermined not by abolishing the distinction but by recognizing it as an *effect* of the work of several thousand years of metaphysics. The difference is not abolished in this move; rather, the two are recognized in their mutually constitutive and irreducible relation that continuously undergoes change—because language continuously lives, and therefore continuously dies.

Throughout this book I enact—and implicitly encourage my readers to enact—close readings of conversations and texts for the purpose of qualifying, modifying, or questioning a theory of language, learning, and context. I do so by means of demonstration, presupposing nothing other than the cultural competencies of an (native) English speaker. I articulate a new way of thinking language by way of close readings of everyday events such as interviews and classroom transactions, and parallel close readings of the philosophical literature from Aristotle to Derrida. But in remaining continuously grounded in the talk of my participants, I walk the walk of talk, that is, I talk the talk—or, which has the same effect, I engage in writing. I do so right into the concluding chapter where I exemplify how to theorize various ways of knowledge and knowledgeable talk (epistemology) on the basis of an ontology of difference. In such an ontology, we think entities not only as different from other entities but also as different within and with respect to themselves: each entity is thought as a singular plural, non-self-identical phenomenon. As such, no entity can exist and be understood on its own because it is only a thread in a complex con/texture. We can then begin by recognizing difference for itself and capitalize on the affordances that derive from bringing difference to the table.

Language, as Ferdinand de Saussure recognizes, means difference, difference that begins at the inside of the sign, *inherently* heterogeneous, thereby opening the very possibility of *différance, khôra,* and *trace.* Thinking difference for itself allows us not only to rethink language, learning, and context, but also to rethink democracy, relations among people, and the dialects and idioms that sustain these relations and the worlds in which they exist and that they constitute. We no longer need to "construct," to draw on the example provided in Chapter 10, the similitude of a tofu-based condiment with another one using egg yolk. In the old way of approaching the two condiments, Tofunaise always remains the substitute, impostor, always in the quest of seeking recognition in the face of the other, legitimate "-aise." Rather than the malaise of Tofunaise, let us celebrate this condiment in its own right, which would begin by designing a new name for a different product (thing). In the same way, rather than using the term "indigenous science," let us recognize in the various languages, idioms, and dialects —aboriginal, mundane, local, feminine, and so on—as actually *legitimate* ways of knowing language and knowing one's way around the world. These ways, rather than coherent and monolithic, are thought to be non-self-identical and useful in different ways in different local contexts, always amenable to change. Let us accept the various forms of indigenous knowing (including Western common sense, mundane knowing) and appreciate them for the contributions they (can) make to render this a better and more livable world.

Tofunaise. But there is another way of looking at the issue. It is an expression of the *métissage* that continuously occurs in cultural context and language. It signifies cultural learning. Rather than looking for a semblance of purity in separating mayonnaise from other condiments on the basis of tofu, Tofunaise simply is the expression and product of a mêlée of words and things. Equivalent mêlées of indigenous knowing and traditional science may, therefore, bring about new forms of knowing that have advantages over the forms of knowing that exist today. Tofunaise is something special, unlike and irreducible to mayonnaise, with its own flavor and taste and use that may bear a family resemblance with the tastes and uses of mayonnaise from which it differs radically, in its very constitution (i.e., ontically).

Appendix

Transcription conventions

All fragments have been transcribed following the conventions of conversation analysis developed for the analysis of prosodic features (Selting et al. 1998).

Notation	Description	Example
(0.14)	Parenthesis enclosing a number: time without talk, in one-tenth of a second	more ideas. (1.03) just
(.)	Period enclosed in parentheses: pause of less than 0.10 seconds	kay. (.) bert
((turns))	Verbs and descriptions in double parentheses are transcriber's comments	((nods to Colby))
[₅mean	Underlining is used to show the extent of a simultaneous process named/described in double parentheses; subscribed appears when there are several cases simultaneously	[₃mean li[₄ke?>]] [₃((touches "his" cube
[₅	Numbered bracket is used to align verbal transcript and video offprint	see [₂from that
::	Colons indicate lengthening of a sound by about one tenth of a second per colon	si::ze
[ ]	Square brackets in consecutive lines indicate the precise beginning and end of overlapping speech	S: s[ize] T: [connor]
.hhh	A row of the letter h prefixed by a dot indicates inbreath, without the dot, the hs indicates outbreath	.hhh it wor[ks]
O(h)kay	A parenthesized h indicates breathiness	o(h)kay
<<p> >	Piano, words are uttered with lower than normal speech volume	<<p>um>
<<pp> >	Pianissimo, words are uttered with very low, almost inaudible volume	<<pp>this>
<<h> >	High pitch (F0) register	<<h>get me out of here>
<<all> >	Allegro, fast	<<all>so you know>

<<rall> >	Rallentando, slowing up	<<rall>well no-no>
<<dim> >	Diminuendo, lowering volume	<<dim>that=s got to be>
<<len> >	Lento, denotes a slower than normal delivery by this speaker	<<len>we can>
<<cresc> >	Crescendo, increasing volume in the course of speaking	<<cresc>when we did the ca=andle>
<<f> >	Forte, high speech volume, intensity	<<f>I=M JUST SAYing just do the number TWO>
ONE bert	Capital letters indicate louder than normal talk indicated in small letters.	no? okay, next ONE bert.
(serial?)	Words followed by question mark in parentheses indicate possible hearings of words	(serial?)
-,?;.	Punctuation is used to mark movement of pitch toward the end of the utterance, flat (-), slightly (,) and strongly (?) upward, and slightly (;) and strongly (.) downward, respectively	T: so can we tell a shape by its color? T: does it ↑belong to another ↑group (0.67) O:r.
=	Phonemes of different words are not clearly separated or there is no gap between the end of one turn and the beginning of the next	loo::ks=similar
↑↓	Arrows indicate shifts to higher or lower pitch in the utterance that immediately follows	↑so can we↓
` ^ ´	Diacritics indicate movement of pitch (F0) within the word that follows: down (`), up-down (^), and upward (´), respectively	`sad ^says `sai:d

Notes

1 Walking the walk

1 Derrida (1988b: 101) notes that this response often has been mistakenly taken as a tautological platitude: "In truth, we have to take note, in a most needed movement, of the fact that language is not the masterable instrument of a speaking being (or subject) and that its essence cannot appear from another instance than language itself that names it, says it, gives it to think, speaks it."

2 This term, as similar ones in other Germanic languages, derives from the preposition *under*, meaning below and amidst, and the verb *stand*. Etymologically, therefore, to *understand* means to stand (put oneself) amidst others, and therefore, in a (social) situation that is shot through with signification.

3 Heidegger (1985) uses the German verb "*nachdenken*," which, in addition to reflect, can also be heard as "to follow/repeat in thinking," and he uses it to suggest that thinking and consciousness only captures what already is in the past.

4 Slow, careful reading is deconstruction (Derrida 1988b), in the form of *Abbau*, the systematic undoing (literally, unbuilding) of a structure for the purpose of understanding it, rather than in the form of destruction. Deconstruction, therefore, also implies the possibility of rebuilding (de Man 1983).

5 For a description and analysis of such a session see Roth and Hsu 2009.

6 Throughout this book, I understand *utterance* in Bakhtin's (1986) way, according to which not only a verbal statement but also a poem, a story, or a novel constitute an utterance, the social evaluation of which comes to be known in and through the recipient's actions.

7 "*Différance*," writes Derrida (1972: 12), "is the non-full, non-simple, structured and differentiating origin of differences. The name 'origin' therefore no longer suits it."

8 A Venn diagram or set diagram consists of an ensemble of closed curves that exhibits all hypothetically possible logical relations between a finite set of groups of things, each represented by a closed curve.

9 If there are identifiable structures *within* some smallest unit of analysis (i.e., an element), then we cannot denote those structures as "elements" or "components." This smallest unit is irreducible, cannot be explained in terms of entities that are smaller or subordinate to it. The term *moment* is used to identify such structures with the understanding that no moment can be reduced to another moment, and that moments cannot be added up to produce the unit. Each moment embodies the unit as a whole, but does so only in a one-sided fashion. A useful analogy is that of light (unit) and its two moments, particle and wave. Neither expresses the whole, neither explains its complement.

10 English translations of German and Russian (critical) social psychology use the term "social" where the original texts employ the term "societal." I retain the

latter, because it embodies all the phenomena of interest to educators and social scientists, including power, social injustice, economic interests, and so forth.

11 I know of the case of an African American teacher, born and raised in the inner city of Philadelphia, who, after receiving his degrees, returned to teach in his old neighborhood. But the students, only a few years younger than he, no longer accepted him as one of theirs.

12 I understand reproduction and transformation to constitute the two parts of the same internally differing (and deferring) phenomenon of production. In acting and producing something, we reproduce and transform culture simultaneously.

13 I make use here of quasi-direct speech that constitutes part of the content of Chapter 8.

14 Bakhtin read *Cours de linguistique générale*, a book on which modern linguistics was founded, but that was not an authorized manuscript but a text posthumously edited and published. A recent finding of original notes (e.g., de Saussure 1996) makes evident that there are many ideas in the book inconsistent with de Saussure's thinking. Bakhtin's critique of de Saussure pertains to the book rather than to the linguist's own ideas.

15 There has been considerable debate about the authorship of *Marksizm I filos-ofija jazyka*. The point here is not to continue this debate. I reference and cite the work using the name as it appears on the French translation, which attributes it to Mikhail Bakhtin (Bakhtine in French) and parenthesizing the name of V.N. Vološinov (Volochinov in French).

16 More technically, the first speaker produces an utterance (locution) with a certain intention (illocution), but the second speaker completes the speech act as he or she makes available the effect (perlocution).

2 Making context in talking

1 This change requires an understanding of the different treatment of negative quantities in biology and physics. In biology, death rate is a positive quantity and therefore has to be subtracted from the birthrate to find the net rate of change. In physics, the convention is to sign quantities so that death rate is a negative quantity and has to be *added* to the birthrate to get the net rate of change.

3 Speaking | thinking as distributed process

1 The technical term that covers all three verbs is G.W.F. Hegel's German verb *aufheben*, which some, as the translator of Derrida (1972), recommend to retain untranslated.

2 Here we find one of the curious differences between the French and the English translation of the Bakhtin/Vološinov book. In the French version, we read about *evolution*, whereas in the English version, we read about "a generative process." But the chapter specifically, and the book generally, is about the history of language and the processes of its continual reproduction and transformation, that is, about the evolution of language.

3 Wikipedia features a number of easy-to-understand articles on the topic, which is also known as magnetocaloric effect. The effect works like this: a sample is put into an electromagnet that is turned off. When the field is turned on, the order within the substance is increased (i.e., entropy is lowered). The field is then turned off again but in such a way that it lowers the temperature while holding the entropy (order) constant. This two-step sequence is repeated until the sample reaches the lowest possible (desired) temperature.

4 In Walter Nernst's formulation of the third law of thermodynamics, the entropy is at a minimum value when $T = 0$. The actual value of this minimum is an arbitrary constant and has been fixed to be zero ($S = 0$) when $T = 0$. In this chapter, I am not concerned with the errors in the physics content that the professor produced while lecturing but focus on the communicative processes during lectures.

5 The BBC carried a documentary feature on the race for absolute zero. Adiabatic demagnetization is the primary means to get at least close to this physical state.

6 Many websites will show temperature–entropy diagrams of the Carnot cycle-based heat pumps, in which the same theory is partially implemented.

7 In most materials available online, the S and T axes are reversed, the former constituting the abscissa, the latter the ordinate (see Figure 3.11 and associated discussion).

8 In school science, there sometimes are claims that the teachers do not know the subject matter sufficiently and make errors because of a lack of competence.

4 Agency|passivity in/of communication

1 *Being* (capitalized) does not refer to any individual but rather precedes all me, you, and we, all (sexual) difference (Derrida 2003b)—"*In the Being* of Being-there lies the 'between' with respect to birth and death" (Heidegger 1977b: 374). For Derrida, this "between" is precisely the one that also characterizes, for example, writing (*écriture*), *différance*, *khôra*, cut (*entame*) trace, hymen, "*phar-makon*," margin (*marge*), "*parergon*," and so on. It is the same phenomenon Bakhtine [Volochinov] (1977) attempts to capture in thinking about the *word*, which, in being uttered, constitutes the between of (a) language as it was and language as it will be, and (b) speaker and listener.

5 Cultured conceptions

1 Heidegger (1985) provided the reverse description in suggesting the humans think *because* they speak.

2 The video was produced by Harvard-Smithsonian Center for Astrophysics and a DVD version is now available under the ISBN: 1–57680–404–6. The documentary features Harvard University graduates who explain, among others, higher summer temperatures in the northern hemisphere by stating that the Earth–Sun distance is shorter than in the winter whereas it is accepted scientific knowledge that increasing the distance from a point-form heat source will decrease the amount of energy that impinges on a certain area—and therefore the temperature—the effect of the changing angle between Earth axis and sun rays due the Earth's revolution around the Sun is much larger. A correct answer, therefore, runs something like this: the lower the angle of sun rays impinging on some area, the fewer rays will strike the area and the smaller the energy received that heats it, and therefore the temperature of the area.

3 In French, language (*la langue*) is of feminine gender. Derrida emphasizes the appropriate reflexive pronoun *elle* [her] twice, and in the first case also emphasizes the verb, it [she] steals [*vole*], which can also take the sense of it [she] flies. The English translation does not use the emphasis, which, qua emphasis, nevertheless was important to the author, who, before and after this quote, highlights words to be understood with *double entendre*.

4 We could also express this fact in this way: conceptual change researchers are blind to the aspects I articulate here, and therefore they are blind to the very facts that make the conceptual change position an untenable one.

6 Talking identity

1 The excerpts are part of a study that extended over a period of 15 months in two consecutive physics courses, the first one of which included three eleventh-grade classes from which about half of the students continued into two twelfth-grade classes. In the course of the study, I collected 3,500 pages of typewritten transcripts of student essays, reflections, and short explanations concerning preferences, whole-class conversations, and interviews on the topic of the nature of science, the nature of knowledge, and learning. In the following, I draw on conversations with one student, Preston, while we were talking about his choices and written explanations to a five-item questionnaire about the nature of science. To make the reader aware and to keep on her/his periphery our institutional relation, I denote the speakers as "Preston" (name) and "Teacher" (a noun that here serves to mark, and therefore name a specific person). Because I focus more on the contents of the talk rather than on its interactive properties, the fragments in this chapter make use of a more traditional transcription form omitting time and using regular punctuation and capitalization.

2 I have had the same experience during a workshop that I attended during the summer of 2009. The organizers asked the 30-odd attendees to talk about why they are science/mathematics educators. Every single response but my own drew on the same pattern of positive childhood influences and experiences facilitated by a family member (parent, uncle, aunt, sibling).

3 The website states: "Our responsibility as Christians is to deal seriously with the theories and findings of all scientific endeavors, evolution included, and to enter into open dialogue with responsible persons involved in scientific tasks about the achievement, failures and limits of their activities and of ours. The truth or falsity of the theory of evolution is not the question at issue and certainly not a question which lies within the competence of the Permanent Theological Committee. The real and only issue is whether there exists clear incompatibility between evolution and the Biblical doctrine of Creation. Unless it is clearly necessary to uphold a basic Biblical doctrine, the Church is not called upon and should carefully refrain from either affirming or denying the theory of evolution. We conclude that the true relation between the evolutionary theory and the Bible is that of non-contradiction and that the position stated by the General Assemblies of 1886, 1888, 1889 and 1924 was in error and no longer represents the mind of our Church." (PCUSA 1969).

7 Culturing emotional *con*texts

1 In technical terms, this first vocal resonance is referred to as $F1$. The second vocal resonance is referred to as $F2$. It turns out, however, that only pitch ($F0$) and $F1$ are strongly correlated with psychological features.

8 When is grammar?

1 Derrida's hyphenation of the German words for presence (*An-wesen*) and absence (*Ab-wesen*) points to the etymological roots of these terms in the Latin prepositions *pr(a)e-* and *ab-* combined with the present participle of the Latin verb *esse*, to be. These connections allow him to show how (Western) language and metaphysics are irremediably tied.

2 Both Deleuze (1990) and Bakhtin (1984b) use obscenities and insults as paradigm cases in which the connection between different orders is clearly evident. Elsewhere I show that these orders are also evident and relevant in talk among students that is studded, precisely, of normally suppressed and repressed obscenities and insults (Roth 2009a).

3 Translations from the French, which permits the use of quasi-direct discourse into English sometimes attempt to maintain its use, not without having to make adjustments such as adding quotation marks as in the following example from Derrida (1972: 303). "*C'est l'histoire du sens 'propre' don't il faudrait, disions-nous plus haut, suivre le détour et le retour*" in the English version becomes "it is the history of 'proper' meaning, as we said above, whose detour and return are to be followed" (Derrida 1982: 254).

4 In the journal to one chapter of the same book, printed in parallel to the chapter text, Derrida (1986: 130) challenges the translators of the work to find an English equivalent for *récit* and then suggests to perhaps leave the word in French, especially because of subsequent repetitions, for example, in the verb form *recite* (I, s/he recites) or in the anagram *écrit* [writing].

5 The composer John Cage revolutionized musical experience and musical theory with his piece 4'33", in which the pianist sits for 4 minutes and 33 seconds at the piano only playing musical pauses/rests—resulting in a piece that features silence in consisting of nothing but silence. He thereby achieves a reflection on the matter of music that Wassily Kandinsky achieved in the visual arts, where abstract painting is a move to make the invisible be seen (e.g. the redness of red) (Henry 2005).

9 Con/textures

1 The English translation uses "meaning" rather than signification, though other translations (e.g., the one into French [e.g., Derrida 1972]) do use signification for the German *Bedeutung* that Wittgenstein uses.

2 The difficulties at heart of the issues immediately become apparent when we look at two "official" translations rendering the same German text "*Den Bedeutungen wachsen Worte zu. Nicht aber werden Wörterdinge mit Bedeutungen versehen.*" The version translated by John Macquarrie and Edward Robinson suggests this English equivalent: "To significations, words accrue. But word-things do not get supplied with significations" (Heidegger 1962: 204). A more recent version reads like this: "Words accrue to significations. But word-things are not provided with significations" (Heidegger 1996: 151). In German, Heidegger uses the definite pronoun before *Bedeutungen*, which neither translation renders in English. The word Bedeutung, here translated by signification, tends to be translated as meaning.

10 Différance

1 Reflexively, classical logical and dialectical logic stand in a relationship similar as use-value and exchange-value in that they are different, one-sided expressions of logic, a form of thinking, which is always wedded to the word (Gr. *logos*) (Vygotsky 1986).

2 Because of these inner workings, "a mixture, therefore, *is* not. It happens, it emerges" (Nancy 1993: 12). Nancy and Derrida therefore are aligned with respect to ontology.

References

Alcoff, L.M. (2006) *Visible identities: Race, gender and the self.* Oxford: Oxford University Press.

Anderson, J.R., Greeno, J.G., Reder, L.M. & Simon, H.A. (2000) 'Perspectives on learning, thinking, and activity'. *Educational Researcher*, 29 (4): 11–13.

Austin, J. (1962) *How to do things with words.* Cambridge, MA: Harvard University Press.

Bakhtin, M.M. [Medvedev, P.N.] (1978) *The formal method in literary scholarship: A critical introduction to sociological poetics.* A.J. Wehrle (trans.), Baltimore: Johns Hopkins University Press.

Bakhtin, M.M. (1981) *The dialogic imagination: Four essays.* M. Holquist (Ed.), C. Emerson & M. Holquist (trans.). Austin: University of Texas Press.

Bakhtin, M.M. (1984a) *Problems in Dostoevsky's poetics.* C. Emerson (Ed. & trans.), Minneapolis: University of Minnesota Press.

Bakhtin, M.M. (1984b) *Rabelais and his world.* Bloomington: Indiana University Press.

Bakhtin, M.M. (1986) *Speech genres and other late essays.* C. Emerson & M. Holquist (Eds.), V.W. McGee (trans.), Austin: University of Texas Press.

Bakhtin, M.M. (1993) *Toward a philosophy of the act.* V. Liapunov & M. Holquist (Eds.), V. Liapunov (trans.), Austin: University of Texas Press.

Bakhtine, M. [Volochinov, V.N.] (1977) *Le marxisme et la philosophie du langage: essai d'application de la méthode sociologique en linguistique.* Paris: Les Éditions de Minuit. An English version has been published under the name of V.N. Vološinov (1973).

Bakhtine, M. (1984) *Esthétique de la création verbale.* A. Acouturier (trans.), Paris: Gallimard.

Basu, S.J., Barton, A.C., Clairmont, N. & Locke, D. (2009) 'Developing a framework for critical science agency through case studying a conceptual physics context'. *Cultural Studies of Science Education*, 4: 345–71.

Benjamin, W. (1972) 'Die Aufgabe des Übersetzers'. In *Gesammelte Schriften Bd. IV.* Frankfurt: Suhrkamp-Verlag; H. Zohn (trans.), 'The task of the translator: An introduction to the translation of Baudelaire's *Tableaux Parisien*'. In L. Venuti (Ed.) *The translation studies reader.* London: Routledge.

Blanchot, M. (1959) *Le livre à venir.* Paris: Gallimard.

Boden, D. (1994) *The business of talk: Organization in action.* Cambridge: Polity Press.

Bourdieu, P. (1997) *Méditations pascaliennes.* Paris: Éditions du Seuil.

Chi, M.T.H. (1992) 'Conceptual change within and across ontological categories: Examples from learning and discovery in science'. In R. Giere (Ed.) *Cognitive models of science: Minnesota studies in the philosophy of science.* Minneapolis: University of Minnesota Press.

Collins, R. (2004) *Interaction ritual chains.* Princeton, NJ: Princeton University Press.

Davidson, D. (1986) 'A nice derangement of epitaphs'. In E. Lepore (Ed.) *Truth and interpretation*. Oxford: Blackwell.

Deleuze, G. (1990) *The logic of sense*. M. Lester (trans.), New York: Columbia University Press.

Deleuze, G. (1994) *Difference and repetition*. P. Patton (trans.), New York: Columbia University Press.

de Man, P. (1979) *Allegories of reading*. Newhaven, CT: Yale University Press.

de Man, P. (1982) 'Sign and symbol in Hegel's Aesthetics'. *Critical Inquiry*, 8: 761–75.

de Man, P. (1983) *Blindness and insight*. Minneapolis: University of Minnesota Press.

Derrida, J. (1967a) *De la grammatologie*. Paris: Les Éditions de Minuit.

Derrida, J. (1967b) *La voix et le phénomène: Introduction au problème du signe dans la phénoménologie de Husserl*. Paris: Presses Universitaires de France; D.B. Allison (trans.), *Speech and phenomena and other essays on Husserl's theory of signs* (1973). Evanston, IL: Northwestern University Press.

Derrida, J. (1972) *Marges de la philosophie*. Paris: Les Éditions de Minuit; A. Bass (trans.), *Margins of philosophy* (1982). Chicago: Chicago University Press.

Derrida, J. (1974) *Glas*. Paris: Galilée; J.P. Leavey, Jr & R. Rand (trans.), *Glas* (1986). Lincoln: University of Nebraska Press.

Derrida, J. (1978) *Éperons: Les styles de Nietzsche*. Paris: Flammarion.

Derrida, J. (1981) *Dissemination*. B. Johnson (trans.), Chicago: University of Chicago Press.

Derrida, J. (1984) *Otobiographies: L'enseignement de Nietzsche et la politique du nom proper*. Paris: Galilée; P. Kamuf (partially trans.), 'Otobiographies: The teaching of Nietzsche and the politics of the proper name'. In *The ear of the Other: Otobiography, transference, translation* (1985). Lincoln: University of Nebraska Press.

Derrida, J. (1986) *Parages*. Paris: Galilée.

Derrida, J. (1988a) *Limited Inc*. Chicago: University of Chicago Press.

Derrida, J. (1988b) *Mémoires: pour Paul de Man*. Paris: Galilée.

Derrida, J. (1991) *Donner le temps: 1. La fausse monnaie*. Paris: Galilée; P. Kamuf (trans.), *Given time: I. Counterfeit money* (1992). Chicago: Chicago University Press.

Derrida, J. (1993) *Passions*. Paris: Galilée.

Derrida, J. (1996) *Le monolinguisme de l'autre ou la prothèse de l'origine*. Paris: Galilée; P. Mensah (trans.), *Monolingualism of the Other; or, The prosthesis of origin* (1998). Stanford, CA: Stanford University Press.

Derrida, J. (2003a) *Psyché: Inventions de l'autre I*. Paris: Galilée; *Psyche: Inventions of the Other vol. 1* (2007a), P. Kamuf & E. Rottenberg (Eds.). Stanford, CA: Stanford University Press.

Derrida, J. (2003b) *Psyché: Inventions de l'autre II*. Paris: Galilée; *Psyche: Inventions of the Other vol. 2* (2007b), P. Kamuf & E. Rottenberg (Eds.). Stanford, CA: Stanford University Press.

Derrida, J. (2005) *Pardonner: L'impardonnable et l'imprescriptible*. Paris: L'Herne.

de Saussure, F. (1996) 'De l'essence double du langage'. *TEXTO! Textes et culture*. Accessed June 22, 2009 at http://www.revue-texto.net/Saussure/Saussure.html.

Durkheim, É. (1893) *De la division du travail social*. Paris: Presses Universitaires de France.

Eckert, P. (1989) *Jocks and burnouts: Social categories and identity in the high school*. New York: Teachers College Press.

Edwards, D. & Potter, J. (1992) *Discursive psychology*. London: Sage.

Elman, J.L. (1993) 'Learning and development in neural networks: the importance of starting small'. *Cognition*, 8: 71–99.

Fish, S. (1982) '"With the compliments of the author" Reflections on Austin and Derrida'. *Critical Inquiry*, 8: 693–721.

Franck, D. (1981) *Chair et corps: Sur la phénoménologie de Husserl*. Paris: Les Éditions de Minuit.

Garfinkel, H. (1967) *Studies in ethnomethodology*. Englewood Cliffs, NJ: Prentice-Hall.

Garfinkel, H. (2002) *Ethnomethology's program: Working out Durkheim's aphorism*. Lanham, MD: Rowman & Littlefield.

Garfinkel, H. & Sacks, H. (1986) 'On formal structures of practical action'. In H. Garfinkel (Ed.) *Ethnomethodological studies of work*. London: Routledge.

Gee, J.J. (2005) 'Language in the science classroom: Academic social languages as the heart of school-based literacy'. In R. Yerrick & W.-M. Roth (Eds.) *Establishing scientific classroom discourse communities: Multiple voices of teaching and learning research*. Mahwah, NJ: Lawrence Erlbaum Associates.

Giddens, A. (1991) *Modernity and self-identity: Self and society in the late modern age*. Stanford, CA: Stanford University Press.

Gilbert, G.N. & Mulkay, M. (1984) *Opening Pandora's box: A sociological analysis of scientists' discourse*. Cambridge: Cambridge University Press.

Goffman, E. (1963) *Behavior in public places: Notes on the social organization of gatherings*. New York: Free Press.

Greeno, J.G., Collins, A.M. & Resnick, L.B. (1996) 'Cognition and learning'. In D. Berliner & R. Calfee (Eds.), *Handbook of educational psychology*. New York: Macmillan.

Haggan, N., Archibald, J-A. & Salas, S. (1998) 'Knowledge gains power when shared'. In D. Pauly, T. Pitcher & D. Preikshot (Eds.) *Back to the future: Reconstructing the strait of Georgia ecosystem*. Vancouver: University of British Columbia.

Hegel, G.W.F. (1979a) *Werke – Band 3: Phänomenologie des Geistes*. Frankfurt: Suhrkamp-Verlag; A.V. Miller (trans.) *Phenomenology of spirit* (1977). Oxford: Oxford University Press.

Hegel, G.W.F. (1979b). *Werke – Band 8: Enzyklopädie der philosophischen Wissenschaften im Grundrisse*. Frankfurt: Suhrkamp-Verlag.

Heidegger, M. (1954) *Was heißt Denken?* Tübingen: Max Niemeyer Verlag.

Heidegger, M. (1957) *Identität und Differenz*. Tübingen: Max Niemeyer Verlag. Reprinted in J. Stambaugh (trans.), *Identity and difference* (2002). Chicago: Chicago University Press.

Heidegger, M. (1977a) *Holzwege*. Frankfurt: Vittorio Klostermann.

Heidegger, M. (1977b) *Sein und Zeit*. Tübingen: Max Niemeyer Verlag; J. Macquarrie & E. Robinson (trans.), *Being and time* (1962). New York: Harper & Row; and J. Stambaugh (trans.), *Being and time* (1996). Albany: State University of New York Press.

Heidegger, M. (1985) *Unterwegs zur Sprache*. Frankfurt: Vittorio Klostermann.

Heidegger, M. (1990) '... Dichterisch wohnet der Mensch ...'. In *Vorträge und Aufsätze*, Pfullingen: Neske; A. Hofstadter (trans.), '... Poetically man dwells ...'. In *Poetry, language, thought* (1971). New York: Harper & Row.

Henry, M. (2005) *Voir l'invisible – sur Kandinsky*. Paris: Presses Universitaires de France.

Holzkamp, K. (1983) *Grundlegung der Psychologie*. Frankfurt: Campus-Verlag.

Ilyenkov, E.V. (1982) *The dialectics of the abstract and the concrete in Marx's 'capital'*, S. Syrovatkin (trans.). Moscow: Progress Publishers.

Indo-European Language Association (2007) *Proto-Indo-European etymological dictionary: A revised edition of Julius Pokorny's Indogermanisches Etymologisches Wörterbuch*. Accessed June 22, 2009 at http://dnghu.org.

Joyce, J. (1986) *Ulysses.* New York: Vintage Books.

Köbler, G. (2000) *Indogermanisches Wörterbuch.* Accessed June 22, 2009 at http://www.koeblergerhard.de/idgwbhin.html.

Lacoue-Labarthe, P. (1975) *Typographie.* Paris: Aubier-Flammarion; C. Fynsk (trans.), *Typography: Mimesis, philosophy, politics* (1998). Cambridge, MA: Harvard University Press.

Latour, B. & Woolgar, S. (1979) *Laboratory life: The social construction of scientific facts.* Beverly Hills, CA: Sage.

Levinas, E. (1971) *Totalité et infini: essai sur l'extériorité.* The Hague: Martinus Nijhoff; A. Lingis (trans.), *Totality and infinity: An essay on exteriority* (1969). Pittsburgh, PA: Duquesne University Press.

Levinas, E. (1978) *Autrement qu'être ou au-delà de l'essence.* The Hague: Martinus Nijhoff; A. Lingis (trans.), *Otherwise than being or beyond essence* (1998). Pittsburg, PA: Duquesne University Press.

Levinas, E. (1982) *Étique et infini.* Paris: Fayard.

Lewis, P.E. (2000) 'The measure of translation effects'. In L. Venuti (Ed.) *The translation studies reader.* London: Routledge.

McDermott, R.P. (1993) 'The acquisition of a child by a learning disability'. In S. Chaiklin & J. Lave (Eds.) *Understanding practice: Perspectives on activity and context.* Cambridge: Cambridge University Press.

McLuhan, M. (1995) *Understanding media: The extensions of man.* London: Routledge.

McNeill, D. (2002) 'Gesture and language dialectic'. *Acta Linguistica Hafniensia*, 34: 7–37.

Merleau-Ponty, M. (1945) *Phénoménologie de la perception.* Paris: Gallimard; C. Smith (trans.), *Phenomenology of perception* (1962). London: Routledge & Kegan Paul.

Merleau-Ponty, M. (1964) *Le visible et l'invisible.* Paris: Gallimard.

Meshcheryakov, A. (1979) *Awakening to life.* Moscow: Progress.

Nancy, J.-L.(1993) 'Éloge de la mêlée'. *Transeuropéennes*, 1: 8–18; S. Miller (trans.), 'In praise of the melee'. In *A finite thinking* (2003). Stanford: Stanford University Press.

Nancy, J.-L. (2000) *Being singular plural.* R.D. Richardson & A.E. O'Byrne (trans.), Stanford, CA: Stanford University Press.

Nietzsche, F. (1954a) *Werke in drei Bänden: Band 2.* München: Carl Hanser Verlag.

Nietzsche, F. (1954b) *Werke in drei Bänden: Band 3.* München: Carl Hanser Verlag.

Noddings, N. (1984) *Caring: A feminine approach to ethics and moral education.* Berkeley: University of California Press.

Nöth, W. (1990) *Handbook of semiotics.* Bloomington: Indiana University Press.

Novalis (2001) *Werke.* München: Verlag C.H. Beck.

Oxford English Dictionary (2009) Online, www.oed.com. Oxford: Oxford University Press.

Pines, A.L. (1985) 'Toward a taxonomy of conceptual relations'. In L.H.T. West & A.L. Pines (Eds.) *Cognitive structure and conceptual change.* New York: Academic Press.

Posner, G.J., Strike, K.A., Hewson, W. & Gertzog, W.A. (1982) 'Accommodation of a scientific conception: Toward a theory of conceptual change'. *Science Education*, 66: 211–27.

Potter, J. (2005) 'Making psychology relevant'. *Discourse & Society*, 16: 739–47.

Presbyterian Church USA (PCUSA) (1969) Theology and worship: Evolution statement. Accessed May 27, 2009 at http://www.pcusa.org/theologyandworship/science/evolution.htm.

Rawls, A.W. (1989) 'Language, self, and social order: A reformulation of Goffman and Sacks'. *Human Studies*, 12: 147–72.

Ricœur, P. (1984) *Time and narrative* vol. 1. K. McLaughlin & D. Pellauer (trans.), Chicago: University of Chicago Press.

Ricœur, P. (1986) *Du text à l'action: Essais d'herméneutique II*. Paris: Seuil; K. Blamey & J.B. Thompson (trans.), *From text to action: Essays in hermeneutics, II* (1991). Evanston, IL: Northwestern University Press.

Ricœur, P. (1990) *Soi-même comme un autre*. Paris: Seuil; K. Blamey (trans.), *Oneself as another* (1992), Chicago: University of Chicago Press.

Ricœur, P. (2004a) *Memory, history, forgetting*. K. Blamey & D. Pellauer (trans.), Chicago: University of Chicago Press.

Ricœur, P. (2004b) *Sur la traduction*. Paris: Bayard.

Rimbaud, A. (1951) *Œuvres complètes*. Paris: Gallimard.

Rorty, R. (1989) *Contingency, irony, and solidarity*. Cambridge: Cambridge University Press.

Roth, W.-M. (2002) 'Gestures: Their role in teaching and learning'. *Review of Educational Research*, 71: 365–92.

Roth, W.-M. (2004) 'Perceptual gestalts in workplace communication'. *Journal of Pragmatics*, 36: 1037–69.

Roth, W.-M. (Ed.) (2005a) *Auto/biography and auto/ethnography: Praxis of research method*. Rotterdam: Sense Publishers.

Roth, W.-M. (2005b) 'Telling in purposeful activity and the emergence of scientific language'. In R. Yerrick & W.-M. Roth (Eds.), *Establishing scientific classroom discourse communities: Multiple voices of research on teaching and learning*. Mahwah, NJ: Lawrence Erlbaum Associates.

Roth, W.-M. (2007) 'Toward solidarity as the ground for changing science education'. *Cultural Studies in Science Education*, 2: 721–45.

Roth, W.-M. (2008a) Bricolage, métissage, hybridity, heterogeneity, diaspora: Concepts for thinking science education in the 21st century. *Cultural Studies in Science Education*, 3: 891–916.

Roth, W.-M. (2008b) 'Knowing, participative thinking, emoting'. *Mind, Culture, and Activity*, 15: 3–8.

Roth, W.-M. (2009a) *Dialogism: A Bakhtinian perspective on science language and learning*. Rotterdam: Sense Publishers.

Roth, W.-M. (2009b) 'Identity and community: Differences at heart and futures-to-come'. *Éducation et Didactique*, 3: 99–118.

Roth, W.-M. & Alexander, T. (1997) 'The interaction of students' scientific and religious discourses: Two case studies'. *International Journal of Science Education*, 19: 125–46.

Roth, W.-M. & Hsu, P.-L. (2008) 'Interest and motivation: A cultural historical and discursive psychological approach'. In J.E. Larson (Ed.) *Educational psychology: cognition and learning, individual differences and motivation*. Hauppauge, NY: Nova Science.

Roth, W.-M. & Hsu, P.-L. (2009) *Analyzing communication: Praxis of method*. Rotterdam: Sense Publishers.

Roth, W.-M. & McRobbie, C. (1999) 'Lifeworlds and the "w/ri(gh)ting" of classroom research'. *Journal of Curriculum Studies*, 31: 501–22.

Roth, W.-M. & Middleton, D. (2006) 'The making of asymmetries of knowing, identity, and accountability in the sequential organization of graph interpretation'. *Cultural Studies of Science Education*, 1: 11–81.

Roth, W.-M. & Pozzer-Ardenghi, L. (2006) 'Tracking situated, distributed, and embodied communication in real time'. In M.A. Vanchevsky (Ed.) *Focus on cognitive psychology research*. Hauppauge, NY: Nova Science.

Roth, W-.M. & Thom, J. (2009) 'The emergence of 3D geometry from children's (teacher-guided) classification tasks'. *Journal of the Learning Sciences*, 18: 45–99.

Roth, W-.M., Tobin, K., Carambo, C. & Dalland, C. 'Coordination in coteaching: Producing alignment in real time'. *Science Education*, 89: 675–702.

Selting, M., Auer, P., Barden, B., Bergmann, J., Couper-Kuhlen, E., Günthner, S., Meier, C., Quasthoff, U., Schlobinski, P. & Uhmann, S. (1998) 'Gesprächsanalytisches Transkriptionssystem'. *Linguistische Berichte*, 173: 91–122.

Sewell, W.H. (1992) 'A theory of structure: duality, agency and transformation'. *American Journal of Sociology*, 98: 1–29.

Sfard, A. (2008) *Thinking as communicating: Human development, the growth of discourses, and mathematizing*. Cambridge: Cambridge University Press.

Smith, D.E. (2005) *Institutional ethnography: A sociology for people*. Lanham, MD: Altamira Press.

Todorov, T. (1984) *Mikhail Bakhtin, the dialogical principle*. W. Godzich (trans.), Minneapolis: University of Minnesota Press.

Treagust, D.F. & Duit, R. (2008) 'Compatibility between cultural studies and conceptual change in science education: There is more to acknowledge than to fight straw men'. *Cultural Studies of Science Education*, 3: 387–95.

Turner, J.H. (2002) *Face to face: Toward a sociological theory of interpersonal behavior*. Stanford, CA: Stanford University Press.

Vološinov, V.N. (1973) *Marxism and the philosophy of language*. L. Mtejka & I.R. Titunik (trans.), Cambridge, MA: Harvard University Press. (First published in 1929.)

Vološinov, V.N. (1976) *Freudianism: A Marxist critique*. I.R. Titunik (trans.). I.R. Titunik & N.H. Bruss (Eds.), New York: Academic Press.

Vygotsky, L.S. (1978) *Mind in society: The development of higher psychological processes*. M. Cole, V. John-Steiner, S. Scribner & E. Souberman (Eds.), Cambridge, MA: Harvard University Press.

Vygotsky, L.S. (1986) *Thought and language*. A. Kozulin (trans.), Cambridge, MA: MIT press. (First published in 1934.)

Waldenfels, B. (2006) *Grundmotive einer Phänomenologie des Fremden*. Frankfurt: Suhrkamp-Verlag.

Walkerdine, V. (1988) *The mastery of reason: Cognitive development and the production of rationality*. London: Routledge.

Wall, T.C. (1999) *Radical passivity: Levinas, Blanchot, and Agamben*. Albany: State University of New York Press.

Weizenbaum, J. (1995) 'The myth of the last metaphor'. In P. Baumgartner & S. Payr, *Speaking minds: Interviews with twenty eminent cognitive scientists*. Princeton, NJ: Princeton University Press.

Wittgenstein, L. (1958) *Philosophische Untersuchungen;* parallel bilingual edition, G.E.M. Anscombe (trans.), *Philosophical investigations*. Oxford: Basil Blackwell.

Index